Music Today and Every Day

Ready-to-Use Music Lessons & Activities for the Elementary Grades

TOD F. KLINE

Artwork by Toya B. Warner

PARKER PUBLISHING COMPANY
Paramus, New Jersey 07652

Library of Congress Cataloging-in-Publication Data

Kline, Tod F.
    Music today and every day : ready-to-use music lessons & activities for the elementary
grades / Tod F. Kline ; artwork by Toya B. Warner.
        p. cm.
    ISBN 0-13-031481-1
    1. School music—Instruction and study—Activity programs. 2. Interdisciplinary
approach in education. I. Title.
MT10.K56 2001

01-058899

Acquisitions Editor: *Win Huppuch*
Production Editor: *Jackie Roulette*
Layout/Interior Design: *Dee Coroneos*

Printed in the United States of America

10 9 8 7 6 5 4 3 2 1   10 9 8 7 6 5 4 3 2 1

ISBN 0-13-031481-1 (spiral)   ISBN 0-13-042589-3 (paper)

PARKER PUBLISHING COMPANY
Paramus, New Jersey 07652

http://www.phdirect.com

ABOUT THE AUTHOR

Tod F. Kline is an instrumental and vocal music teacher at Hooverville Elementary School in the Waynesboro, Pennsylvania, Area School District. He earned his Bachelor of Music and Master of Science degrees from the North Carolina School of the Arts and Western Maryland College, respectively, and also attended Gettysburg College. Tod has been an adjunct faculty member for Shippenburg University, Penn State University, and Mercersburg Academy and is also the author of *Classic Tunes & Tales: Ready-to-Use Music Listening Lessons & Activities for Grades K–8* (Paramus, NJ: Parker Publishing Co., 1997).

ABOUT "MUSIC TODAY AND EVERY DAY"

This practical resource gives elementary music teachers a unique store of stimulating, tested lessons and activities for developing music literacy and linking music to the regular classroom curriculum. The lessons introduce children to the basic elements of music and include a variety of hands-on activities that build their understanding of music concepts and relate them to other content areas. While the study of music certainly needs no justification, it is beneficial to have other means to promote it. Complementing the academic curriculum can only yield positive rewards.

For easy use, the lessons and activities are printed in a big spiral-bound format that folds flat for desktop use and for photocopying of music, story and activity sheet pages. Lessons are organized into three grade-level sections:

Level 1 (Grade Levels K–2) provides 15 ready-to-use lessons for teaching music concepts such as contrast, loud/soft, AB/ABA, So-Mi, same/different pitches, beats per measure, slow/fast, and instrument families. The music concepts are tied to integrated subjects such as antonyms, size, animals, geometric shapes, habitats, weather, transportation, families and storytelling. In the lesson "Same/Different (The Farm)," for example, children identify same and different pitches in a melody through songs such as "I Got Me a Cat" and "Old MacDonald." An activity page entitled "Same-Different/Animals Playing Instruments" invites them to circle the animals playing the same instrument.

Level 2 (Grade Levels 3–4) offers ten detailed lessons focusing on the concepts of note names, note values, music symbols, African music instruments, two- and three-section forms, American composers and more. These are connected to regular classroom concepts such as vowels, fairy tales, fractions, exaggeration, African/world culture, geometric shapes, biographies and fiction/nonfiction. The lesson entitled "Note Values," for example, helps students learn to recognize the whole note, half note, and quarter note through the song "Riding in a Buggy" and an excerpt from Beethoven's Piano Sonata No. 8, identifying fractions/notes on a Music Pizza page, writing the notes, and sorting notes in a "Pick 'n Put" activity.

Level 3 (Grade Levels 5–6) presents ten detailed lessons featuring concepts such as bass clef notation, 6/8 and 3/8 meter, minor key signatures, voice, Civil War music, opera and women composers. Classroom ties touch upon suffixes, speed measuring devices, countries, the role of women, the Civil War, technology, the human body, mystery and others. In the lesson "The Vocal Instrument (Health)," for example, students perform various singing tasks such as diction, breathing, posture, voice care, range and quality as they sing the song "Rocky Mountain" at different tempos, volumes and keys, and then circle healthy practices for singing on an activity page.

Each grade-level section also provides a store of "Supplementary Materials," including reproducible games, information sheets, activity pages, puzzles and more that can be used to reinforce and extend the lessons in that section or in any other way you wish. This is followed by 50 "Daily Music Skill-Builders" for daily practice in singing and rhythm skills and a reproducible Interdisciplinary Planner form to help you integrate music with the academic curriculum at each grade level.

You'll find that all of the lessons in this resource are illustrated, complete, and ready for use with minimal preparation on your part. Each lesson is spelled out in a similar, easy-to-follow format, including:

Title: a title identifying the music concept and related academic concepts to be developed

Objective: the lesson objective in behavioral terms

Materials: specific materials needed to carry out the lesson, including reproducible music pages, patterns, gameboards, and worksheets

Procedure: step-by-step activities for developing the lesson, including an opening activity, a listening activity, a singing or performance activity, and a game or composition activity

Activity Pages: one or more reproducible activity sheets to give students practice in applying what they have learned

Additional reproducible games or activities for reinforcing a particular lesson may also be found in the supplementary materials at the end of the section.

In short, this resource places at your fingertips a wealth of exciting music activities, games, activity sheets, songs, and skill-building exercises for daily use and reference. It will help you save preparation time, make teaching and learning music more fun for you and your students, and connect music concepts with the classroom curriculum. My hope is that you will find many of the lessons adaptable to all grade levels and that the easy step-by-step approach will help you create your own integrated lesson plans—making this resource truly useful today and every day.

Tod F. Kline

CONTENTS

LEVEL 2
(Grade Levels 3–4)

LEVEL 3
(Grade Levels 5–6)

LEVEL 1
(Grade Levels K-2)

ELEMENT	MUSIC CONCEPT	INTEGRATED LINK	PAGE
Contrast			
Contrast	Contrast	Antonyms	91
Instruments	Contrast Size/Sound	Size	45
Dynamics			
Soft/Loud	Soft/Loud	Animals in the Zoo	23
Form			
Form	AB/ABA	Geometric Shapes	109
Melody			
So-Mi	So-Mi	Capital Letters	76
Same/Different	Same/Different Pitches	The Farm	30
Low/Middle/High	Low/Middle/High	Habitats	58
High/Low	High/Low Pitches	Thermometer	70
So-Mi-La	So-Mi-La	Maps	101
Mood			
Mood	Dramatic/Calm	Weather	19
Rhythm			
Meter	Beats per Measure	Addition	120
Tempo			
Fast/Slow	Fast/Slow	Transportation	10
Timbre			
Instruments	Instrument Families	Families	82
Other			
The Magic Flute	Appreciation	Retelling a Story	2
Rhyming	Rhyming Words	Rhyming Words	63

Supplementary Materials (K–2)   **127**

Appreciation of *The Magic Flute*
(Retelling a Story)

LESSON PLAN

Objective: Students will be able to retell the story of *The Magic Flute.*

Materials: Piano
Story of *The Magic Flute*
Copy of the music pages
Copies of: Papa Gayno page
      The Magic Flute Characters page
      The Magic Flute Story Sequence page
Scissors
Glue
Crayons or markers

Procedure: 1. *Opening Activity:* Tell the story of *The Magic Flute.*

        2. *Singing Activity:* Teach "Honor Is Better Than Prize." Ask the students in what part of the story this song would occur.

        3. *Imagination Activity:* Teach "The Birdcatcher." Ask: "Who is Papa Gayno? What did he do during the story?" After discussing Papa Gayno, hand out a copy of the Papa Gayno page to each student. Have the students draw what they believe Papa Gayno would look like.

        4. *Listening Activity:* Teach "Power of the Kingdom." Ask: "Who would sing this song? Why? How does he think he is going to get the power?"

        5. *Storytelling Activity:* Using *The Magic Flute* Characters page, arrange the students into groups. Have each group put on a puppet show of *The Magic Flute.* Allow the students to cut, color, and glue the characters to Popsicle sticks. Give them time to review, retell, and rehearse the story. Finally, have each group perform their play for you. Each student could play one or more parts.

Activity Page: Give each student a copy of *The Magic Flute* Story Sequence page. Have the students cut out the story circles and place them on the story sequence page in the order in which the picture occurs in the story.

STORY OF *THE MAGIC FLUTE*

Long, long ago a man named Thomas wanders from his homeland into a strange, faraway land while hunting. As he searches for his prey, he encounters a serpent. Not having the ability to slay the serpent, he hides behind a rock. The serpent remains for hours. It is so long that Thomas falls asleep. Three ladies then stroll into the countryside and see the situation the stranger is in, and decide to help.

Suddenly, a beautiful flute sound echoes through the trees. The serpent freezes in its place, and the ladies help Thomas to safety. The three heroines take Thomas back to their home, the Queen of the Night's castle, where the ladies work as assistants to the queen.

On the way into the castle, a man can be seen jumping, climbing, and running around carrying a net trying to catch birds. A peculiar fellow he certainly is.

After the ladies get Thomas inside, they leave him alone, still asleep, and sitting on a chair. Soon after the ladies leave the room, the birdcatcher, Papa Gayno, as he is known, comes inside snooping around to see what is going on. Thomas suddenly wakes up. He asks Papa Gayno if he has saved him from the will of the serpent. Papa Gayno proudly responds: "Why, yes. I certainly did." While Papa Gayno boasts about his bravery and cleverness in saving Thomas, the three ladies return with the queen.

The queen asks Thomas and Papa Gayno to rescue her daughter Princess Pamina from the evil knight Sarastro. Sarastro has kidnapped the princess in order to gain the power of the kingdom. If Thomas and Papa Gayno are successful, Thomas will be guided home and the kingdom will be safe. However, Papa Gayno wants a reward, too. So, the queen offers the post of "Official Guide of the Land." To help the two men save the princess, the queen gives them a flute, a magic flute to play when they are in trouble.

Thomas and Papa Gayno arrive at the evil knight Sarastro's castle. They peek through the window and hear Sarastro and his helper, Monty, telling the princess that they will control the kingdom as long as they keep her captive.

The two heroes plan a surprise rescue, but it backfires and they are both captured by Sarastro's men. However, Thomas reminds Papa Gayno of the magic flute. Papa Gayno plays the magic flute and beautiful music is heard, and Sarastro, Monty, and his men are frozen in place until the queen's guards arrive to escort the heroes back to the castle for a big celebration.

MUSICAL EXCERPTS
FROM *THE MAGIC FLUTE*
Honor Is Better than Prize

Mozart

When du - ty calls the gal - lant will re-spond with

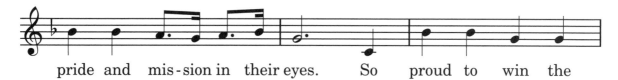

pride and mis - sion in their eyes. So proud to win the

hearts of eve - ry - one for hon - or's bet - ter than a prize.

The Birdcatcher

Oh, I am the res - i - dent - ial bird - catch - er, and I know birds head to foot fea - thers. I've caught ro - bins, owls, eag - les, and con - dors. Name them all in the trees and bush - es tall or small. For the coun - try - side is the home you see. Who could know this land __ an - y bet - ter than me? An - y cir - cum - stance I can catch a fowl. Come to Pa - pa Gay - no 'cause he real - ly knows how.

Power of the Kingdom

For me to be in pow - er of the king-dom, my peo-ple will hear and o - bey my word. When I speak, peo-ple lis - ten to me. All that I want plus all that is due me. All that I want is all there will be.

Papa Gayno

The Magic Flute Characters

Papa Gayno
(birdman w/flute)

Thomas the Hunter

The Queen

Sarastro

Monty

Princes Pamina

The Serpent

Ladies in Waiting

Queen's Guards

The Magic Flute Story Sequence

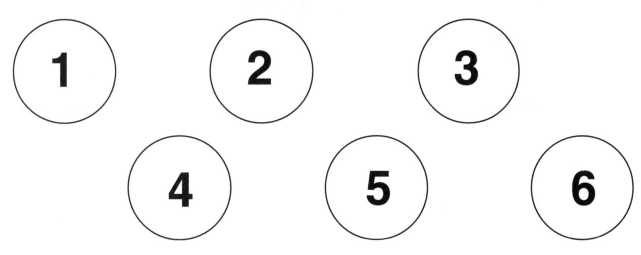

Cut out the circles below and glue each one in the numbered circles in the order it happened during the story. Circle 1 was the first thing to happen. Circle 6 was the last.

Queen with three ladies talk to Papa Gayno and Thomas

Man walking with bow and arrow

Three ladies and one blows the magic flute

Serpent with man hiding behind rock

Men frozen in a room. Thomas, Princess, and Papa Gayno escape.

People celebrate: Queen, Princess, Papa Gayno, Thomas, etc.

Fast/Slow
(Transportation)

LESSON PLAN

Objective: Students will distinguish between fast and slow music.

Materials: Piano
Recording of the *William Tell Overture,* if available
Copy of the Fast/Slow Music pages
Rhythm sticks
Copies of: Transportation activity page
                Transportation Objects game pages

Procedure: 1. *Opening Activity:* Play and sing the song "Walk to School" for the class. Have the students walk while you sing the word *walk,* run when you sing the word *run,* etc. (any other form of transportation to school). After you finish, ask the students to name or point out things or animals that are fast and things and animals that are slow. Substitute the motion word (e.g., walk, run, skip, jog, etc.) which the students name. Do the motions and sing the song. After awhile, the students will learn the song quite well.

2. *Listening Activity:* Point out or ask the students whether or not the *tempo,* or how fast the song went, changed when singing about walking or running. Play a recording of the *William Tell Overture,* and have the students gallop, and a recording of "Brahm's Lullaby," and have the students cradle their arms as though they are holding and rocking a baby to sleep. Ask, "Which music is fast and which is slow?"

3. *Instrument Activity:* Teach the song "My Truck" to the students. Ask the students what a truck is and what it is used for. Then, have them discover what happens when you get on a truck and how the truck works. Finally, have them snap to the beat of the song as everyone sings. After each verse, stop the song and ask if the words indicate to slow the truck down or speed it up. Then sing the song faster or slower for the appropriate verse. Later, you may want to teach the song as "The Bus" and use the appropriate motions (i.e., The people on the bus go up and down).

Procedure:
(Continued)

4. ***Game:*** You will need a copy of the Transportation Objects game pages. Cut out the objects and laminate each for best practice. Discuss the different speeds of the objects on the page with the students. Teach "The Passenger Song." With the class in a circle or at their seats, pick a student to be the passenger. The passenger will pick a card and sing the song fast or slow for the appropriate object. This activity can be a good evaluation tool for pitch recognition, slow/fast, etc.

Activity Page:

Hand out a copy of the Transportation activity page for each student. Instruct the students to circle all the things under section one that move fast. Section two is a listening exercise. Play three music selections of any combination of slow and fast and ask the students to circle the racing horse if the song is fast. This activity page is another good slow/fast evaluation.

FAST/SLOW MUSIC
Walk to School

Walk, walk, walk to school. Walk to school to - geth - er.
Run   .   .   .
Skip   .   .   .
Jog   .   .   .
Crawl   .   .   .
Hop   .   .   .

Walk, walk, walk to school. Walk to school to - geth - er.

William Tell Overture

Rossini

Will-iam Tell   Over - ture,   Will-iam Tell _ Over - ture,

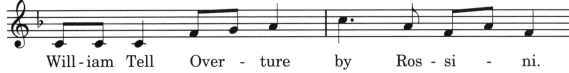

Will - iam Tell   Over - ture   by   Ros - si - ni.

Lullaby

Brahms

Lul-la - by,   lul-la - by,   Go to sleep lit - tle   ba - by, slum-ber

well my   lit - tle   one   as you   dream plea - sant   things.

12

My Truck

Traditional
Adapted

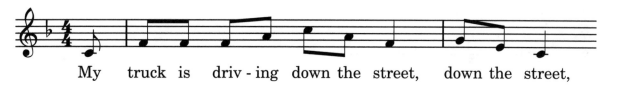

My truck is driv-ing down the street, down the street,

down the street. My truck is driv-ing down the street. Down, down, down.

2. My truck is driving up the hill, up the hill, up the hill.
   My truck is driving up the hill, up, up, up.

3. My truck is moving down the hill, down the hill, down the hill.
   My truck is moving down the hill, down, down, down.

4. My truck is really loaded down, loaded down, loaded down.
   My truck is really loaded down, down, down, down.

FAST/SLOW MUSIC
The Passenger Song

I am rid - ing in a race - car.

I am go - ing ver - y fast.

I am fly - ing in a jet. _____

I am go - ing ver - y fast.

I am sail - ing in a sail - boat.

I am go - ing ver - y slow.

I am travel - ing in a freight train.

I am go - ing ver - y fast.

FAST/SLOW MUSIC
The Passenger Song (Continued)

Transportation Objects

Heavy Loaded Truck

Empty Truck

Motorcycle

Race Car

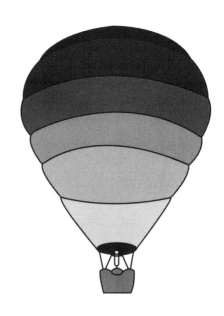

Jet Ski

Hot Air Balloon

Transportation Objects

Sailboat

Freight Train

Covered Wagon

Walking Horse

Race Horse

Passenger Train

17

Transportation
(Slow/Fast)

Circle the pictures of the things that move fast.

Circle the covered wagon when you hear a slow tune or the racing horse when you hear a fast tune.

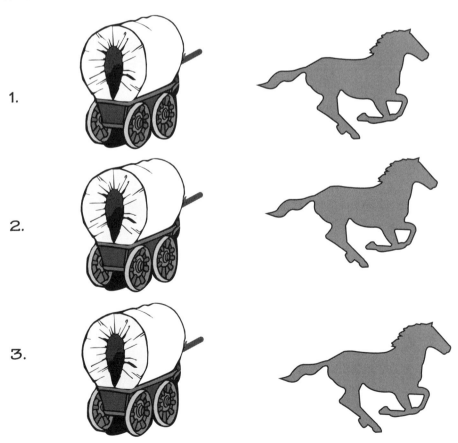

1.

2.

3.

Mood of the Music
(Weather)

LESSON PLAN

Objective: Students will be able to identify mood (dramatic/calm) in music.

Materials: Piano
Copies of: Mood Music page
            Calm or Stormy Moods activity page
Pencils/crayons
Various classroom instruments

Procedure:

1. *Opening Activity:* Sing "Rain, Rain Go Away." Ask the students: "Do you think of stormy or calm weather when you hear this song?" You will hear a variety of responses. Explain that the music can be stormy or calm. Teach and sing the song.

2. *Listening Activity:* Sing "Twinkle, Twinkle Little Star." Ask the students if this song makes them think of calm—at night. Play "Twinkle, Twinkle Little Star" in the piano's extreme lower register. Ask: "Does this song sound calm or stormy?" You may want to try this activity on various instruments. Discuss with the students why the song sounds as it does.

3. *Performance Activity:* Place the students into groups of two or three. Pass out various rhythm or tonal instruments. Have the groups compose a calm weather song and a stormy weather song.

4. *Another Activity:* Give each student a pair of the weather cards. Play a variety of music that depicts stormy and/or calm weather. Have the students raise the correct card in response.

5. *Final Note:* Discuss other types of weather. Ask the students how the music for such weather would sound.

Activity Page: Play Wagner's "Ride of the Valkyries" and Grieg's "Morning." Have the students draw a picture to show a stormy scene for Wagner's piece and a calm scene when they hear Grieg's piece.

MOOD MUSIC
Rain, Rain, Go Away

Rain, rain   go   a - way.   Come a - gain a - no - ther day.
I   want the rain   to   stop.   Eve - ry   lit - tle   drip-py drop.

Twinkle, Twinkle Little Star

Mozart

Twin-kle, twin-kle,   lit - tle star,   how I   won-der   what you are?

Up   a - bove the   world so   high.   Like a   dia-mond   in   the sky.

Ride of the Valkyries

Wagner

Morning

Grieg

Calm

Grieg wrote a qui - et tune from his Peer Gynt _ Suite.

It kind of goes _ like this. It is called "Morn-ing," so

qui - et and sun - ny. Just start-ing a new _____ day.

Calm or Stormy Moods
(Weather)

Draw a picture for the calm music you hear.

Draw a picture for the stormy music you hear.

Soft/Loud
(Animals in the Zoo)

LESSON PLAN

Objective: Students will be able to distinguish loud and soft music.

Materials: Piano
Soft/Loud Music page
Copies of: Singing Loud and Soft activity page
Zoo Animals pages
Scissors
Pencils

Procedure: 1. *Opening Activity:* Ask the students what a lion sounds like; or, a bird. Students will make various sounds. Ask: "Would you say a lion or a bird speaks louder? Just as animals, music can be big or little, loud or soft. In music, we usually say soft instead of quiet."

2. *Performing Activity:* Teach "This Time I Am Singing Loud." Select a student to stand in front of the class and direct the class singing loud or soft. Have the director spread his/her arms out for loud and move hands closer for soft. As the class sings the song, the director motions the class whether to sing loud or soft on the appropriate words.

3. *Singing Activity:* Teach the short melodies of Saint-Saëns's *Carnival of Animals.* Have the students put their pointer fingers over their mouths in a position for quiet when singing a quiet melody. When singing a louder melody, have the students cup their hands around their mouths in a shouting position. Remind the students that this gesture is only a signal. One should never shout—just sing loudly.

4. *Game:* Copy, laminate, and cut out the figures on the Zoo Animal pages. Teach the song "Zookeeper" (first, echo clap the rhythm, then the words and the tune). Select a student to stand up and cover his or her eyes. Allow another student to select an animal card and give it to another student—every student should pretend to have the card. Tell the student what the animal is and ask him/her if it is a soft or loud speaking animal. Have the student walk around while the class sings "Zookeeper." The class will sing and get louder or softer for the appropriate animal as

Procedure:
(Continued)

the student comes nearer to the hidden card. The student tries to guess who has it. The student with the animal card is next. The student who just finished will pick a card and give it to another student to hide.

Activity Page:

Give each student a copy of the Zoo Animals (singing loud and soft) page. Have the students draw a line from the animals they feel sound loud to the word "Loud" and a line from the animals that sound soft to the word "Soft." At the bottom of the page, play a melody familiar to the class loudly or quietly. Direct the students to circle the flute if the melody is played softly and circle the electric guitar if the melody is played loudly. After an example or two, play three loud or soft melodies.

SOFT/LOUD MUSIC
This Time I Am Singing Loud

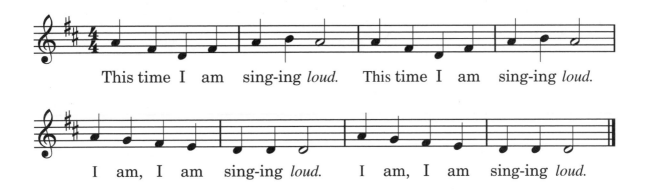

This time I am sing-ing *loud.* This time I am sing-ing *loud.*

I am, I am sing-ing *loud.* I am, I am sing-ing *loud.*

Zookeeper

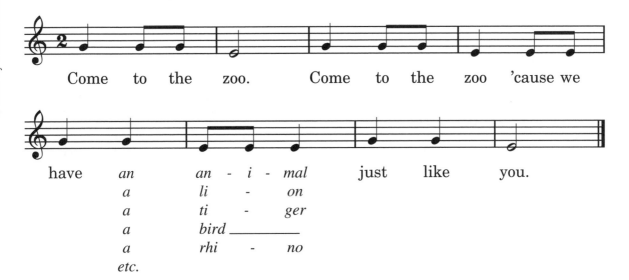

Come to the zoo. Come to the zoo 'cause we

have	*an*	*an* - *i* - *mal*	just	like	you.
	a	*li* - *on*			
	a	*ti* - *ger*			
	a	*bird* _____			
	a	*rhi* - *no*			
	etc.				

Carnival of Animals

Saint-Saëns

Zoo Animal Cards

Lion

Elephant

Monkey

Bird

Snake

Kangaroo

Zoo Animal Cards *(Continued)*

Bear

Alligator

Seal

Gorilla

Name _____

Singing Loud and Soft
Zoo Animals

Draw a line from the animal to the word *loud* for loud-sounding animals and to *soft* for soft-sounding animals.

Animals

lion

snake

kangaroo

elephant

giraffe

alligator

monkey

ostrich

Loud

Soft

Circle the flute if the music sounds soft, and circle the electric guitar if the music sounds loud.

1.

2.

3.

Same/Different
(The Farm)

LESSON PLAN

Objective: Students will identify same and different pitches.

Materials: Piano
Bells or xylophone
Same/Different Music page
Copies of: Same/Different Animal Barns page
Farm Animal Cards
Writing Music page
Same/Different activity page
Crayons or pencils
Scissors
Glue

Procedure: 1. *Opening Activity:* Sing "I Got Me a Cat." Ask the students: "Who might have or where might you find all these animals?" Help lead the students to the desired answer of a farmer or a farm. Teach the song to the students. Have the students make up other verses to the song.

2. *Listening Activity:* Give a copy of the Same/Different Animal Barns page to each student. Play the various same/different measures from the music page. Instruct the students to point to the barn with the same animals when they hear the same pitches and to the barn with different animals when they hear different pitches played. When the activity is over, the student may color the page.

3. *Game:* Copy, cut out, and laminate the animal cards (different colored cards work best). Form a rectangle or square with the students. Place the cards on the floor outside the rectangle of students. Place in order the farmhouse, the animals, and the barn. Choose a student to stand on the farmhouse. Place two or three tone bells (xylophone or set of bells will do) in the center of, or somewhere near, the rectangle. Have another student play same or different tones on the bells. The first student guesses same or different. The student will move one card forward for each correct answer until he/she reaches the barn. The bell player becomes the next player. See how many students can end up in the barn!

Procedure:
(Continued)

4. *Listening Activity:* Teach and/or sing "Old MacDonald." Add verses, if possible. Point out the repeated or same pitches during the animal sounds. Have the students raise their hands each time they sing the animal sounds (chick-chick here, moo-moo here, etc.).

5. *Writing Activity:* Give each student a copy of the Writing Music page. Have the students cut out the four birds and glue two of the birds on the same fence rail under *same* and on different fence rails under the *different* heading.

Activity Page:

Give a copy of the Same/Different Animals Playing Instruments page to each student. Instruct the students to circle the animals playing the same instruments. They may color the animals or the entire page, if you wish, after finishing.

SAME/DIFFERENT MUSIC
I Found Me a Cat

I found me a cat and my cat pleased me. I

fed my cat un-der yon-der tree. *Cat* goes fid-dle-ei - fee.

2.
Hen goes chim-my chuck, chim-my chuck.
go back to one

3.
Duck goes quack, quack.
go to *2.* then *1.*

4.
Cow goes moo, moo.
4,3,2,1

5.
Horse goes neigh, neigh.
5,4,3,2,1

6.
Goose goes his-sy, his - sy.
6,5,4,3,2,1

Same/Different Examples

Same Possibilities

Different Possibilities

Old MacDonald

1. Old Mac-Don-ald had a farm. Ee - i - ee - i - o. And on his farm he had some chicks. Ee - i - ee - i - o. With a *chick   chick* here and a *chick   chick* there. Here a *chick.* There a *chick.* Eve - ry - where a *chick   chick.* Old Mac-Don-ald had a farm. Ee - i - ee - i - o.

2. Ducks—*quack, quack*

3. Pigs—*oink, oink*

4. Cows—*moo, moo*

5. Sheep—*baa, baa*

Same/Different

Animal Barns

Farm Animal Cards

Farmhouse

Farm Animal Cards

Cow

Farm Animal Cards

Horse

Farm Animal Cards

Pig

Farm Animal Cards

Chicken

Farm Animal Cards

Sheep

Farm Animal Cards

Cat

Farm Animal Cards

Barn

Writing Music
Same/Different

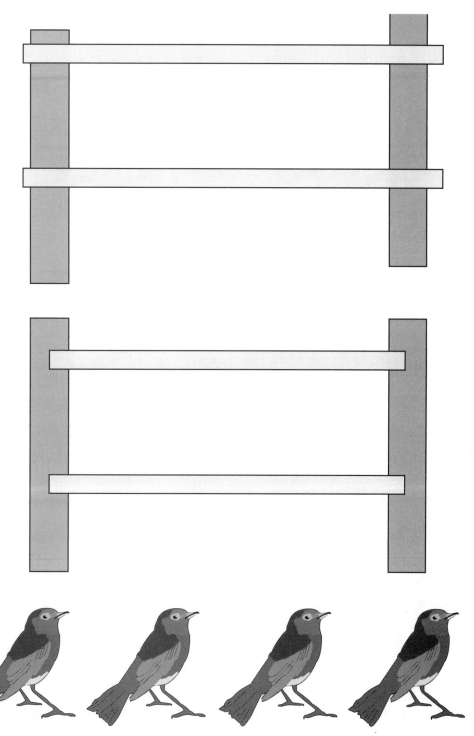

Animals Playing Instruments
Same/Different

Circle the same two animals playing the same two instruments in one corral.

Instruments
(Size)

LESSON PLAN

Objective: Students will identify instrument characteristics by size (i.e., big/little, large/small, and fat or wide/narrow).

Materials: Piano
Flute, Clarinet, Trumpet, Sax, Trombone, Snare drum, and Bass
   drum or substitutions that may be available
Set of Bells
Various classroom instruments
Copies of: Music page
          Instrument pages
          Sizes of Instruments activity page
Pencils
Chalkboard

Procedure:

1. *Opening Activity:* Sing "Tall, Small" for the class. Ask: "What is the difference between tall and small?" Answers will vary. Help lead the students to the word *size*. Teach the song to the students. Add standing and squatting motions on the appropriate words of the song.

2. *Discussion Activity:* Ask: "What other words for size do we use? For what do we use these words? What things in this room can we describe by using these words?" Write the examples on the board. Ask the students how the words can be used in music.

3. *Demonstration Activity:* Demonstrate a major scale on a set of bells. Ask: "What happens to the sound? Why?" Explain to the students how the larger bars produce a lower sound and the smaller bars produce a higher sound. Thus, the bigger the instrument, the lower the sound. The smaller the instrument, the higher the sound. Compare variously sized instruments—flute, clarinet, sax, trumpet, trombone, snare drum, and bass drum. If you do not have these instruments at your disposal, use posters or draw a rough idea of the instruments' sizes on the board or large paper. Use words such as fat/narrow, large/small, big/little, and long/short. Finally, play a glissando on the piano. "The notes go low to high. The piano uses strings inside to produce its sound. So, what length strings do the low notes use? How thick or long are the high note strings?"

Procedure:
(Continued)

4. ***Discovery Activity:*** Copy enough of the instrument pages for each student (possibly, use folders for all the pages). Have the students separate the instruments into piles according to sizes of large and small, then have them segregate the instruments into narrow and fat. Perhaps, try big/little and long/short, too. Finally, allow the students an opportunity to color each of the instruments.

5. ***Hands-On Activity:*** Place variously sized classroom instruments at stations around the room. Team the students into groups of two or three, and have them discuss the size and shape of the various instruments and how they sound.

Activity Page:

Give each student a copy of the Sizes of Instruments page. Instruct the students to correctly describe each instrument using the words in the boxes designated for each quadrant of the page.

Tall, Small

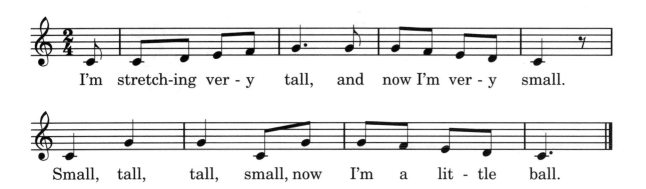

I'm stretch-ing ver - y tall, and now I'm ver - y small.

Small, tall, tall, small, now I'm a lit - tle ball.

Flute

Clarinet

Saxophone

Trumpet

Trombone

Tuba

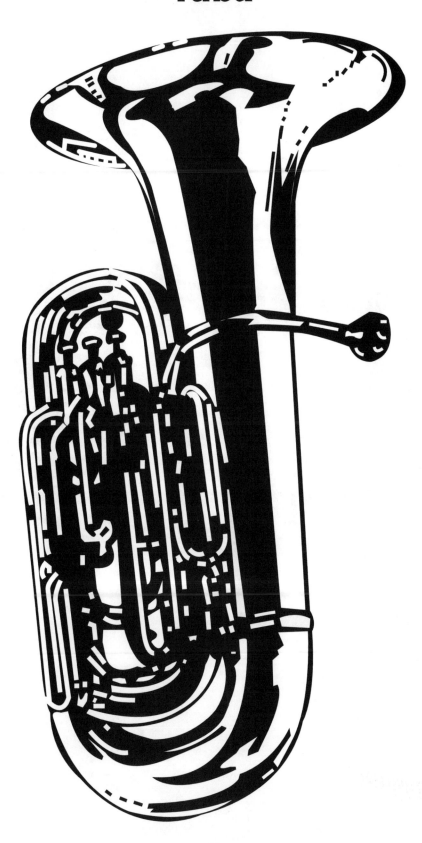

Snare Drum

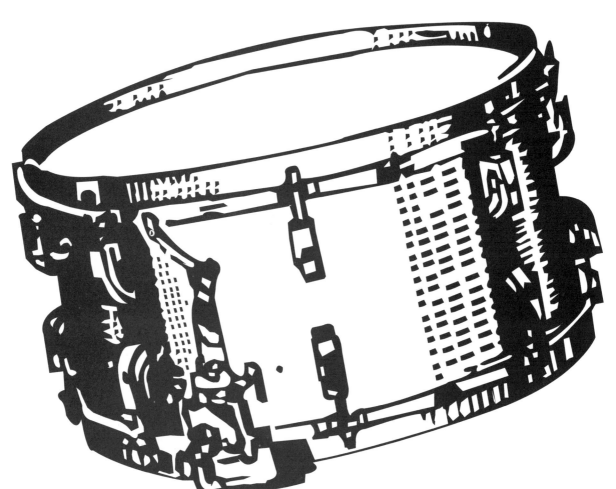

Bass Drum

Harp

Sizes of Instruments

Place the word under the instrument that best describes it.

Fat/Narrow   Large/Small

Tuba   Flute   Snare Drum   Bass Drum

_____   _____   _____   _____

Long/Short   Big/Little

Trumpet   Trombone   Violin   String Bass

_____   _____   _____   _____

Low/Middle/High
(Habitats)

LESSON PLAN

Objective: Students will identify high, middle, and low pitches.

Materials: Piano
                      Bells or xylophone
                      Copies of: Music page
                              Low/Middle/High Habitats page
                              Composing a Habitat Song page
                              Low, Middle, High Stairs page
                      Pencils

Procedure: 1. *Opening Activity:* Teach "Head, Tummy, Toes." Also, teach the motions to the students (*Head*—touch head, *Tummy*—touch tummy, etc.). Replace the words *head* with high, *tummy* with middle, and *toes* with low, and continue with the same motions. Ask the students what animals live in the sky. Ask what animals live on the ground, and what animals live in the ocean/water. Repeat the song again, and use the words *sky* for high, *land* for middle, and *ocean* for low. Ask: "What do we call these places where animals live?" "Habitats."

                      2. *Singing Activity:* Teach "Habitat"; the first four measures and then the second four measures. Ask the students to name examples of animals that live in the sky, on the land, and in the ocean and replace the words with names of animals. Be sure to use sky animals for high notes, land animals for middle-range notes, and fish or marine mammals for the lowest notes.

                      3. *Listening Activity:* Using bells, piano, or xylophone, play a low "C" (or middle C, G above, and C octave above) to demonstrate low, middle, and high. Hand out a copy of the Low/Middle/High Habitats page to each student. Continue to play examples of low, middle, and high notes in various orders and have the students point to the corresponding habitat.

                      4. *Composition Activity:* Give each student a copy of the Composing a Habitat Song page. Instruct the students to draw an animal for each of the habitat boxes. Each box should contain only one animal. Example: a bird for sky (high), a cow for land (middle), and a fish for the ocean (low). Play each song for the class or mark (or use tape) low, middle, and high tone bars on an xylophone and allow students to play the compositions on their own. A piano can be substituted for an xylophone.

Activity Page: Hand out a Low, Middle, High Stairs page to each student. Have the students write *low, middle,* or *high* on the line of each given example. At the bottom of the page, students may write their own examples.

Head, Tummy, Toes

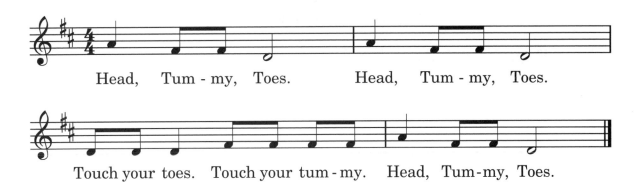

Head,   Tum - my, Toes.   Head,   Tum - my, Toes.

Touch your toes.   Touch your tum - my.   Head, Tum-my, Toes.

HABITAT

(Hot Cross Buns)

Ha - bi - tat,   Ha - bi - tat.   A - ni - mals live

in this place called Ha - bi - tat.   Sky, land, o - cean, sky, land, o - cean,

Fish in the o - cean. Cows on the land.   Ha - bi - tat.

Low/Middle/High

(Habitats)

Point to the correct box.

High

Middle

Low

Name _____

Composing a Habitat Song

Draw an ocean animal, a land animal, or a sky animal for each box. Only one for each box.

Low, Middle, High Stairs

Write low for low steps, middle for medium-high steps, or high for high steps on the line below each example.

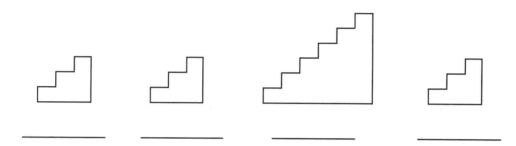

_____   _____   _____   _____

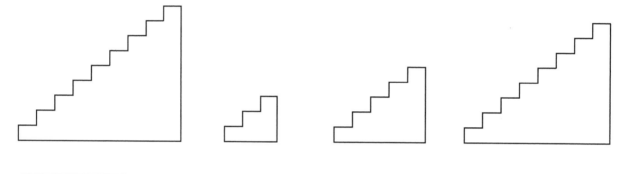

_____   _____   _____   _____

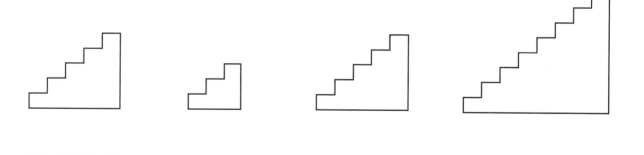

_____   _____   _____   _____

Try drawing your own high, middle, or low stairs.

_____   _____   _____

Rhyming Words
(Rhyming)

LESSON PLAN

Objective: Students will identify rhyming words in songs.

Materials: Piano
Copies of: Music pages
"Twinkle, Twinkle Little Star"
"So-Mi Song" and "Hip-Knee Song" page
Rhyming Words activity page

Procedure: 1. *Opening Activity:* Have the students sing the "A B C Song" and ask them to name the letters in the song that rhyme. Sing "Twinkle, Twinkle Little Star" and, using Twinkle, Twinkle Little Star Rhyming Words cards, stop the song at the end of each phrase before singing the final word for the end of each phrase.

2. *Listening Activity:* Sing "Baa, Baa Black Sheep" for the students. Instruct the students to find the rhyming words.

3. *Reading Activity:* Give a copy of the "So-Mi Song" to each student, and teach it to the class. Sing the "So-Mi Song" and the "Hip-Knee Song." Have the students create new words that rhyme with So and Mi.

4. *Listening Activity:* Sing "Mary Had a Little Lamb" to the students. Ask the students what words rhyme. Ask: "Does the last word of the song, *snow*, rhyme with any other word of the song?"

5. *Writing Activity:* Give each student a copy of the Rhyming Words for a Song page. Instruct the students to fill in the last word of each phrase with the best word from the Word Bank, and be sure that the pairs of phrases rhyme.

Activity Page: Choose a favorite song of the class, or use "Eency, Weency Spider." Give each student a copy of the Writing About Rhyming Words page. Instruct the students to write about the words that rhyme, using the space allowed.

ABC Song
(Twinkle, Twinkle Little Star)

A B C D   E F G   H I J K   L M N O P

Q R S   T U V   W ___ X   Y and Z

Now I've said my   A B C's,   Tell me what you   think of me.

Baa, Baa, Black Sheep

Baa, baa, Black Sheep, have you any wool?
Yes, Sir, Yes, Sir, three bags full.
One for my master, one for my mate.
One for the little boy who lives down the lane.
Baa, baa, Black Sheep, have you any wool?
Yes, Sir, yes, Sir, three bags full.

Mary Had a Little lamb

Ma - ry had a   lit - tle lamb,   lit - tle lamb,   lit - tle lamb.

Ma - ry had a   lit - tle lamb whose fleece was white as   snow.

Hip-Knee Song

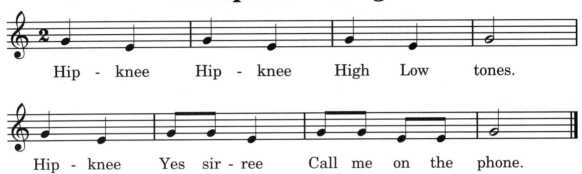

Hip - knee   Hip - knee   High   Low   tones.

Hip - knee   Yes sir - ree   Call me   on   the   phone.

So Mi Song

So   mi,   so   mi   my   lit - tle   song.

I   like   to   sing   my   so   mi   song.

Eency Weency Spider

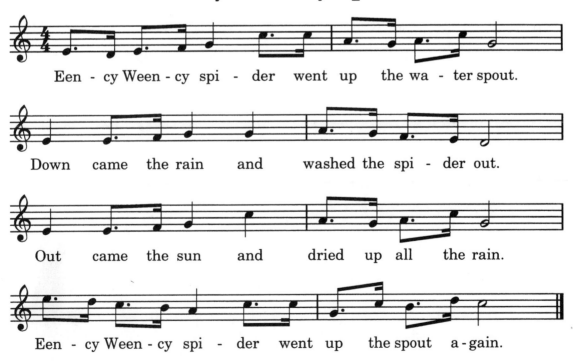

Een - cy Ween - cy spi - der   went up   the wa - ter spout.

Down   came   the rain   and   washed the spi - der out.

Out   came   the sun   and   dried   up   all   the rain.

Een - cy Ween - cy spi - der   went up   the spout a - gain.

Twinkle, Twinkle Little Star
Rhyming Words Cards

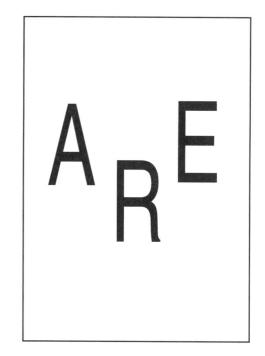

So-Mi Song*

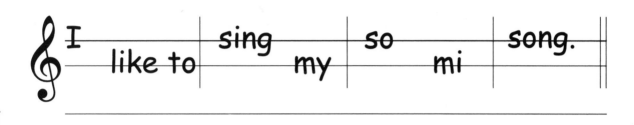

Your words: _____

_____

_____

_____

Hip-Knee Song

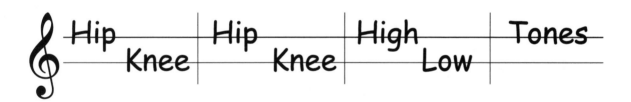

Your words: _____

_____

_____

*Try using other words that rhyme with So and Mi!

Rhyming Words for a Song
(Twinkle, Twinkle Little Star)

Fill in the blanks with the words that best fit the phrases below. Be sure the words rhyme.

I can count from one to _____.

Five cows, four pigs, and a _____.

Reading, writing, math and _____.

My report card was not _____.

I like school for it is _____.

It makes my day bright like the _____.

© 2001 by Parker Publishing Company

```
┌─────────────────────────────────────┐
│            Word Bank                 │
│                                      │
│   fun          ten          more     │
│                                      │
│   poor         sun          hen      │
└─────────────────────────────────────┘
```

Writing About Rhyming Words

Write about the words that rhyme in the song.

High/Low
(Thermometer and Temperature)

LESSON PLAN

Objective: Students will be able to recognize high and low pitches.

Materials: Piano and/or bells or xylophone
A ball
Copies of: High and Low Music page
             Music Thermometers page
             Composer Thermometers page
             Music and Thermometers page
Pencils and crayons

Procedure:

1. *Opening Activity:* Sing the "Thermometer Song" to the students. Have them mime fanning themselves and stand when you sing "Reading a thermometer as it goes up" and "When the temperature is hot it goes very high." Have the students shiver and sit when you sing "Reading the thermometer as it goes down" and "When it gets cold it goes very low."

2. *Listening Activity:* Continuously play "C" below middle "C" on the piano or on the tone bells. Have the students bend their knees or sit on their ankles when you play the low "C." Have the students stand up when they hear the high "C." Continue playing either high or low "C," but change the number of times you play each one.

3. *Singing Activity:* Sing "Bounce High, Bounce Low." Using a ball, or an imaginary one, have the students pass the ball around standing in a circle. When singing the word *high,* pass the ball high. When singing the word *low,* pass the ball low. Also, try "See-Saw, Margery Daw." Teach and sing the song. Have the students move to the pitches, pretending to see-saw (high for high notes and low for low notes).

4. *Listening Activity:* Give a Music Thermometers page to each student. Play various high and low pitches on the piano, xylophone, or bells. Direct the students to place a finger on the top line when they hear a high pitch or on the low line for a low pitch. (Add three more lines to the thermometer and you can use it for other music activities.)

Procedure:
(Continued)

5. ***Composition Activity:*** Give each student a copy of the Composer Thermometers page. Have the students color the glass tube part of the thermometers halfway up for a low pitch and the whole way up for a high pitch. Ask the students to try singing the song. Use bells, xylophone, or a piano (using only the two pitches So and Mi) to present the opportunity for the students to perform their own compositions. Mark the pitches on the instruments that students are permitted to use.

Activity Page:

Hand out a copy of the Music and Thermometers page to each student. Ask students to color only the thermometers that show notes high on the gauge.

HIGH AND LOW MUSIC
Thermometer Song

Read-ing   a   ther-mom - e - ter   as   it   goes right up.

Read-ing   a   ther-mom - e - ter   as   it   goes right down.

When your temper-a - ture   is   hot,   it   goes ver - y   high.

When your temper-a - ture   is   cold,   it   goes ver - y   low.

Bounce High, Bounce Low

Bounce high, bounce low.   Bounce the   ball   to   Shi - loh.

See-Saw, Margery Daw

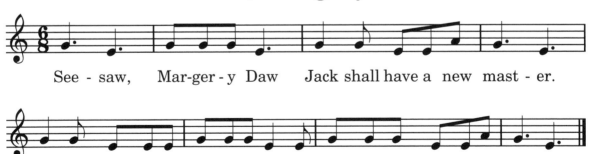

See - saw,   Mar-ger - y Daw   Jack shall have a new mast - er.

He shall have but a   pen-ny a day, be-cause he can't work a-ny fast-er.

Name _____

Music Thermometers

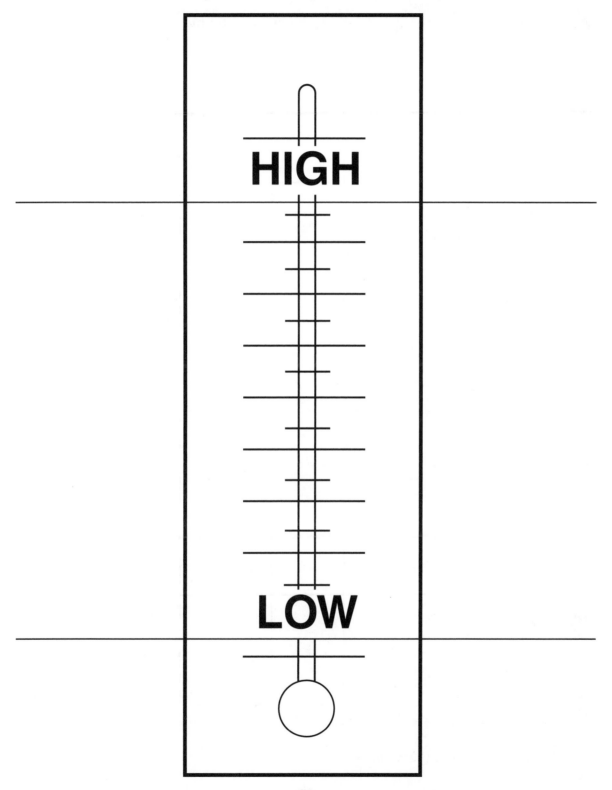

HIGH

LOW

Composer Thermometers

Color the four thermometers. Fill in the whole thermometer for high notes and fill in only half for low notes.

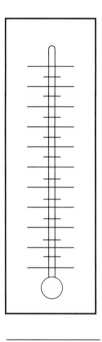 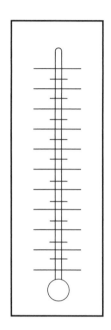

_____ _____

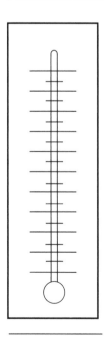 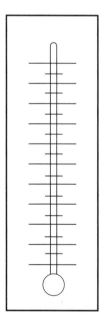

_____ _____

*Try adding words to your thermometer song!

© 2001 by Parker Publishing Company

Music and Thermometers

Color only the thermometers that have high notes.

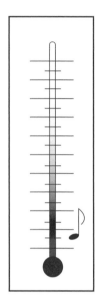
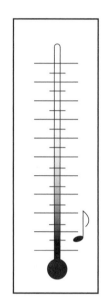
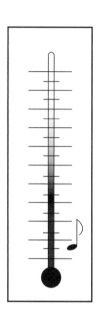
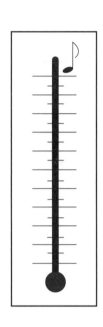

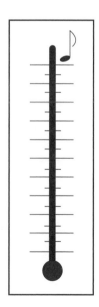
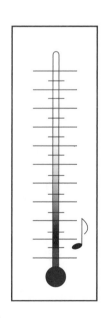
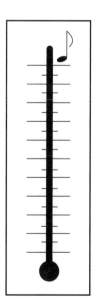
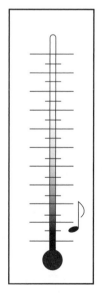

So and Mi
(Capital Letters)

LESSON PLAN

Objective: Students will be able to identify the So and Mi syllables.

Materials: Piano
Copies of: So and Mi Music page
Capital Letter Song page
So and Mi Hand Signals page
So and Mi Fill-In page
Song of _____ page

Procedure:
1. *Opening Activity:* Teach the class "Greeting Song." Have the class go round robin for the solo, so you can assess each student's ability to match pitches.

2. *Singing Activity:* Teach the students "Bumblebee." Have the students stand when singing So and crouch when singing Mi. Teach and sing "Color Song." Do the suggested motions.

3. *Hand Signal Activity:* Teach the student the hand signals to So and Mi. Use "Greeting Song" and "Bumblebee" for practice. Echo each phrase or measure with the class one at a time.

4. *Writing Activity:* Hand out a copy of the So and Mi Fill-in Page to each student. Ask the students to fill in the blanks with the correct music symbol using capital letters.

5. *Song Activity Page:* Give each student a copy of the Capital Letter Song Page. Have the students circle the lower-case letters of each song. Later, sing the song on So and Mi.

Activity Page: Give each student a copy of the Song of _____ activity page. Have the students write a sentence for the music line. Insist they use capital letters for the beginning of each sentence. It is important they capitalize the first letter of their first and last names. Finally, be sure to help them sing their song. Perhaps put the students into small groups and allow each one to sing his/her own song for the group.

SO AND MI MUSIC
Greeting Song

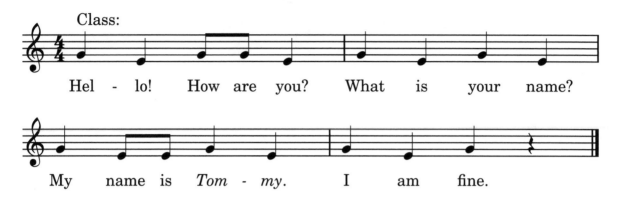

Hel - lo! How are you? What is your name?

My name is *Tom - my.* I am fine.

Bumblebee

Bee, bee, Bum-ble - bee, Tell me where your wed-ding be.

Color Song

Those who are wear-ing *red,* please *stand up.*
Those who are wear-ing *blue,* please *stand and jump.*
Those who are wear-ing *white,* please *turn a - round.*
An - y - one wear-ing *black,* please *bend your knees.*

So and Mi

Hand Signals

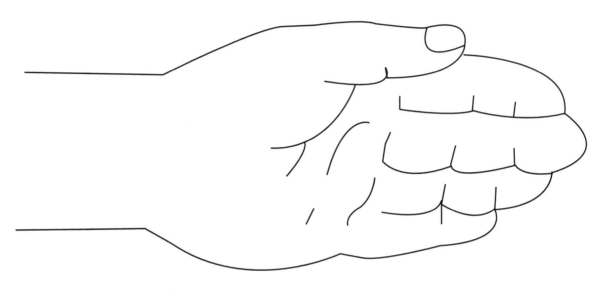

So
(Palm faces self)

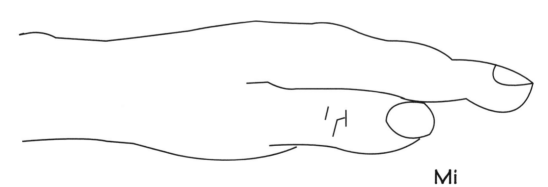

Mi
(Hand salute from upper chest)

So and Mi Fill-In Page

Using capital letters, fill in the blanks with the music syllables.

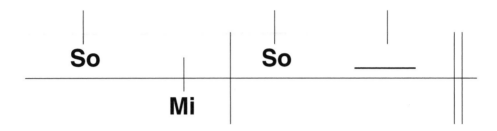

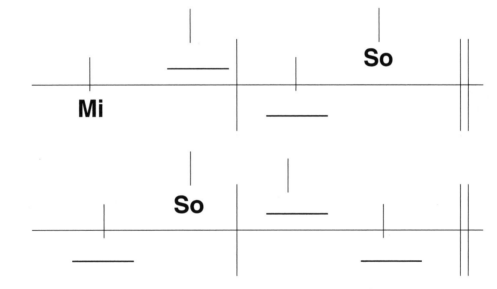

Name _____

Capital Letter Song Page

Circle the lower-case letters of each song.

Bumblebee

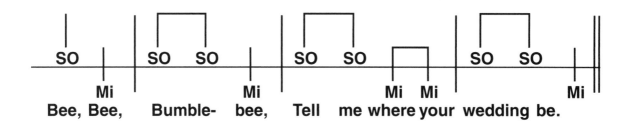

Greeting Song

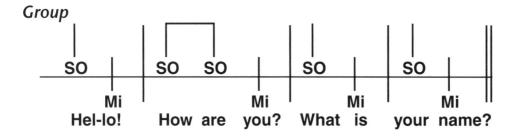

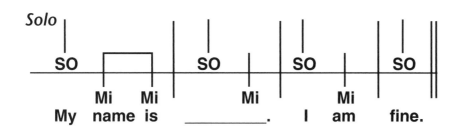

Song of _____
(Your Name)

Write a two-sentence song. Begin each sentence with a capital letter.

So | **So**
Mi | **Mi**

_____ _____ _____ _____ ∎

So | **So**
Mi | **Mi**

_____ _____ _____ _____ ∎

Instrument Families
(Families)

LESSON PLAN

Objective: Students will be able to identify and distinguish the instrument families.

Materials: Piano
Copies of: Music page
            nine instrument drawings from the Instruments lesson
            Instrument Page
            Brass Family Circle page
            Woodwind Family Circle page
            String Family Circle page
            Percussion Family Circle page
            Instrument Family Tree

Procedure: 1. *Opening Activity:* Sing "Ten Little Flutes." Ask the students to name other instruments. Sing the song again using the instruments named by the students. You may want to add the playing motions of each instrument.

2. *Discovery Activity:* Using the nine instrument drawings from the Instruments/Size Lesson, mix up the instruments and place them at various stations in the room. Be sure to copy enough instruments for groups of two to four students. Discuss the instrument families and their characteristics. Make comparisons between human and instrument families. After grouping the students, have them divide the instruments into families. Have each group explain why they chose the groupings they did.

3. *Cut-Out Activity:* Give each student a copy of the Instrument Page and the Brass, Percussion, Woodwind, and String Family Circles pages. Have the students cut out and glue each instrument and place it in the correct family circle.

4. *Instrument Construction Activity:* This activity can be done individually or in groups. Have the students choose to make a string family instrument or a percussion family instrument. Various ideas for instruments are listed on the next page.

Procedure:
(Continued)

a. String instruments:

- a decorated box with tight and loose or long and short rubber bands

- a can with strings or rubber bands stretched across the open end

- a frame of wood with strings stretched across

b. Percussion instruments:

- a decorated can with a plastic lid head

- long and short metal pipes or bars dangling from strings

- a can or cup with seeds or pebbles with paper glued over the open end to create a shaker

- jars containing different amounts of water with a stick to tap the rims of the jars

5. ***Performance Activity:*** Using the instruments made during the previous activity, have the students play their instruments. Perhaps have the students write out their music. The string instrument makers can write out simple high, middle, and low notation on two lines of music by placing dots on the spaces.

Activity Page: Give a copy of the Instrument Family Tree to each student. Have them use the instruments given to assist in placing the instruments on the lines under the correct instrument families.

Ten Little Flutes

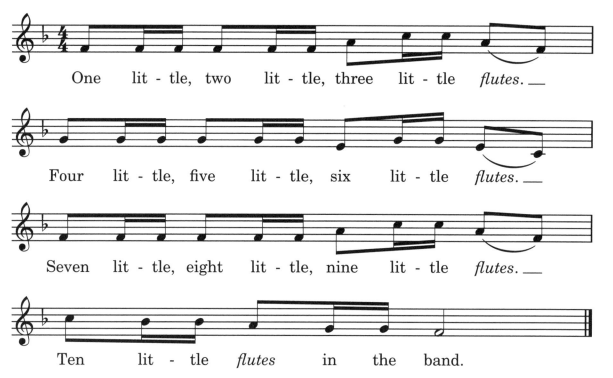

One   lit - tle, two   lit - tle, three   lit - tle   *flutes.* __

Four   lit - tle, five   lit - tle, six   lit - tle   *flutes.* __

Seven   lit - tle, eight   lit - tle, nine   lit - tle   *flutes.* __

Ten   lit - tle   *flutes*   in   the   band.

Instrument Page

Cut out each instrument below and glue it in the correct instrument family circle.

Trumpet

Flute

Cymbals

Clarinet

Trombone

String Bass

Cello

Violin

Bass Drum

French Horn

Tuba

Bassoon

Saxophone

Viola

Snare Drum

Name _____

Brass Family Circle
Characteristics and Traits

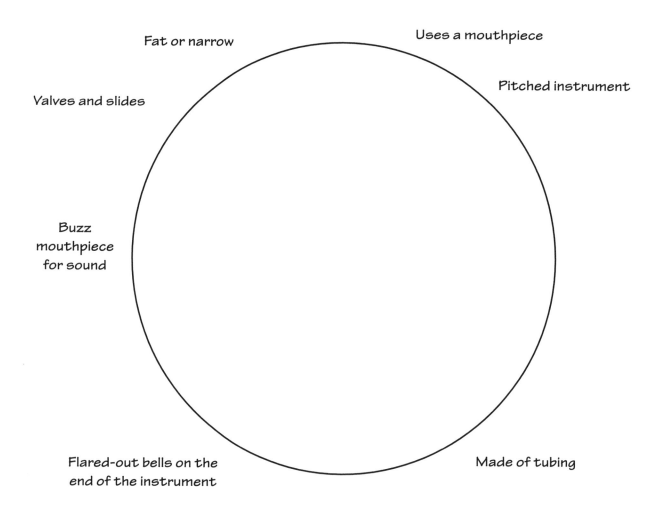

Made of brass

Can play very loud

Fat or narrow

Uses a mouthpiece

Valves and slides

Pitched instrument

Buzz
mouthpiece
for sound

Flared-out bells on the
end of the instrument

Made of tubing

Name _____

Woodwind Family Circle
Characteristics and Traits

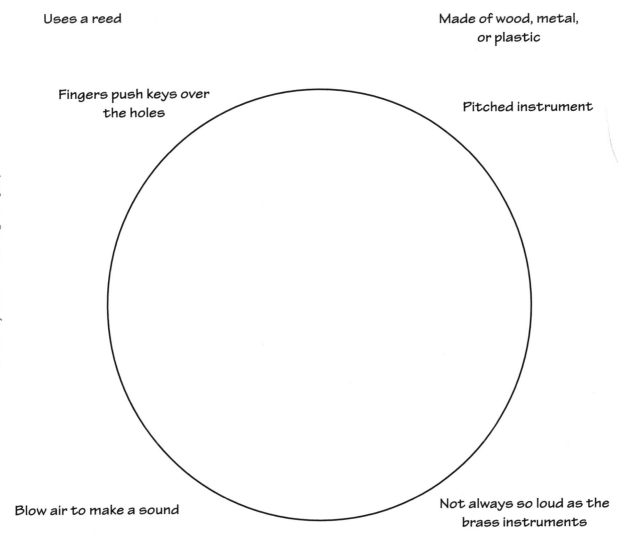

Uses a reed

Made of wood, metal,
or plastic

Fingers push keys over
the holes

Pitched instrument

Blow air to make a sound

Not always so loud as the
brass instruments

As you cover more holes, the
pitch usually goes lower

String Family Circle
Characteristics and Traits

Made of Wood

Can be plucked or bowed

Uses strings

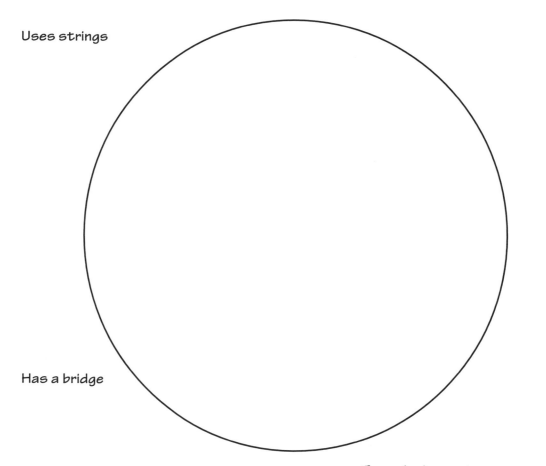

Has a bridge

Tunes by loosening or stretching

Has a post inside to help produce the sound

Percussion Family Circle
Characteristics and Traits

Is played by striking, shaking, or scraping

Pitched or non-pitched

Can be big or small

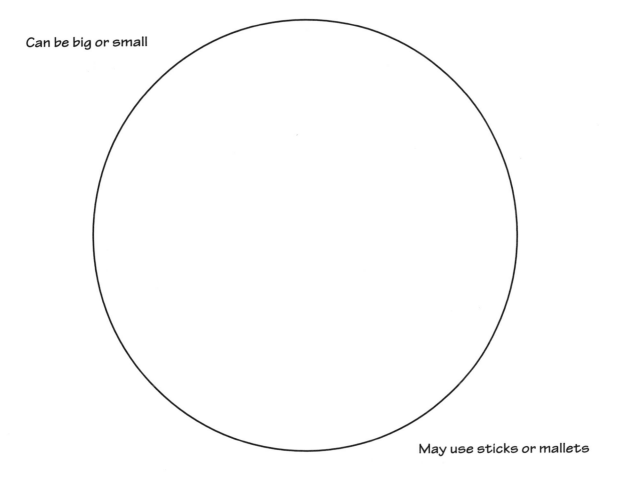

May use sticks or mallets

Made of wood, metal, or plastic

Instrument Family Tree

Place the instrument names on the lines under their instrument family.

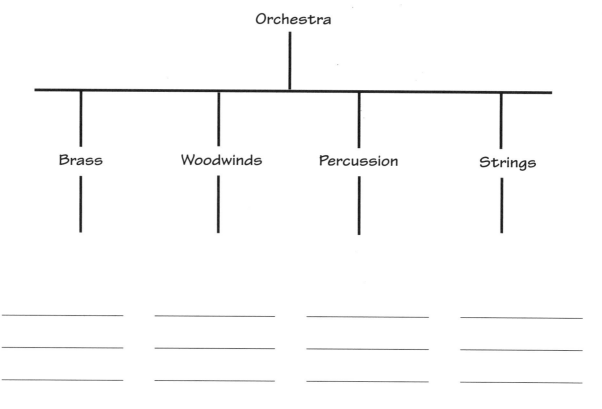

WORD BOX

Clarinet	Snare Drum	Trombone	Violin
Trumpet	Flute	String Bass	French Horn
Saxophone	Tuba	Bass Drum	Cello
Viola	Cymbals	Triangle	Harp

Contrasts
(Antonyms)

LESSON PLAN

Objective: Students will identify contrasts in music.

Materials: Piano
Copies of: Contrasts Music page
           Music Boy Song page
           Music Antonym Treasure Map
           Antonyms and Music Contrasts pages
           Find the Antonyms or Contrasts page
           Contrast Wordsearch

Procedure: 1. *Opening Activity:* Sing "All Night, All Day" for the students. Ask the students: "What is the song about? What is the difference between night and day? They are opposites or complete contrasts, yes? What is another word for opposites? . . . Antonyms." Teach the song, and possibly, add motions. Sing the song.

2. *Listening Activity:* Teach "Walking, Walking" to the students. Then use the words *running, running,* but play the song faster. Ask the students what the opposites or antonyms are in the song.

3. *Listening Activity:* Teach "Teddy Bear" to the students. Give each student a copy of the Music Boy Song page. Have the students sing the first song at the top of the page together. At the bottom of the song, have the students fill in the blanks with the antonyms of the top song.

4. *Map Activity:* Give each student a Music Antonym Treasure Map. Instruct the students to draw a line down the path that passes over all music antonyms. If the words are not antonyms, then one cannot pass. The path that goes through all music antonyms leads to the treasure.

5. *Identification Activity:* Give each student a copy of the Antonyms and Music Contrasts page and the Find the Antonyms or Contrasts pages. Instruct the students to write the antonym or contrasting word to each picture. Have the student draw a straight line from one word to its antonym or contrasting word on the Antonyms and Contrasts pages. These pages can be used by students to help complete each one.

Activity Page: Give each student a copy of the Contrast Wordsearch. Have the students search for each antonym or contrasting word.

CONTRASTS MUSIC
All Night, All Day

All night, all __ day an-gels watch-ing ov-er me my Lord.

All night, all __ day an-gels watch-ing ov-er me.

Walking, Walking

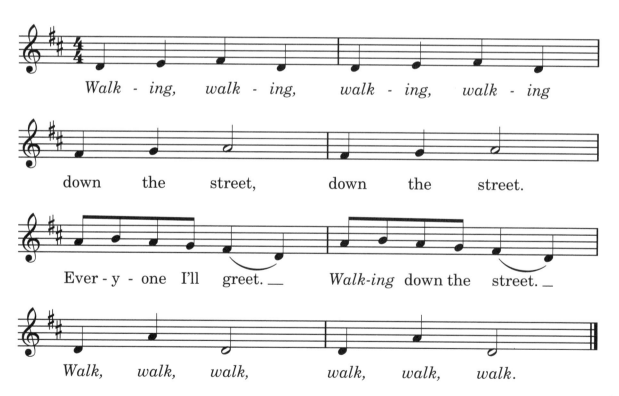

Walk - ing, walk - ing, walk - ing, walk - ing

down the street, down the street.

Ever - y - one I'll greet. __ Walk-ing down the street. __

Walk, walk, walk, walk, walk, walk.

Music Boy

Mu - sic *Boy*, Mu - sic *Boy*, play ver - y *loud.* __

Mu - sic *Boy*, Mu - sic *Boy*, play ver - y *slow.*

Mu - sic *Boy*, Mu - sic *Boy*, play ver - y *short.* __

Mu - sic *Boy*, Mu - sic *Boy*, play ver - y *low.*

Teddy Bear
(Music Boy)

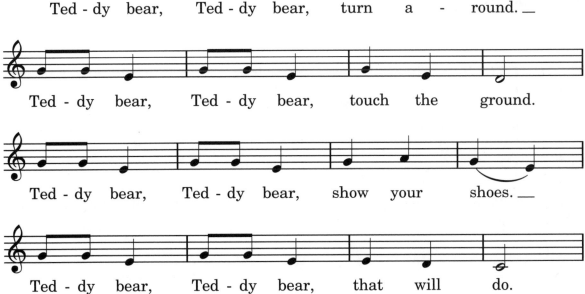

Ted - dy bear, Ted - dy bear, turn a - round. __

Ted - dy bear, Ted - dy bear, touch the ground.

Ted - dy bear, Ted - dy bear, show your shoes. __

Ted - dy bear, Ted - dy bear, that will do.

Music Boy Song

Music Boy, Music Boy, play very loud.

Music Boy, Music Boy, play very slow.

Music Boy, Music Boy, play very short.

Music Boy, Music Boy, play very low.

Fill in the blanks with the antonyms listed below the song.

Music Boy Song

Music Boy, Music Boy, play very _____.

Music Boy, Music Boy, play very _____.

Music Boy, Music Boy, play very _____.

Music Boy, Music Boy, play very _____.

© 2001 by Parker Publishing Company

| long | fast | quiet | high |

*What other antonyms or contrasting words could be used in the words or title of the song?

Name _____

Music Antonym Treasure Map

Find the treasure by using the antonyms in the map directions. Find the antonyms in the order of the map directions.

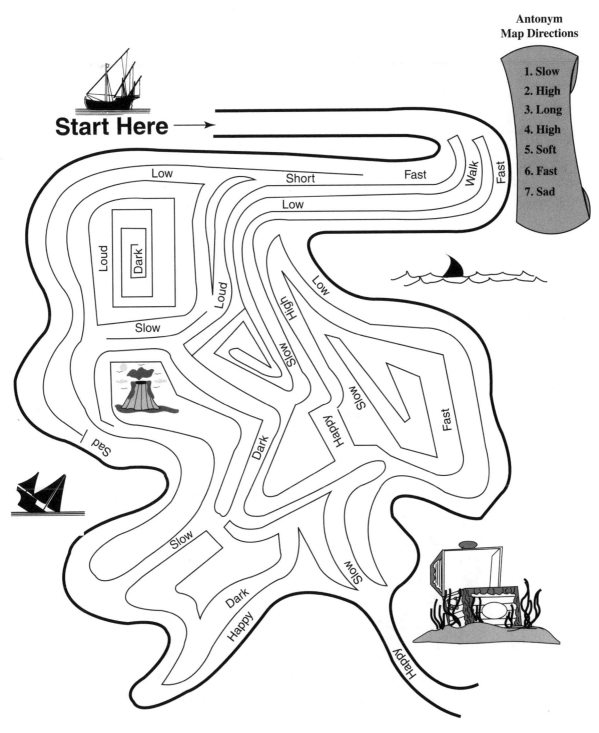

Antonym Map Directions

1. Slow
2. High
3. Long
4. High
5. Soft
6. Fast
7. Sad

Start Here →

© 2001 by Parker Publishing Company

95

Antonyms and Music Contrasts

Put an "X" beside each picture that is an antonym or opposite of the word below it.

Loud

High

Dark

Long

Slow

Little

Antonyms and Music Contrasts

Put an "X" beside each picture that shows antonyms or opposites.

_____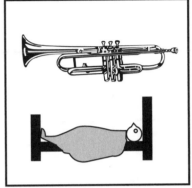

Loud/Quiet

 _____

High/Low

_____

Bright/Dark

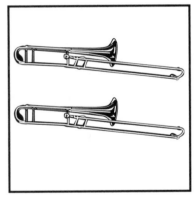 _____

Short/Long

_____

Fast/Slow

 _____

Big/Little

Find the Antonyms or Contrasts

Draw a line between the antonyms or contrasts below.

1. Loud   High

2. Fast   Little

3. Low   Soft

4. Big   Slow

5. Dark   Happy

6. Sad   Thin

7. Up   Run

8. Walk   Down

9. Tall   Light

10. Fat   Short

Contrast Wordsearch

Find each word in this puzzle and circle it.
The words can be found forward and backward.

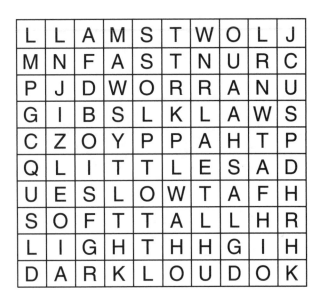

L	L	A	M	S	T	W	O	L	J
M	N	F	A	S	T	N	U	R	C
P	J	D	W	O	R	R	A	N	U
G	I	B	S	L	K	L	A	W	S
C	Z	O	Y	P	P	A	H	T	P
Q	L	I	T	T	L	E	S	A	D
U	E	S	L	O	W	T	A	F	H
S	O	F	T	T	A	L	L	H	R
L	I	G	H	T	H	H	G	I	H
D	A	R	K	L	O	U	D	O	K

Big	Little
Loud	Soft
Dark	Light
Tall	Small
High	Low
Fast	Slow
Happy	Sad
Fat	Narrow
Run	Walk

Contrast Wordsearch

(Answer Key)

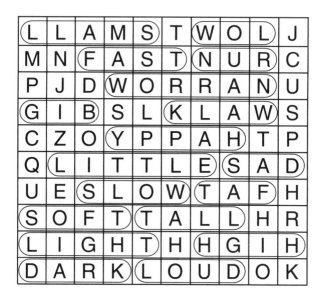

So-Mi-La
(Maps)

LESSON PLAN

Objective: Students will identify the melodic syllable "La."

Materials: Piano
Scissors
Pencils
Copies of: So-Mi-La Music page
So-Mi-La Cards page
Music Class Map
La La Land page
Music Stairs page
A Song With LAs page
Chalkboard

Procedure: 1. *Opening Activity:* Teach "Doggie, Doggie." Play the game: Choose a student to stand and hide his/her eyes, or use a blindfold. Give the bone (from the So-Mi-La page) to another student in the class. Sing the song with the appropriately assigned parts, and the blindfolded student must guess who has the bone. The blindfolded student selects the next student by giving the bone out to someone. The student who had the bone is now blindfolded.

2. *Singing Activity:* Teach "Where Is the La?" Give each student a copy of the Music Class Map page and a "La" card from the So-Mi-La page. Put the students into pairs. Have one student cover his/her eyes while the other hides the card somewhere in the room. The student who hid the card must make a map to help the other student find the card. The map-making student sings the first part of the song, and the other student sings the second part. Once the student finds the La card, the students switch roles. Continue the game as often as you wish; perhaps, switch pairs.

3. *Singing Activity:* Teach and sing "One, Two, Tie My Shoe." Add motions. Possibly, teach the La hand signal and have the students raise it when singing even numbers.

4. *Reading Activity:* Using the Music Stairs and the So-Fa syllable notes, place SO on the fifth stairstep and MI on the third. Show the students where LA falls in relation to SO and MI. Teach the rule: If SO is on a space, LA is on the line above SO. If SO is

Procedure:
(Continued)

on a line, then LA is on the space above SO. Place SO on a different step. Have the students locate MI and LA on the stairs. After using the music stairs, put a music staff on the board and show the students how to read LA. Move SO around and continue the activity.

5. ***Writing Activity:*** Hand out a copy of the La, La Land page to each student. Have the students write in LA on the correct line or space. Remind the students of the rule from activity #4.

Activity Page:

Give each student a copy of "A Song With LAs." Have the students write in SOs, MIs, and LAs to complete the composition. Encourage the students to sing the song and perform it on an instrument. Perhaps put the song on an opaque projector or overhead so the entire class can try singing each other's songs.

SO-MI-LA MUSIC
Doggie, Doggie

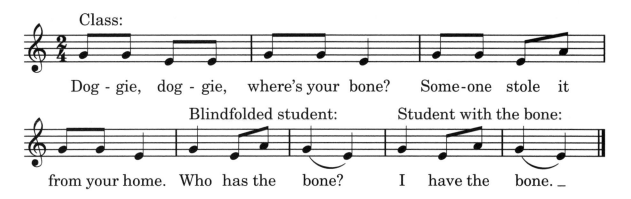

Class:

Dog - gie, dog - gie, where's your bone? Some-one stole it

Blindfolded student: Student with the bone:

from your home. Who has the bone? I have the bone. _

Where Is the "La"?

Mapmaker   "La" Searcher

Where is the "La"?   Is the "La" here?

Responses:

No, the "La" is not.   Yes, the "La" is there.

One, Two, Tie My shoe

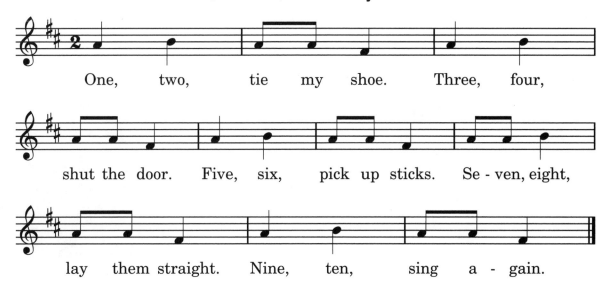

One, two, tie my shoe. Three, four,

shut the door. Five, six, pick up sticks. Se - ven, eight,

lay them straight. Nine, ten, sing a - gain.

So-Mi-La

Cards

Music Class Map

Draw windows, doors, shelves, desks, and anything else you think will help your partner find the missing syllable.

La La Land

Place LA on the staff as you walk around La La Land.

Music Stairs

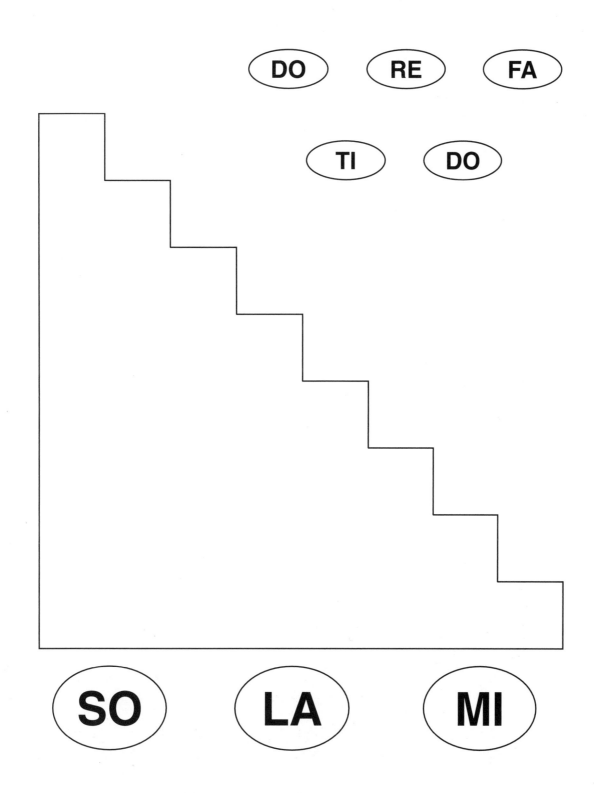

A Song with LAs

Using two tahs (♩) in a measure, compose a song with SOs, MIs, and LAs.

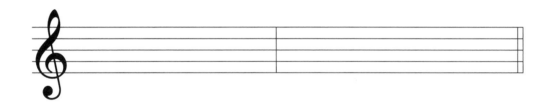

*Try singing your song. Perhaps try playing your song on a set of bells. Extra idea—add words to your song.

Form
(Geometric Shapes)

LESSON PLAN

Objective: Students will identify and perform AB and ABA forms.

Materials: Piano
Scissors
Pencils
Copies of: Form Music page
        Form Shapes page
        Other Form Shapes page
        Find the Sections page
        Shapes and Music Form page

Procedure: 1. **Opening Activity:** Sing "Good Night, Ladies" to the class. Teach "Merrily We Roll Along." Then, sing "Good Night, Ladies" again. Immediately after, have the class sing "Merrily We Roll Along." Explain to the class that music has form, a design. It can be made up of sections. Ask: "How many sections did the song we sing have?" Lead the class to the correct answer. Using the triangle and the circle from the Form Shapes page, have a student raise the triangle for "Good Night, Ladies" and the circle for "Merrily We Roll Along," and split the class and sing the songs.

2. **Listening Activity:** Teach "Bluebird" to the students. Also teach the motions. Have the students sit, form hands into a bird, use pointer fingers to shape a window, and spread out arms in a question position for section A. Have the girls stand and tap a boy on the shoulder for the words "Choose a little boy" and vice versa during section B. Use the triangle and circle to explain the form of this song. But before using the shapes, ask the students if they know how many sections the song has. Explain to the class that it has two sections and we call it AB form.

3. **Listening Activity:** Teach "Oh, Susanna" to the class. Put the students into small groups. Ask the students if the song is in two sections, could we call it AB form, and if it is not AB, then what is the name of the form? Be sure they can distinguish the second section from the first. Make enough copies of the Form Shapes page with the triangle and circle for each student. Cut out and laminate the shapes. Sing the songs and have the students raise the triangle for section A at the beginning, and the circle at section B. Be sure to count off before students raise the cards or close their eyes, so they don't copycat their fellow students' responses.

Procedure:
(Continued)

4. ***Movement Activity:*** Teach "Looby Loo." Form a circle with the students. Have the students move around in the circle while they sing the chorus, and do the body motions while standing still during the verses. Focus on the ABA form. Ask the students how many sections make up the song. "Do any sections repeat? Which part?"

5. ***Movement Activity:*** Teach "Shoo, Fly." Put the students into groups of four or five. Have each group form a circle. During the verse, have the groups reverse the circle. When returning to the first section of the song, have the group return the circle to its original direction. Using the form shapes of the triangle and the circle, have the students determine the sections of the song and raise the correct form shape as they sing the song.

6. ***Listening Activity:*** Give each student a copy of the Find the Sections of an AB Song page. Have each student draw a shape where section A begins and a different shape where section B begins. Review the song first, but have the students think the song silently to find the sections.

Activity Page:

Hand out a copy of the Shapes and Form page to each student. Have the students circle the groups of shapes that represent AB form. At the bottom section of the page, have the students draw their own combinations of shapes to represent ABA form.

FORM MUSIC
Good Night, Ladies; Merrily We Roll Along

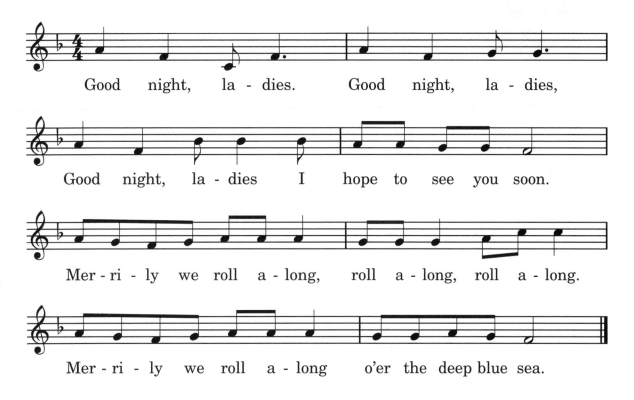

Good night, la - dies. Good night, la - dies,

Good night, la - dies I hope to see you soon.

Mer - ri - ly we roll a - long, roll a - long, roll a - long.

Mer - ri - ly we roll a - long o'er the deep blue sea.

Bluebird

112

Oh, Susanna

Foster

Verse

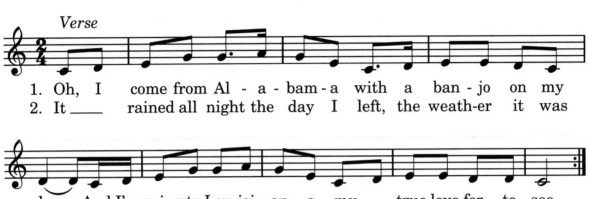

1. Oh, I come from Al - a - bam - a with a ban - jo on my
2. It ___ rained all night the day I left, the weath-er it was

knee. And I'm going to Lou-isi - an - a my ___ true love for to see.
dry. The _ sun so hot I froze to death Su - san - na don't you cry.

Refrain

Oh, Su - san - na, oh, don't you cry for me. ___ I ___

come from Al - a - ba - ma with a ban - jo on my knee.

Looby Loo

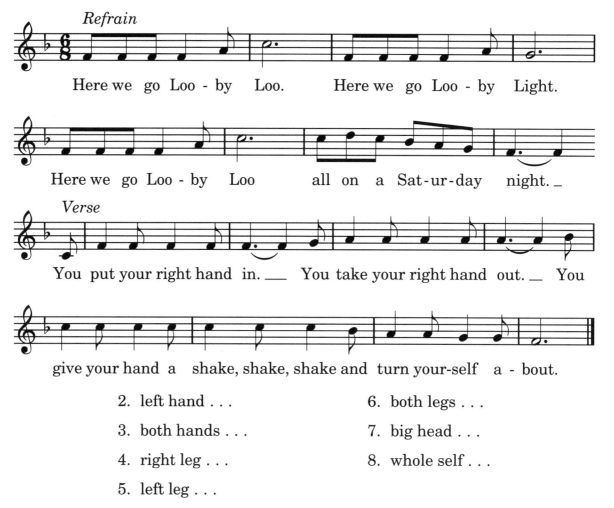

Refrain

Here we go Loo - by Loo. Here we go Loo - by Light.

Here we go Loo - by Loo all on a Sat-ur-day night. _

Verse

You put your right hand in. _ You take your right hand out. _ You

give your hand a shake, shake, shake and turn your-self a - bout.

2. left hand . . .	6. both legs . . .
3. both hands . . .	7. big head . . .
4. right leg . . .	8. whole self . . .
5. left leg . . .	

Shoo, Fly!

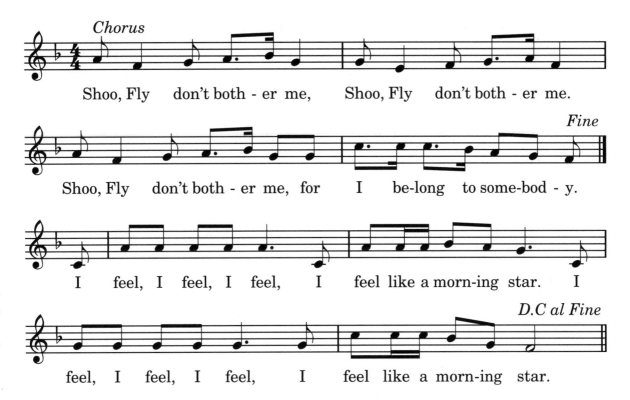

Shoo, Fly don't both - er me, Shoo, Fly don't both - er me.

Shoo, Fly don't both - er me, for I be-long to some-bod - y.

I feel, I feel, I feel, I feel like a morn-ing star. I

feel, I feel, I feel, I feel like a morn-ing star.

Form Shapes

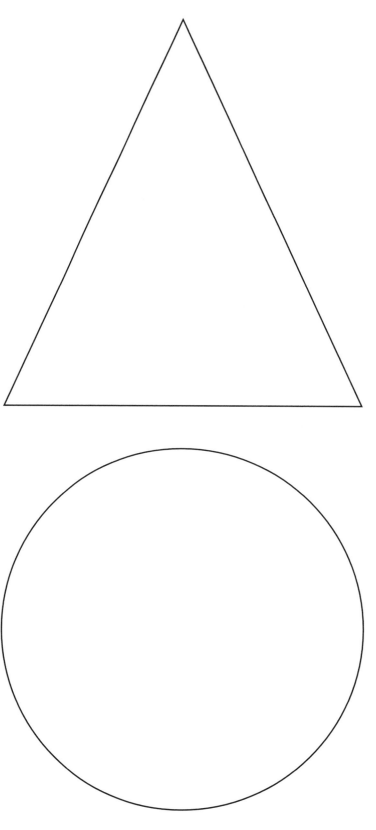

Other Form Shapes

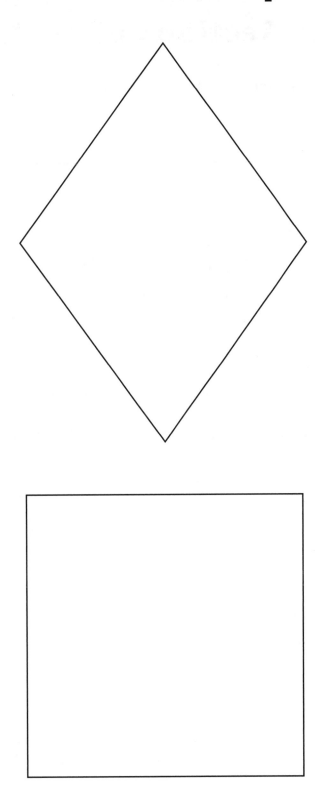

Find the Sections of an AB Song

Place a shape at section A of this song. Place a different shape at the beginning of section B.

Yankee Doodle

Yankee Doodle went to town a-riding on a pony.

Stuck a feather in his cap and called it macaroni.

Yankee Doodle keep it up. Yankee Doodle dandy.

Mind the music and the step and with the girls be handy.

Name _____

Shapes and Music Form

Circle the groups of two shapes that could be an AB form.

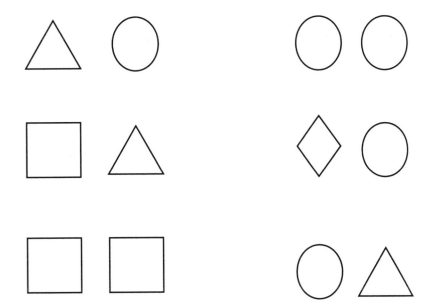

Draw three (3) examples of ABA form. Use any shapes.

Beats per Measure
(Addition)

LESSON PLAN

Objective: Students will recognize the number of beats per measure.

Materials: Piano
Pencils
Tape or magnet tape
Chalkboard
Copies of: Music page
     Large Rhythm Cards
     Small Rhythm Cards
     Adding Notes page

Procedure:

1. *Opening Activity:* Echo clap the rhythms on the music page.

2. *Singing Activity:* Teach and sing "Bingo." Have the students tap their legs to the beat. Sing the numbers one and two to the melody of the song to emphasize the number of beats in a measure.

3. *Singing Activity:* Teach and sing "Yankee Doodle." Again, reword the song with the numbers 1, 2, 3, and 4 to emphasize four beats in a measure.

4. *Review Activity:* Using the Large Rhythm Cards, display each rhythm card to the students and ask how many beats each one gets. Teach and sing "Adding Song." In call-and-response style, allow the class to sing the group line, and the teacher sings the teacher line. Vary the numbers for adding and the soloists. Have the soloist pick the next person during the last line of music.

5. *Note-Adding Activity:* Photocopy numerous copies (eight to ten) of the Large Rhythm Cards page. Using magnets or tape, attach combinations of rhythm cards on the board for the students to add the number of beats.

    Examples: quarter note + quarter note = 2 beats.
        (1 beat)   (1 beat)
        quarter note + half note = 3 beats.
        (1 beat)   (2 beats)

Procedure:
(Continued)

6. ***Partner Activity:*** Photocopy two to four of the Small Rhythm Cards page (put the number of beats the note is worth on the back of each card). Be sure to have enough copies for each student to have a pack of cards. Put the students into groups of two. Have one student place notes into an addition problem. The other student figures out the answer, or the sum, of the problem. Depending on the level of the class, try using more than two numbers to add. Draw a minus sign on the back of the plus sign, and this activity can be used for subtraction.

Activity Page:

Give each student a copy of the Adding Notes page. Instruct the students to find the sum, or answer, to each note-addition problem.

Adding Song

Class:

Can you add two num - bers?

Solo:

I can add two num - bers.

Teacher:

One plus *one* e - quals what? _____

Solo:

One plus *one* e - quals *two.* _____

1.   2.   3.

4.   5.

Solo:

Now I pick _____ _____
(next person's name)

Bingo

There was a far-mer had a dog and Bin-go was his name - o.
One, two   One, two   One, two   One, two

B - I - N - G - O   B - I - N - G - O
One, two   One, two   One, two   One, two

B - I - N - G - O and Bin - go was his name - o.
One, two   One, two   One, two   One, two

Yankee Doodle

Verse

Yan-kee Doo-dle   went to town a - rid-ing on a   po - ny.

Stuck a fea-ther   in his cap and called it ma-ca - ro - ni.

Chorus

Yan - kee Doo-dle   keep it up,   Yan - kee Doo-dle   dan - dy.

Mind the mu - sic   and the steps and   with the girls be   han - dy.

123

Large Rhythm Cards

Small Rhythm Cards

Name _____

Adding Notes

Add the following notes.

Example 1: ♩ + ♩ = <u>2</u>

Example 2: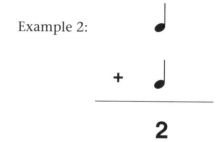

1. ♩ + Z = _____

2. ♩ + ♩ = _____

3. ♩ + ♩ = _____

4. ♩ + Z = _____

5. ♩ + ♩ + ♩ = _____

6. ♩   7. ♩   8. ♩   9. Z   10. ♩

+ ♩   + ♩   + ♩   + Z   + Z

_____   _____   _____   _____   _____

11. ♩ + ♫ = _____   13. ♫
                              + ♩
12. ♫ + ♩ = _____   _____

Supplementary Materials
(K–2)

Famous Americans in Music

Careers in Music

Music and George Washington (1732–1799)

Music and Abraham Lincoln (1809–1865)

Strong & Weak Beats and Number of Beats (activity sheet)

Playing Instruments by Push and Pull (activity sheet)

Instrument Family Word Finds
    Instrument Family Word Finds (answer key)

Instrument Family Sandwiches

Instrument Connect-the-Dots

Adding Beats and Notes (activity sheet)

Note Values & Time (activity sheet)

Beats per Measure Trains (pattern)

Music Dice Games and Activities
    Music Die, Point Note and Composer Pieces
    Musicland (gameboard)

Notes & Beats and Subtraction (activity sheet)

So-Mi (exercise sheet)

So-Mi-La (exercise sheet)

Treble Clef Puzzle

Barlines, Beats, and Measures (activity sheet)

Musical Antonym Treasure Map

Daily Music Skill Builders
    Daily Singing (Pitch) Skill Builders 1–25
    Daily Rhythm Skill Builders 1–25

Interdisciplinary Planner

FAMOUS AMERICANS IN MUSIC

Aaron Copland (1900–1992), born in New York City, New York, was one of America's greatest composers. His music used melodies from well-known American folk songs. He was best known for his ballets: *Rodeo, Billy the Kid,* and *Appalachian Spring.*

Stephen Foster (1826–1864), born near Pittsburgh, Pennsylvania, was a composer of the pop music of his day. His music was influenced by the working slaves singing spirituals, everyday workers singing work songs and folk songs, and the enjoyment he got from singing and playing the guitar and piano with his sisters. He was best known for his songs: "My Old Kentucky Home," "Swanee River," "Jeannie with the Light Brown Hair," and "Oh! Susanna."

George Gershwin (1898–1937), born in Brooklyn, New York, was the American composer who combined jazz with classical music. Aside from his jazz and classical style, he and his brother Ira wrote for many Broadway shows. He was best known for: *Rhapsody in Blue, Summertime, Porgy and Bess,* and *Swanee.*

Scott Joplin (1868–1917), born in Texarkana, Texas, was known as the "King of Ragtime." His "honky tonk" style became popular during the turn of the twentieth century. He was one of the first African-American composers to gain such popularity among all people in America. His music includes: "Maple Leaf Rag" and "The Entertainer."

John Philip Sousa (1854–1932), born in Washington, D.C., son of a band director, was known as the "March King." He became the director of the United States Marine Corps Band. Among his best known works were: "Stars and Stripes Forever," *El Capitan,* and "The High School Cadets."

Careers in Music

Composer

A composer writes music for orchestras, groups of instruments, individual instruments, singers, movies, television, churches, recordings, and many other purposes.

Musician

A musician plays or performs music for movies, television, shows, recordings, concerts, churches, weddings, special events, and just for him-/herself.

Music Salesperson

A music salesperson sells music and musical instruments at a store, through the mail or the Internet, or by traveling to schools and businesses.

Music Teacher

Music teachers include teachers at elementary schools, middle schools, high schools, colleges; music stores; professional musicians; band, orchestra, and chorus directors; and private tutors.

Other Music Careers

Other music careers include music directors, musician management/agents, sound engineers, electronic music engineers, music instrument manufacturers, music historians, music arrangers, music transcribers, and music publishers.

Music and George Washington
(1732–1799)

What was going on in music during George Washington's life?

- Bach, Mozart, and Beethoven lived, performed, and composed music throughout Europe.

- The orchestra included the four families of instruments: brass, woodwinds, percussion, and strings.

- Opera was becoming more popular during this time.

- The piano was overtaking the harpsichord and clavichord in popularity.

- Mozart used the "Twinkle, Twinkle Little Star" melody for one of his compositions.

- Music, like buildings and other forms of architecture, was often symmetrical. What one could see or hear on one side could be seen or heard on the other side.

Can you name other famous Americans who lived during the lifetimes of Bach, Mozart, and Beethoven?

What were some famous events that took place during the time all the people listed above were living?

Name _____

Music and Abraham Lincoln
(1809–1865)

Below are the people who lived and events that took place during the life of Abraham Lincoln, the sixteenth President of the United States.

- Beethoven (German), Tchaikovsky (Russian), Stephen Foster (American), and John Philip Sousa (American) were a few of the composers who lived during Lincoln's lifetime.

- Ballet was quite popular (*The Nutcracker, Swan Lake,* and *Giselle*).

- Music became very emotional and passionate. This period of time was called "Romantic."

- Very soft, very loud, very low, very high, very slow, and very fast were characteristics of the exaggerations in music at the time.

- The concert harp, as we know it today, became more popular.

- The piano was very popular. The world's finest and greatest composers were composing for the piano. Some of the world's all-time great pianists performed on the piano at this time.

What were some famous events that took place during the time all the people listed above were living?

Strong & Weak Beats
and Number of Beats

Color the strong beats of the following song.

Rain, Rain Go Away

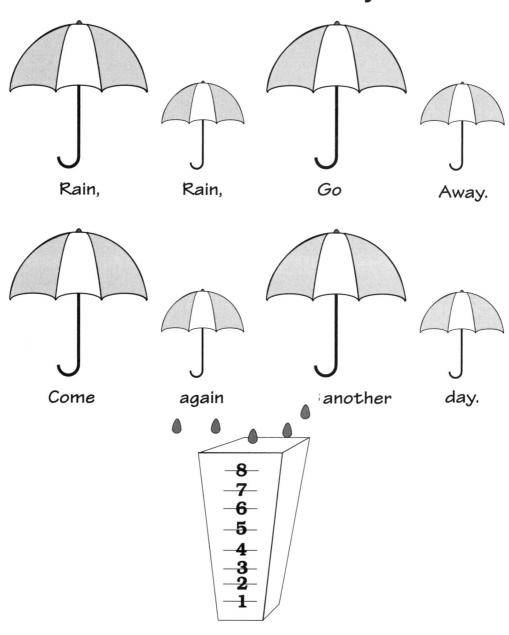

Rain,   Rain,   Go   Away.

Come   again   another   day.

8
7
6
5
4
3
2
1

Circle the number of beats in "Rain, Rain Go Away" on your rain gauge.

Name _____

Playing Musical Instruments by Push and Pull

How do these instruments work? Do you push or pull or bow?

Trumpet

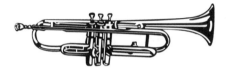

Tuba

Trombone

Clarinet

Saxophone

Gong

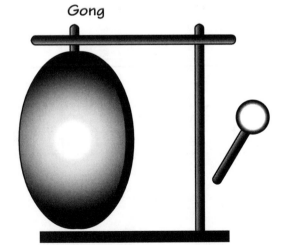

Instrument Family Word Finds

Brass

T	R	U	M	P	E	T	A	B	N
C	C	T	R	O	P	R	F	N	R
H	R	O	N	W	V	O	P	H	O
Z	F	G	I	T	T	M	A	O	H
C	Y	X	N	E	V	B	A	C	H
E	R	H	N	I	U	O	W	U	C
T	R	R	U	T	P	N	O	N	N
K	O	P	U	I	R	E	K	W	E
C	C	T	W	C	B	F	A	Z	R
F	R	E	N	T	H	Q	R	I	F

TRUMPET
TROMBONE
TUBA
FRENCH HORN
CORNET

Woodwinds

S	A	X	O	P	H	O	N	E	K
T	S	N	P	B	H	C	F	D	G
R	W	O	F	R	E	N	C	K	R
P	C	C	L	A	R	I	N	E	T
I	A	O	U	Q	J	F	O	T	B
C	O	M	T	I	U	N	O	R	A
C	T	E	E	P	R	I	S	U	S
O	N	O	E	R	N	E	S	M	C
L	B	R	G	Z	N	U	A	B	O
O	B	U	U	N	T	W	B	Z	N

FLUTE
PICCOLO
CLARINET
SAXOPHONE
BASSOON
OBOE

Strings

S	N	H	V	O	E	A	N	W	M
C	E	L	L	O	N	L	U	R	O
A	R	L	U	N	J	A	R	E	P
S	Q	E	V	T	R	N	D	R	E
S	T	R	I	N	G	B	A	S	S
O	F	C	O	N	E	H	L	B	R
N	C	R	L	B	A	S	O	O	A
W	G	U	I	T	A	R	I	V	N
M	N	N	N	R	O	E	V	I	U
P	P	E	F	G	A	H	I	K	R

VIOLIN
VIOLA
CELLO
STRING BASS
HARP
GUITAR
BANJO

Percussion

J	N	O	W	H	B	O	M	R	Q
U	U	T	R	I	A	N	G	L	E
F	C	S	B	V	S	C	D	T	N
K	Z	L	U	N	S	S	R	I	O
S	N	A	R	E	D	R	U	M	H
P	W	B	N	O	R	H	C	P	P
N	G	M	H	T	U	Y	I	A	O
R	V	Y	S	U	M	S	R	N	L
E	I	C	L	B	A	P	L	I	Y
T	Z	R	A	R	C	Q	Z	F	X

SNARE DRUM
BASS DRUM
CYMBALS
TRIANGLE
XYLOPHONE
TIMPANI

Instrument Family Word Finds
(Answer Key)

Brass

T	R	U	M	P	E	T	A	B	N
C	C	T	R	O	P	R	F	N	R
H	R	O	N	W	V	O	P	H	O
Z	F	G	I	T	M	A	O	H	
C	Y	X	N	E	V	B	A	C	H
E	R	H	N	I	U	O	W	U	C
T	R	R	U	T	P	N	O	N	N
K	O	P	U	I	R	E	K	W	E
C	C	T	W	C	B	F	A	Z	R
F	R	E	N	T	H	Q	R	I	F

Woodwinds

S	A	X	O	P	H	O	N	E	K
T	S	N	P	B	H	C	F	D	G
R	W	O	F	R	E	N	C	K	R
P	C	C	L	A	R	I	N	E	T
I	A	O	U	Q	J	F	O	T	B
C	O	M	T	I	U	N	O	R	A
C	T	E	E	P	R	I	S	U	S
O	N	Q	E	R	N	E	S	M	C
L	B	R	G	Z	N	U	A	B	O
O	B	U	U	N	T	W	B	Z	N

Strings

S	N	H	V	O	E	A	N	W	M
C	E	L	L	O	N	L	U	R	O
A	R	L	U	N	J	A	R	E	P
S	Q	E	V	T	R	N	D	R	E
S	T	R	I	N	G	B	A	S	S
O	F	C	O	N	E	H	L	B	R
N	C	R	L	B	A	S	O	O	A
W	G	U	I	T	A	R	I	V	N
M	N	N	N	R	O	E	V	I	U
P	P	E	F	G	A	H	I	K	R

Percussion

J	N	O	W	H	B	O	M	R	Q
U	U	T	R	I	A	N	G	L	E
F	C	S	B	V	S	C	D	T	N
K	Z	L	U	N	S	S	R	I	O
S	N	A	R	E	D	R	U	M	H
P	W	B	N	O	R	H	C	P	P
N	G	M	H	T	U	Y	I	A	O
R	V	Y	S	U	M	S	R	N	L
E	I	C	L	B	A	P	L	I	Y
T	Z	R	A	R	C	Q	Z	F	X

Instrument Family Sandwiches

Color Paper

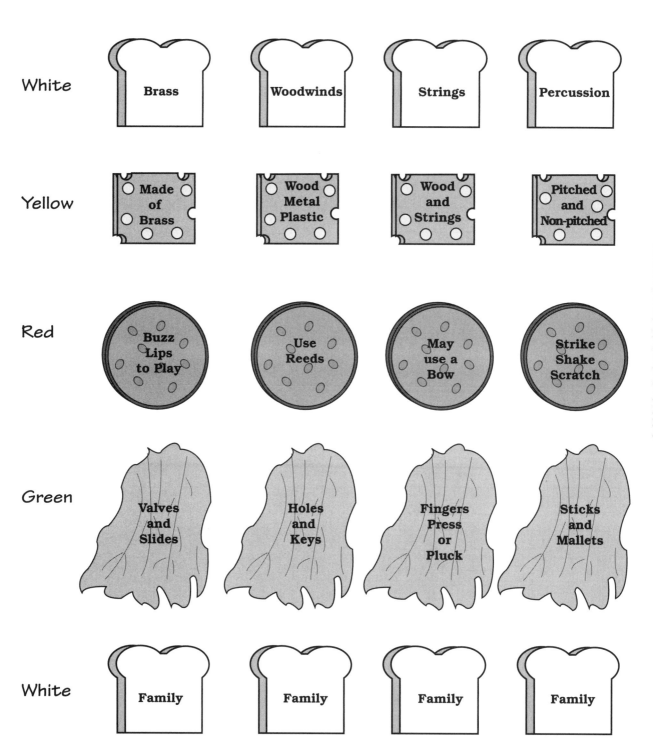

White   Brass   Woodwinds   Strings   Percussion

Yellow   Made of Brass   Wood Metal Plastic   Wood and Strings   Pitched and Non-pitched

Red   Buzz Lips to Play   Use Reeds   May use a Bow   Strike Shake Scratch

Green   Valves and Slides   Holes and Keys   Fingers Press or Pluck   Sticks and Mallets

White   Family   Family   Family   Family

Name _____

Instrument Connect-the-Dots

This instrument is the ____ ____ ____ ____.

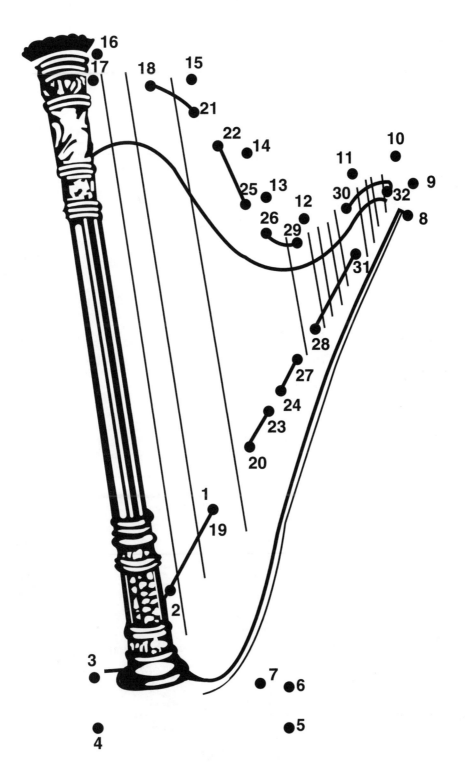

Name _____

Adding Beats and Notes
(Buying Fast Food)

Add the beats of the notes. If your answer is correct, the coin beside the answer will be added with the total number of cents you have. You can color the item at the bottom of the page.

♩ + ♩ = _____

♩ + ♩ = _____

♩ + ♩ = _____

♩ + 𝄽 = _____

♩ + 𝄽 = _____

You can buy . . .   *Specials*   **Total** _____

Drink
51¢

Ice cream cone
5¢

Shake
16¢

Fries
41¢

Hamburger
91¢

138

Note Values & Time

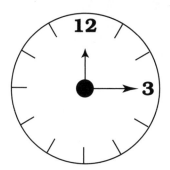

The Quarter Hour

The Quarter Note

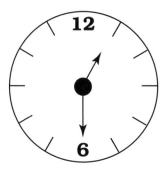

The Half Hour

The Half Note

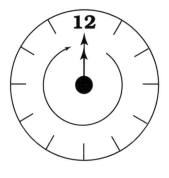

The Whole Hour

The Whole Note

Write the name of the notes on the lines below.

Draw the notes on the line of the words below.

The Whole Note _____   Quarter Note _____   Half Note _____

Beats per Measure Trains

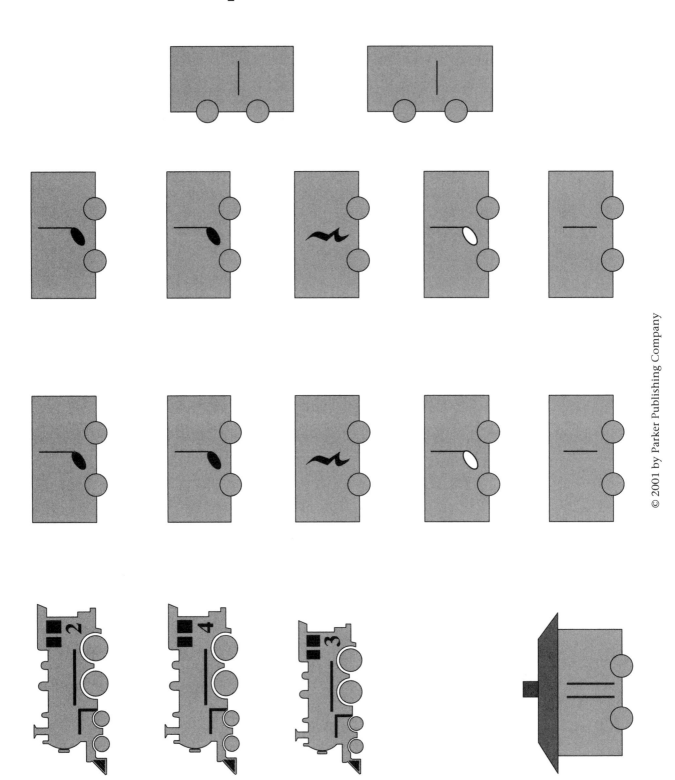

MUSIC DICE GAMES
AND ACTIVITIES

The music die on the next page can be used in a variety of music activities and games, and can yield many educational benefits. Below, you will find a few suggestions.

1. **Completing the Measures**—Copy numerous music dice. Put two or four incomplete measures of whatever meter and rhythm you wish to focus on on the board. Group the class into small teams having each student roll the die. If the note rolled will complete the measure, the next student rolls to complete the next measure. If the note does not fit, then the next student takes a turn. When a student completes a measure successfully, the student gets a point. The student with the most points wins. Use the quarter note on the dice page to hand out to students when they earn a point. To elongate the game, continue to add measures.

2. **Walk-a-Note**—Make five to ten large quarter note, half note, quarter rest, and double eighth note cards. Place the cards on the floor around the room. Allow each student to role the die. If the die note matches the note on the floor, the student walks to that card (provided he/she can name the note). Continue with all the students or copy the small rhythm cards in the Beats per Measure lesson and play the game in small groups. The first student to reach the end wins.

3. **Musicland Game Board**—Using the Musicland Gameboard following the die pattern and the composer pieces from the die page, prepare enough copies for the groups playing. Allow each student to choose a composer piece. Each student rolls the die. If the die matches the first note space and the student can name the note correctly, the student moves the piece to the first space of the gameboard. If it does not match or the student does not name the note correctly, the next student takes a turn. The one who reaches the conductor first wins.

Music Die

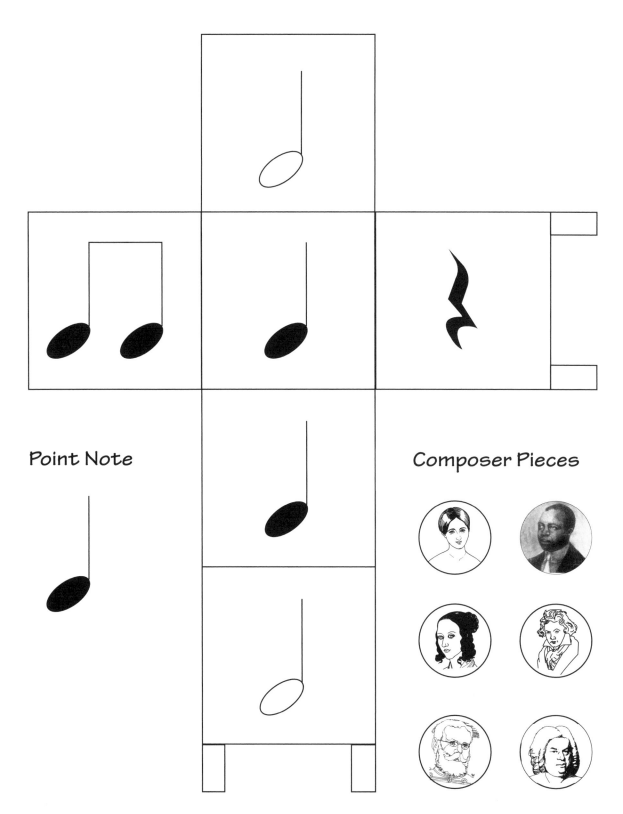

Point Note

Composer Pieces

Musicland

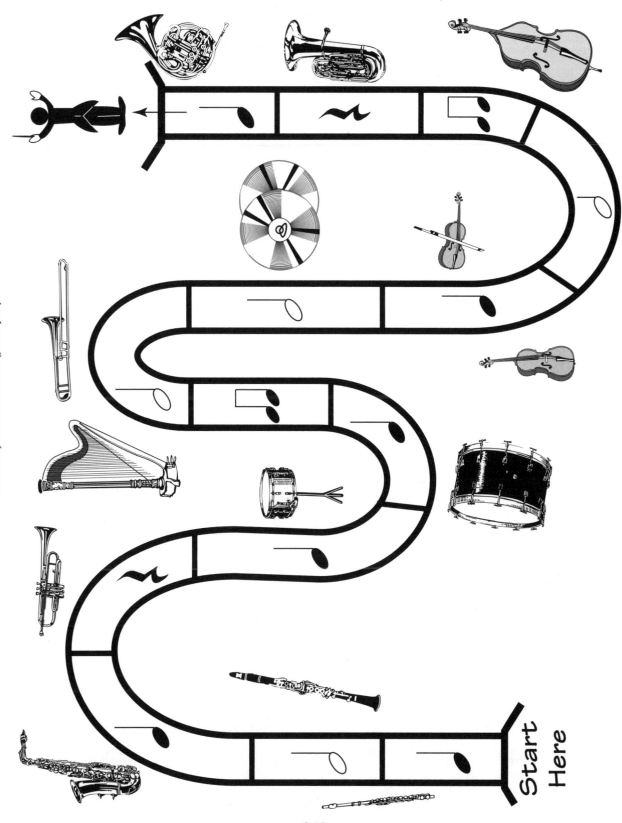

143

Notes & Beats
and Subtraction

Circle the notes that do not belong.

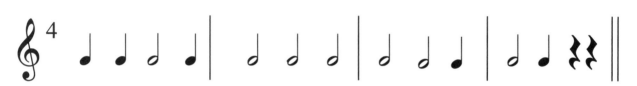

Add notes to complete the measures.

So-Mi

Complete the following So-Mi exercises.

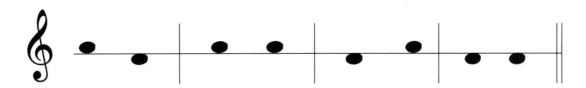

So ___ ___ ___ ___ ___ ___ ___

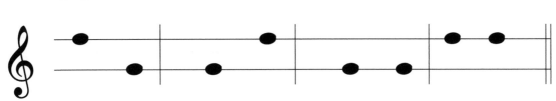

So ___ ___ ___ ___ ___ ___ ___

So Mi   So Mi   So Mi   So Mi

Mi So   So So   Mi Mi   So Mi

So-Mi-La

Do the following So-Mi-La exercises.

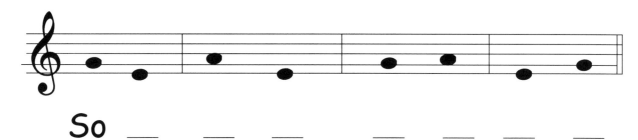

So ____ ____ ____ ____ ____

So ____ ____ ____ ____ ____

So La   So Mi   La Mi   So Mi

So Mi   La Mi   So La   Mi So

Treble Clef Puzzle

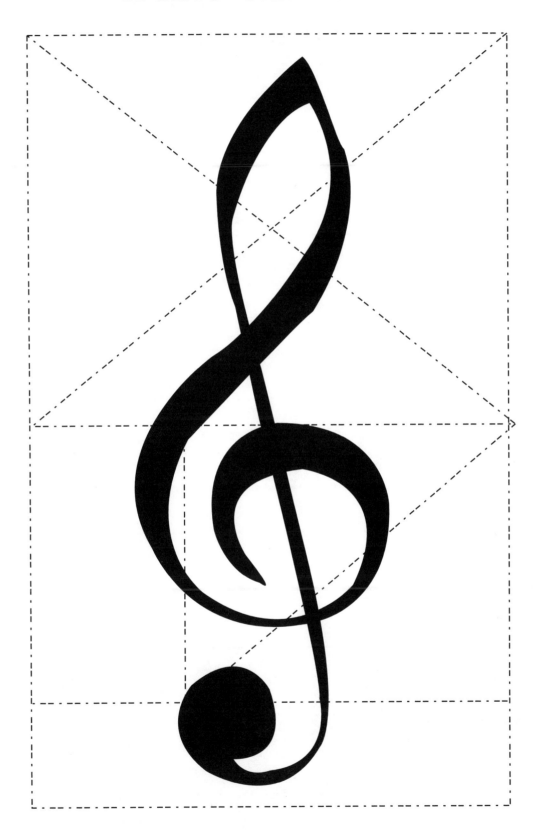

Barlines, Beats, and Measures

Add the barlines after each 2 beats.

Circle the measure that does not have 2 beats.

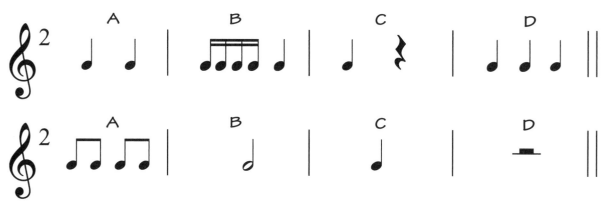

Write your own 2-beat measures.

Name _____

Musical Antonym Treasure Map

Find the treasure by following the antonyms.

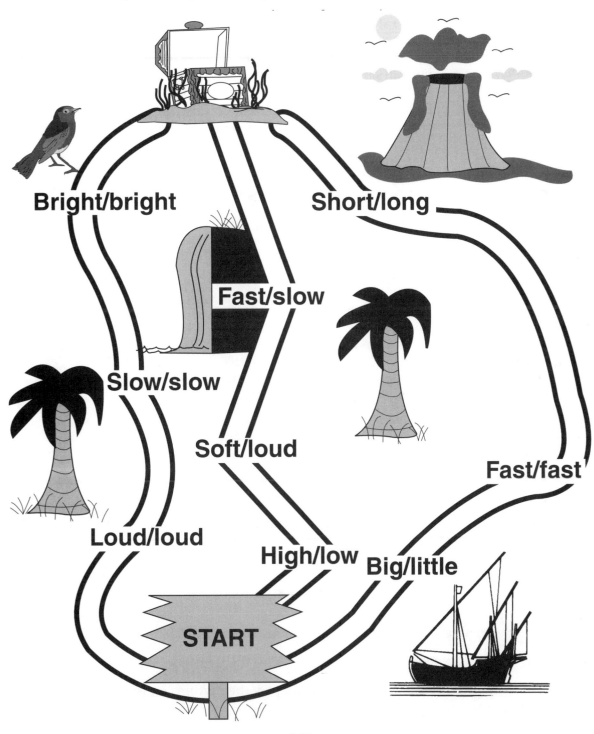

Daily Music Skill Builders
Activities

Directions: The Daily Music Skill Builders are intended to give teachers a daily resource for building singing and rhythm skills. These skill builders may be used in a variety of ways. They certainly are not all-inclusive, but can give one a start. Also, they should be used in conjunction with songs of similar elements in order to bring practice into performance.

Following are some suggested activities for using the skill builders.

Singing

1. Put the exercise(s) on the chalkboard and name the syllables.

2. Put the exercise(s) on the chalkboard and sing the syllables.

3. Photocopy or enlarge the skills.

4. Write the skills on large strips and name and/or sing.

5. Add repeats.

6. Add words.

7. Echo sing: Teacher sings, class echoes.

8. Play on instruments.

9. Write the exercise(s) on the chalkboard or on paper. Leave some notes blank. Allow the students to fill in the blanks.

10. Allow students to compose their own exercises.

11. Teacher sings, students dictate on music paper or on the board. Use the syllables do, re, mi, so, and la.

Rhythm

1. Put the exercise(s) on the chalkboard and say the rhythms.

2. Put the exercise(s) on the chalkboard and clap the rhythms.

3. Put the exercise(s) on the chalkboard and play the rhythms on instruments.

4. Photocopy or enlarge the skills.

5. Write the skills on large strips and say and/or clap.

6. Add repeats.

7. Add words.

8. Play on instruments.

9. Write the exercise(s) on the chalkboard or on paper. Leave some notes blank. Allow the students to fill in the blanks.

10. Echo clap: Teacher claps, class echoes.

11. Allow the students to compose their own exercises.

12. Dictation—Teacher claps, students write the rhythm down on paper, the chalkboard, or using Popsicle sticks.

Rhythm syllables: ♩♩ = ta-ah, ♩♩ = ta-ah-ah, ▬ = rest-rest-rest-rest,

▬ = rest-rest, ♩ = tah, ♫ = ti-ti, ♩ = ta-ah, ♩. = ta-ah-ah, o = ta-ah-ah-ah,

𝄽 = rest.

DAILY SINGING SKILL BUILDERS
So-Mi

So-Mi-La

© 2001 by Parker Publishing Company

So-Mi-La *(Continued)*

So-Mi-La-Re

So-Mi-Do

So-Mi-Do-Re

DAILY RHYTHM SKILL BUILDERS
Tah

Tah, Rest

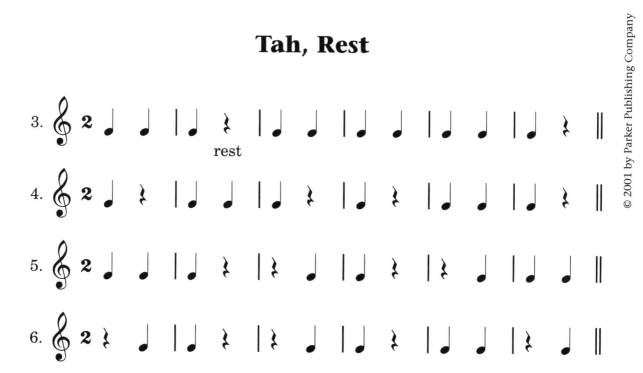

156

Tah-ah

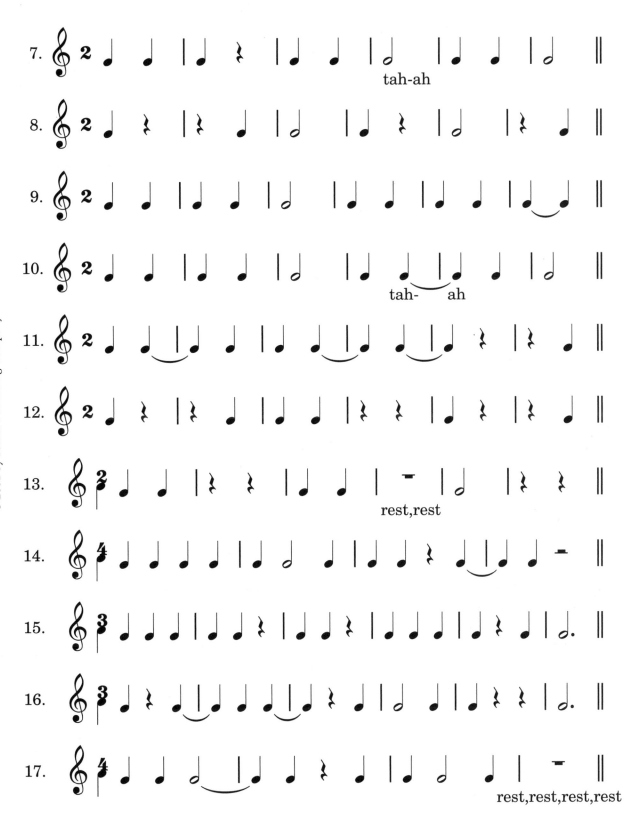

157

Ti-Ti (Tee-Tee)

18.

19.

20.

21.

22.

23.

© 2001 by Parker Publishing Company

Tah-ah-ah

24.

Tah-ah-ah

25.

Tah-ah-ah-ah

Interdisciplinary Planner

A record of the regular classroom's units, content, and concepts to be integrated with music.

Date _____

INTEGRATED SUBJECT	KINDERGARTEN	FIRST	SECOND
Literature Arts			
Math			
Science			
Health			
Social Studies			
Art			
Physical Education			
Other			

LEVEL 2
(Grade Levels 3-4)

Note Names
(Blends, Digraphs, Squ-Ph, and Long Vowels)

LESSON PLAN

Objective: Students will identify the names of tonal music notation on a treble clef staff.

Materials: Piano
Bells, xylophone
Chalkboard
Pencils
Copies of: Music page
Note Page
Learning to Read Music page
Music Crossword Puzzle
Playing the Long-legged Sailor page
Music Dog activity page

Procedure: 1. *Opening Activity:* Teach and sing "Little Sally Walker." Remind students that song melodies move up, down, and stay the same. Tell students that, aside from so, mi, and la syllables, there is another way to distinguish pitches. Discuss the advantages of reading music (playing an instrument, singing, playing someone else's music, the skill of decoding symbols, etc.). Point out that reading music is similar to reading words, sentences, and stories. Reading music is decoding symbols, and it takes time and practice like reading the English language.

Place a music staff on the chalkboard. Using the notes from the Note Page (copy, cut out, laminate, tape or glue a magnet to the backs), place three notes on the staff; one on the second line, one on the first line, and one on the second space. If your students recognize these notes in so/fa syllables, then refer to these notes as such. If not, refer to these as a particular numbered line or space. Proceed by explaining the lines and spaces on the staff as having letter names. Use the sentence and word *Every Good Boy Does Fine* (lines) and *FACE* (spaces).

2. *Reading Activity:* Give a copy of Learning to Read Music to each student. Have the students write the correct letter to the notes and the note to the correct letter for each exercise.

Procedure:
(Continued)

3. ***Practice Activity:*** Give each student a copy of the Music Crossword Puzzle. First, have the students figure out the names of the notes and fill in the blanks to complete the words. Then have the students place the word in the correct places in the puzzle.

4. ***Performance Activity:*** Teach "Long-legged Sailor." Also, create and teach some obvious motions to the song. Hand out a copy of the Playing the Long-legged Sailor activity page. Have the students write the name of the notes in the note circles on the staff. Have them try playing the song on the keyboard at the bottom of the page.

5. ***Extension Activity:*** Use the Long-legged Sailor activity page and have the students try the song on bells, xylophones, or a keyboard.

Activity Page:

Give each student a copy of the Music Dog page. Instruct them to complete the story by filling in the missing letters and using the music notes to complete the words.

Long-legged Sailor

1. Did you ev-er, ev-er, ev-er in your long-leg-ged life meet a long-leg-ged sail-or with a long leg-ged wife? No, I nev-er, nev-er, nev-er in my long-leg-ged life met a long-leg-ged sail-or with a long-leg-ged wife.

    2. Short-legged

    3. Bow-legged

    4. Knock-kneed

Little Sally Walker

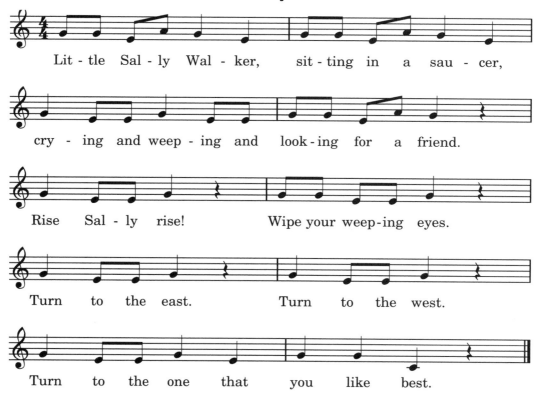

Lit-tle Sal-ly Wal-ker, sit-ting in a sau-cer, cry-ing and weep-ing and look-ing for a friend.

Rise Sal-ly rise! Wipe your weep-ing eyes.

Turn to the east. Turn to the west.

Turn to the one that you like best.

Note Page

These notes can be used on black paper or a variety of colors. It is sometimes helpful to label some with so/fa syllables to use for other activities.

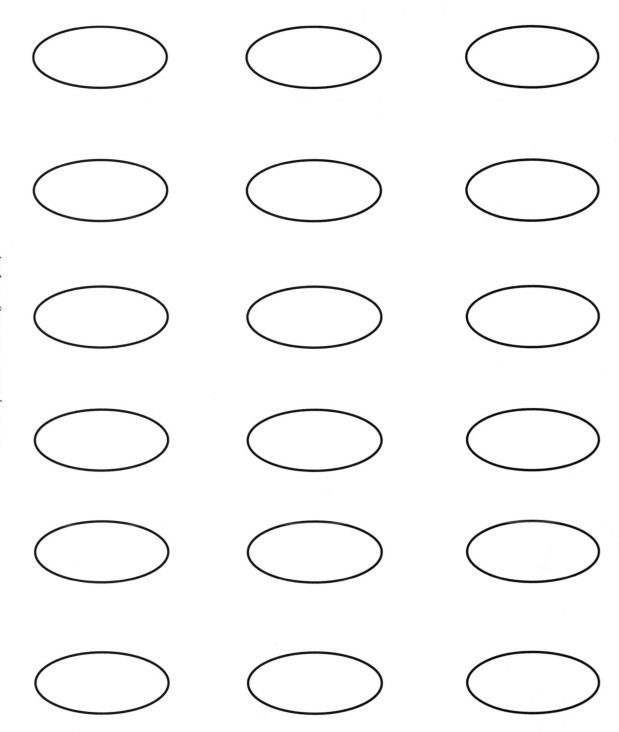

Learning to Read Music

Write the correct name of each note in the circle or diamond.

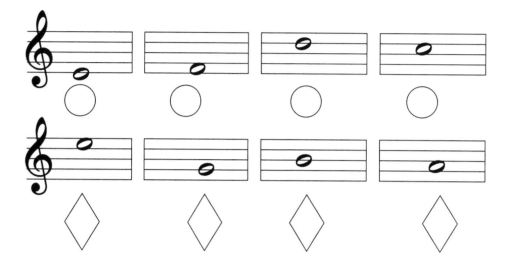

Place the note on the correct line or space of the staff.

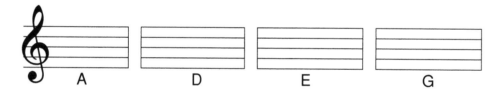

A   D   E   G

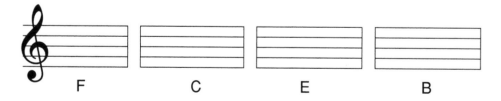

F   C   E   B

Write the correct letter of the notes in the spaces below to complete each word.

GR__PH   SQU__EZE   __ATE   __ITE

© 2001 by Parker Publishing Company

Music Crossword Puzzle

Complete the crossword puzzle by figuring out the names of the notes and filling in the words below each note.

ACROSS

1.  TUN__

2.  S__HOOL

3.  __BOVE

4.  SQU__AL

5.  SQU__WS

6.  __INE

DOWN

1. T__IL

2. SQUE_K

3. ROP__

4. 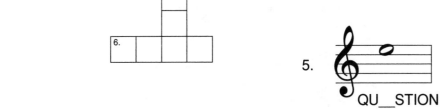 __E__S

5. QU__STION

6.  __ __ __ __

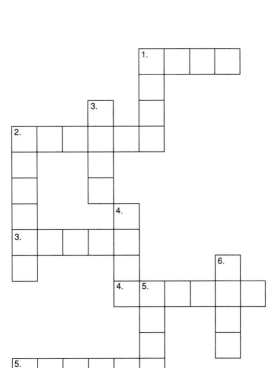

Playing the Long-legged Sailor

Write the letter name for each note below the song words.

Did you ev-er, ev-er, ev-er, in your long-leg-ged life meet a

long - leg-ged sail-or with a long - leg-ged wife?

Try playing the song on this keyboard!

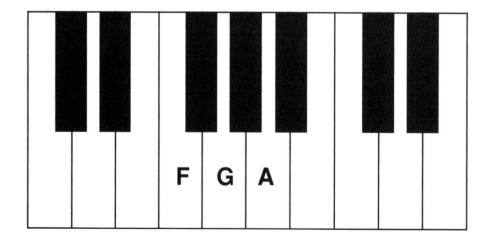

F G A

Music Dog

Complete the story by filling in the spaces with the name of each given note.

On__e upon __ tim__ th__re w__s a

__og n__m__d Moz__rt. He w__s a

musi__ __o__. __v__rytime he h__ __r__ his

fri__ n__ Bo__ __y pl__y his s__xophon__, Moz__rt

woul__ sin__. W__ll, m__y__ __ h__

woul__ squ__ __l.

Note Values
(Basic Fractions)

LESSON PLAN

Objective: Students will identify and recognize the whole note, half note, and quarter note.

Materials: Piano
Copies of: Music page
    "Riding in a Buggy" refrain page
    Music Pizza pages
    Piano Sonata No. 8 activity page
    Writing Practice page
    Pick 'n Put activity page
Pencils
Crayons or markers

Procedure: 1. *Opening Activity:* Sing "Riding in a Buggy" for the students. Bring attention to and emphasize the whole notes. Ask students to listen for the longest notes and raise their hands when they hear them. Ask the students to listen for other rhythms—short or long. Give each student a copy of "Riding in a Buggy" refrain page. Have the students point to the notes they believe are the longest notes, the long notes, and the shorter ones.

2. *Demonstration Activity:* Using the Music Pizza pages (Whole Notes, Half Notes, and Quarter Notes), identify the whole note, half note, and quarter note by explaining the fraction name for each note. Use the pizzas to show how two halves equal a whole and how four quarters equal a whole. Refer back to "Riding in a Buggy," and ask students to point out whole notes, half notes, and quarter notes.

3. *Singing and Reading Activity:* Hand out copies of Beethoven's piano sonata page to all the students. Teach the song to the students. While singing the song, have the students point to the whole notes when singing them, to the half notes when singing them, and, finally, to the quarter notes when singing them. Ask the students to circle the whole notes in red, the half notes in blue, and the quarter notes in green.

4. *Writing Activity:* Give each student a copy of the Writing Practice page. Have the students practice making whole notes, half notes, and quarter notes.

Activity Page: Hand out a copy of the Pick 'n Put activity page to each student. Have the students put the whole notes, half notes, and quarter notes in the appropriate baskets. The students may cross out or color each note they place. This is also a good music penmanship activity.

**Follow-Up
Activity:**   Continue the lesson by adding the numbers of beats to whole notes, half notes, and quarter notes.

Riding in a Buggy

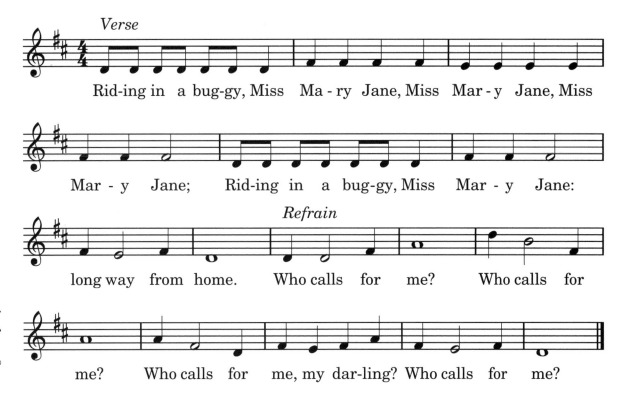

Verse

Rid-ing in a bug-gy, Miss Ma - ry Jane, Miss Mar - y Jane, Miss

Mar - y Jane; Rid-ing in a bug-gy, Miss Mar - y Jane:

Refrain

long way from home. Who calls for me? Who calls for

me? Who calls for me, my dar-ling? Who calls for me?

Piano Sonata No. 8
(Pathetique)

van Beethoven

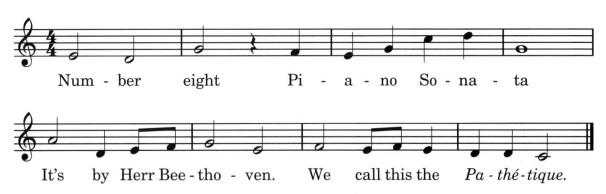

Num - ber eight Pi - a - no So - na - ta

It's by Herr Bee - tho - ven. We call this the *Pa - thé - tique.*

Riding in a Buggy

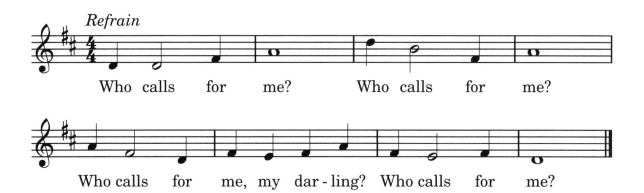

Refrain

Who calls for me? Who calls for me?

Who calls for me, my dar-ling? Who calls for me?

Music Pizzas

Whole Note

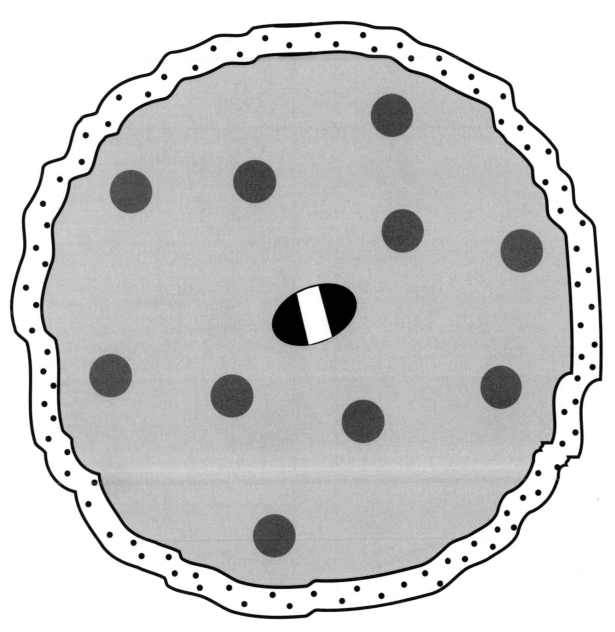

Music Pizzas

Half Notes

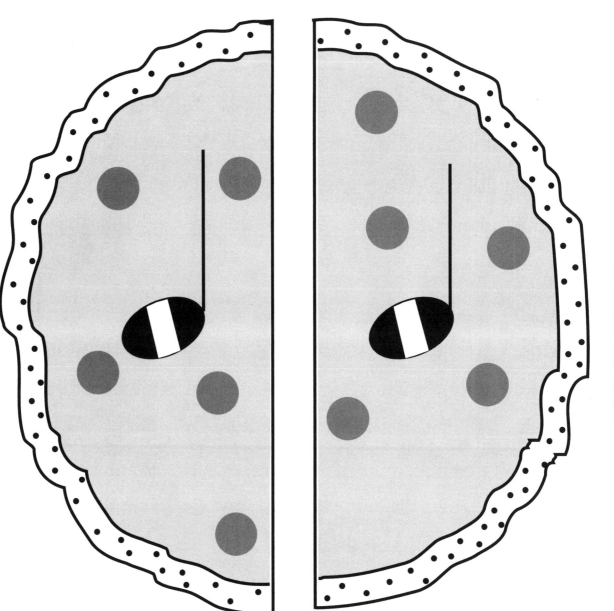

Music Pizzas

Quarter Notes

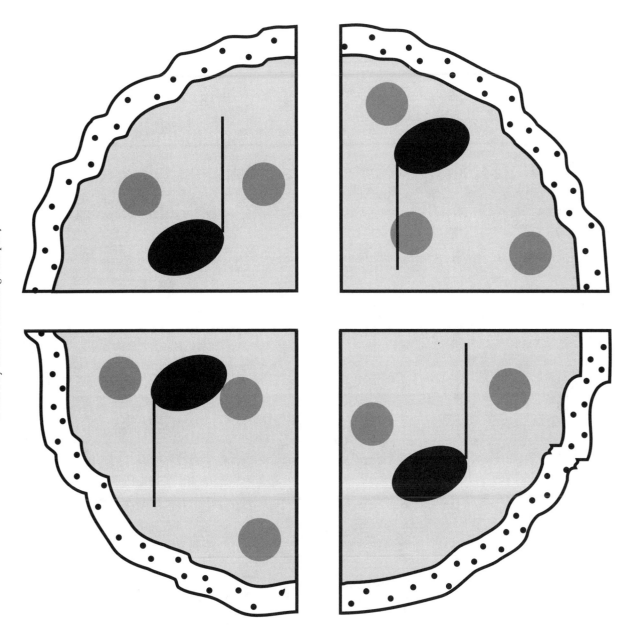

Music Pizza

Eighth Notes

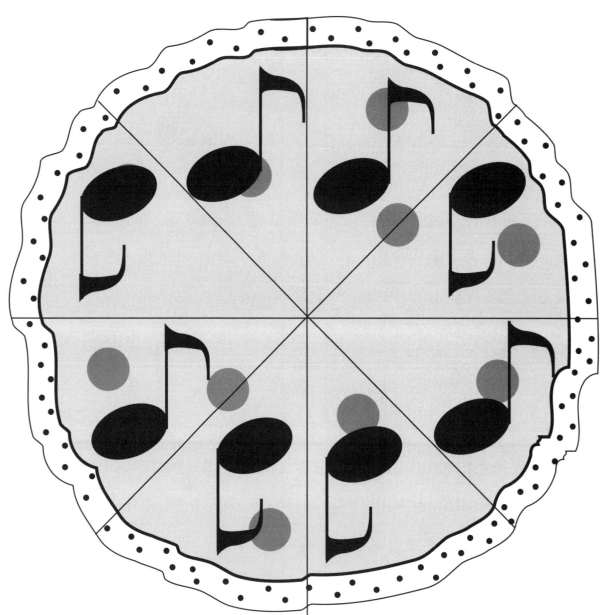

Name _____

Piano Sonata No. 8

(Pathétique)

Circle the whole notes in red, half notes in blue, and quarter notes in green.

Num - ber eight Pi -

a - no So - na - ta.

It's by Herr Bee - tho - ven.

We call this the "Pa - thé - tique."

Writing Practice

Practice making whole notes, half notes, and quarter notes.

Whole Notes

Half Notes

Quarter Notes

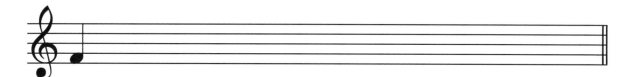

You Decide!

Pick 'n Put

You are an orchard owner. It is your job to find the whole notes, half notes, and quarter notes in the fruit trees. Place the notes in the matching basket. Cross out or color the note you put in the baskets.

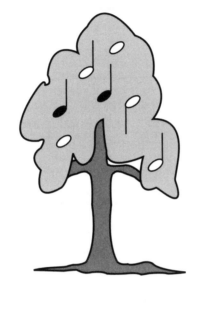

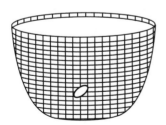

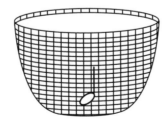

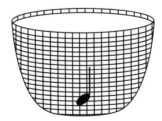

Dynamics
(Exaggeration)

LESSON PLAN

Objective: Students will be able to distinguish the music dynamics pp, p, mp, mf, f, and ff.

Materials: Piano
Hand drums, rhythm sticks, or rhythm instruments
Copies of: Music page
        Dynamics Puzzle page
        Volume/Dynamics Button page
        Changing Dynamics page
        Dynamics Marking page

Procedure: 1. *Opening Activity:* Sing "Russian Sailor's Dance" for the students in a quiet/soft voice. Sing it again, but noticeably louder, and ask the students how it was different from the first time. Teach the song to the students and have them perform the song in soft and then loud voices. Using the Dynamics Puzzle page, copy the puzzle to an enlarged size. Be sure they realize p = soft and f = loud. Perhaps sing and use the "p" and "f" again to tell students how to sing the dynamics.

2. *Singing Game:* This game is like turning up the volume button on the stereo, but we call it the *dynamics* ("This means *energy, in motion,* or *active.*") button. Copy the Volume/Dynamics Button page, cut out the button and place it on the board. Teach the song "Keys to Dynamics." To play the game, select a student to hide his/her eyes. Select another student to give the dynamic key, from the Volume/Dynamics Button page, to someone. After hiding the key, have the student (the pointer) stand at the chalkboard where the Dynamic Button is placed. As the student who hid his/her eyes begins to walk around the room, the pointer will point to the pianissimo part of the button and the class begins singing the song very softly. As the walking student gets closer to the student with the key, the class sings louder. As the walking student gets farther away from the student with the key, the class sings softer. The walker gets one guess. The pointer points to the dynamic level the class should be singing. Be sure all the students know that the louder the class gets, the closer the walking student is to the key.

Procedure:
(Continued)

3. ***Performance Activity:*** Ask the students what can be done to dynamics if you don't want exaggerated dynamics. "What could this be called?" Lead the students to the answer of *medium loud* and *medium soft*. Ask them what the letters could be, and then explain *mezzo* (half or medium) to the students. Give the students a copy of the Changing Dynamics page. Teach the students the song, then sing it. Be sure to sing the given dynamics. Follow the song, and use the Dynamics Where You Want exercise. Have the students write in the dynamic marking where they want. Then, have the students try to perform their own arrangements of the dynamics on hand drums, rhythm sticks, or any other rhythm instruments.

4. ***Recognition Activity:*** Copy enough Dynamic Puzzle pages for each student in the class. Cut out each puzzle and the dynamic division pieces (plastic sandwich or snack bags make good storage containers for the puzzle pieces). With the pieces mixed up, have the students put the pieces in the correct order from very soft to very loud and vice versa for the other puzzle.

Activity Page: Give each student a copy of the Dynamics Marking page. In the first section, have the students write the abbreviation letters that best describe the picture. In the lower section, have the students draw a picture that best describes the dynamic.

Key to Dynamics

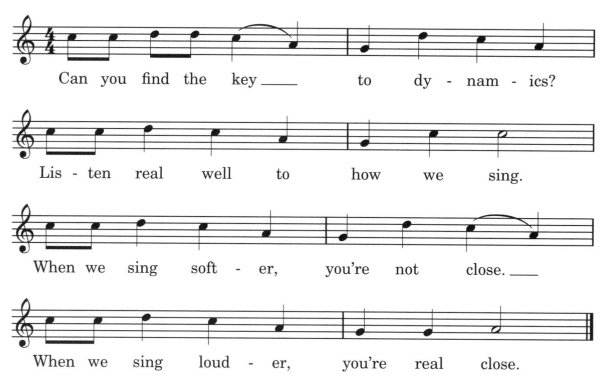

Can you find the key ___ to dy - nam - ics?

Lis - ten real well to how we sing.

When we sing soft - er, you're not close. ___

When we sing loud - er, you're real close.

Russian Sailor's Dance

Glière

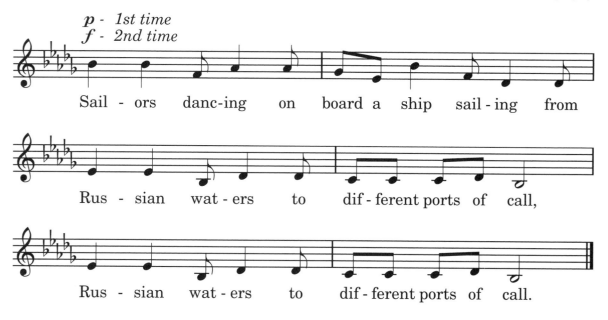

p - 1st time
f - 2nd time

Sail - ors danc-ing on board a ship sail - ing from

Rus - sian wat - ers to dif - ferent ports of call,

Rus - sian wat - ers to dif - ferent ports of call.

Changing Dynamics

Torch Dance

This is called the Torch Dance by Mi - chael Prae - tor - i - us.

He com-posed in six - teen hun-dred. I - ta-ly was his home.

Write the dynamic markings to this song. **ff** = very loud, **f** = loud, **mf** = medium loud, **mp** = medium soft, **p** = soft, and **pp** = very soft.

Dynamics Where You Want

Volume/Dynamics Button

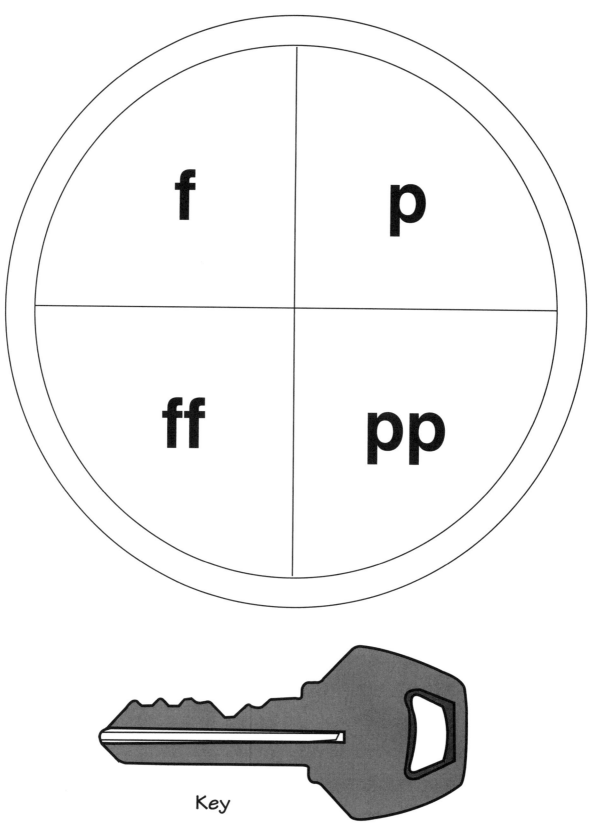

Key

Dynamic Puzzles

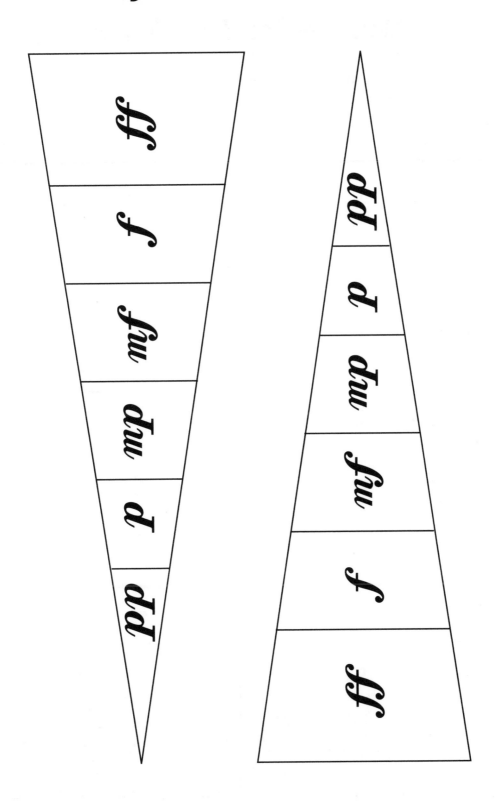

Dynamics Marking

Write the dynamic marking that describes the picture.

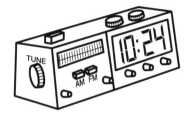

_____ _____ _____

_____ _____ _____

Draw a picture of something very loud and something very soft.

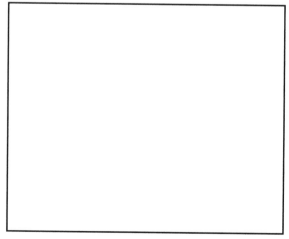

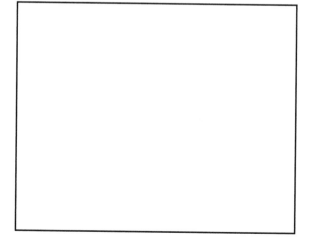

Very Loud   **Very Soft**

Billy the Kid
By an American Composer
(Famous Americans/Role Playing)

LESSON PLAN

Objective: Students will be able to identify Aaron Copland and his ballet, *Billy the Kid*.

Materials: Piano
Copies of: Music page
                 Aaron Copland page
                 Billy the Kid Story page
                 Billy the Kid Story Sequence page
                 Aaron Copland and *Billy the Kid* Crossword Puzzles
Pencils

Procedure:
1. *Opening Activity:* Sing "Simple Gifts" to the students. Ask: "Does anyone know or recognize this song?" Teach the song to the students. Explain to the students that "Simple Gifts" was a Shaker dance, and that Shakers were plain, religious people. Also, explain that the American composer Aaron Copland took this American folk tune and used it as a theme for his ballet, *Appalachian Spring*.

2. *Reading Activity:* Give each student a copy of the Aaron Copland page. Sing *Appalachian Spring* and read the Copland biography. After reading and singing, ask the students where Copland was from, to name something he composed, who were the significant people in his life, and what was a feature or characteristic of his music. You may want to break the students up into groups and give them the questions before they read the biography. Then, as a whole class, ask the students the questions above.

3. *Listening and Singing Activity:* Teach the songs of *Billy the Kid* to the students. Hand out copies of the *Billy the Kid* Story page. Read the story as a class and sing the songs at the appropriately noted spots. After finishing, review with the students the characters and their roles, the story plot and sequence of events, and possible props needed to produce the story.

4. *Writing Activity:* Give each student a copy of the *Billy the Kid* Story Sequence page. Instruct the students to write the main ideas of each segment of the story in order using the cowboy hat story sequence. At the bottom half of the page, students are to list the characters and props needed to produce the story.

Procedure:
(Continued)

5. *Role-Playing Activity:* Depending on the size of your class, assign a character of the story to each student by dividing the students into groups or acting companies. Have the students review the story and devise their own play. Props, scenery, etc., may be used to enhance the productions. Be sure to give the students an opportunity to perform the plays for each other. Discuss the differences between the various productions. This activity may take some time, so perhaps you may want to extend the lesson into several class periods.

Note: This story does have a violent and sad theme, so it would be wise to make sure this activity would be acceptable in your school. Nevertheless, the story does give a good depiction of the frontier life in the American West.

Activity Page:

Give a copy of the Aaron Copland and *Billy the Kid* Crossword Puzzle page to the students. Have them complete the puzzles by filling in the correct answers to the questions.

Simple Gifts

Tis the gift to be sim-ple, tis the gift to be free. Tis the
gift to come down where you want to be.
When we find our-selves in the place just right 'twill
be in the val - ley of love and de - light.
When true sim - pli - ci - ty is gained, to
bow and to bend we shan't be a - shamed. To
turn, turn will be our de - light, 'til by
turn - ing, turn - ing we come 'round right.

Billy the Kid

Copland

Great Grand-Dad was a bus-y man. Cooked his food with a fry-ing pan and

picked his teeth with a hunt-ing knife and wore the same suit all his life.

It's whoop-ing and yell - ing and driv - ing the do - gies you

know that Wy - om - ing is where I call home.

Yes, this is a sto - ry of Bil - ly the kid. ___

Shoot-ing by the cow - boys had shot his moth - er dead.

Bil-ly turned his life in-to a crime rid-den life in the west. ___

Good - bye, Old Paint, I'm off for Mon -

ta - na. Good - bye, Old Paint, I'm leav - ing Chey-enne.

AARON COPLAND

Born in Brooklyn, New York, in 1900, Aaron Copland was the predominant composer in America during the 1920s and 1930s. He began his musical life studying the piano at age eight. By the time he was fifteen, Copland had demonstrated an ability to play and compose and decided to pursue a career as a composer.

Copland traveled to Paris in 1921 to study with the great teacher of music composition Nadia Boulanger. In 1924, Copland returned to America to continue his composing career.

Using jazz and folk tunes in his music, Copland developed a unique American sound. His compositions include *Appalachian Spring, Rodeo, Billy the Kid, El Mexico Salon,* and *Red Pony.*

Appalachian Spring

Copland

Aa-ron Cop-land, com-pos-er born in Nine-teen hun-dred. He com-

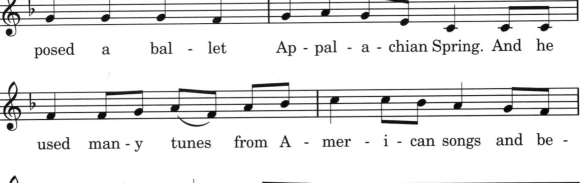

posed a bal - let Ap-pal - a - chian Spring. And he

used man - y tunes from A - mer - i - can songs and be -

came a fa - mous com - pos - er soon.

191

BILLY THE KID
Story Page

Pat Garrett, a sheriff who symbolizes the pioneer spirit of the frontier, begins his trek to the West. People begin to follow him to a frontier town in New Mexico.

Soon cowboys begin to ride their horses and herd cattle, and businesses begin to start in the western frontier town. Billy (as a boy), his real name being William Bonney, appears on the scene with his mother. Billy and his mother witness an argument between two cowboys. A stray bullet hits Billy's mother. In a panic and rage, Billy pulls out a knife and stabs her killer.

Many years later, Billy, who has become a dangerous man, is hunted and captured. Soon, he escapes. He hides in the desert and dreams about his girlfriend. Pat Garrett searches for him in the desert. After seeing Billy light a cigarette, Garrett fires a shot and kills him. A group of Mexican mourners appear and lament the death of Billy the Kid.

Name _____

Billy the Kid

Story Sequence Page

Write the sequence of events for *Billy the Kid* in the story sequence hats below.

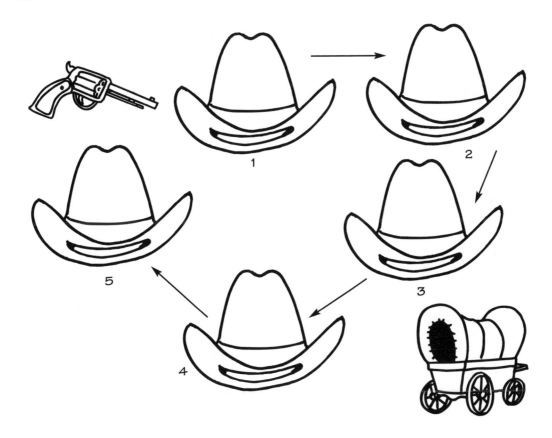

List the characters and props needed to produce the story.

CHARACTERS

_____

_____

_____

_____

_____

PROPS

_____ _____

_____ _____

_____ _____

_____ _____

_____ _____

Aaron Copland
and *Billy the Kid*

CROSSWORD PUZZLES

Aaron Copland

ACROSS

1. How old was Copland when he first studied a musical instrument?

2. Copland began with this instrument.

3. This was one of Copland's ballets. It was about the west.

4. Copland composed the ballet *Appalachian* _____.

DOWN

2. Copland traveled here to study composition.

5. Copland studied with this teacher (last name).

6. This was Copland's home state.

7. He used jazz and _____ in his music.

Billy the Kid

ACROSS

1. What was Billy the Kid's last name?

2. Who was killed that turned Billy to a life of crime?

3. Who argued when Billy's mother was killed?

DOWN

1. Billy was one when his mother was killed.

4. Where did Billy live with his mother?

5. Who was Pat Garrett?

6. This person shot Billy the Kid.

7. Billy died here.

Adding Note Values
(Fractions)

LESSON PLAN

Objective:	Students will identify, recognize, and perform the whole note, half note, quarter note, and eighth note.
Materials:	Piano A variety of rhythm instruments Copies of: Music Page Pizza Note Slices Note Values and Math Completing Measures page Subtracting Notes page Table Song page Baseball Game page Pencils
Procedure:	1. ***Opening Activity:*** Echo clap the following rhythms. Clap the quarter notes, tap the half notes, and stomp the whole notes.

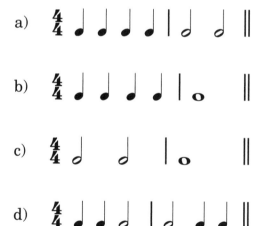

2. ***Singing Activity:*** Teach "Note Value Song" to the students. Have the students step in place for each quarter note. Then, have each student stop in place for each half note and whole note. Teach "Oh, Come Little Children." Have the students clap the quarter notes, tap the half notes, and stomp the whole notes while singing the song.

Procedure:
(Continued)

3. ***Dictation Activity:*** Copy enough Pizza Note Slices pages for each student (oaktag and lamination work well). Have each student cut out the pizza shapes. Echo clap a variety of two- or four-meter measure rhythms or have the students use the shapes and notes to write the rhythm of "Oh, Come Little Children" or "Note Value Song." Possibly, enlarge the Pizza Note Slices page. For advanced classes, use the Pizza Note Slices Rest page to add to the difficulty.

4. ***Composition Activity:*** Give a copy of the Completing Measures page to each student. Using whole notes, half notes, quarter notes, and eighth notes, have the students complete the measures in 2 and in 4 by writing in the rhythms. Afterwards, try allowing the students to perform the rhythms. Perhaps have the students perform each other's compositions.

5. ***Writing Activity:*** Give each student a copy of the Note Values and Math page. Instruct the students to add the values of the notes for each problem.

6. ***Writing Activity:*** Give each student a copy of the Subtracting Notes page. Ask the students to subtract the note values for each problem.

7. ***Composition Activity:*** Give each student a copy of the Table Song page. Have each student write a rhythm composition in 2. Partner each student with another, and have a student at the top of the composition and one at the bottom. Each student will perform (clap) the composition's rhythms from his/her standpoint simultaneously.

Activity Page:

Give each student a copy of the Baseball Game activity page. Have the students add or subtract the beats for each problem at each base. If a student renders the correct answer for each problem, four runs are scored, beating the visitor's score of 3. Three correct problems = three runs; two correct = two runs; one correct = one run; and none correct = no runs. Color in or check the bases that the student reached.

Note Value Song

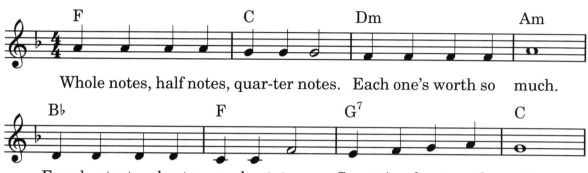

Whole notes, half notes, quar-ter notes.   Each one's worth so   much.

Four beats, two beats, one beat, too.   Count-ing beats and   such.

When you sing or   play a song,   each note must be   read.

Whole notes, half notes, quar-ter notes.   Count all notes as   said.

Come Little Children

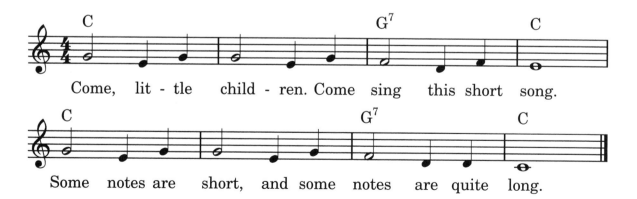

Come, lit - tle   child - ren. Come sing   this short   song.

Some   notes are   short, and some notes   are quite   long.

Pizza Note Slices

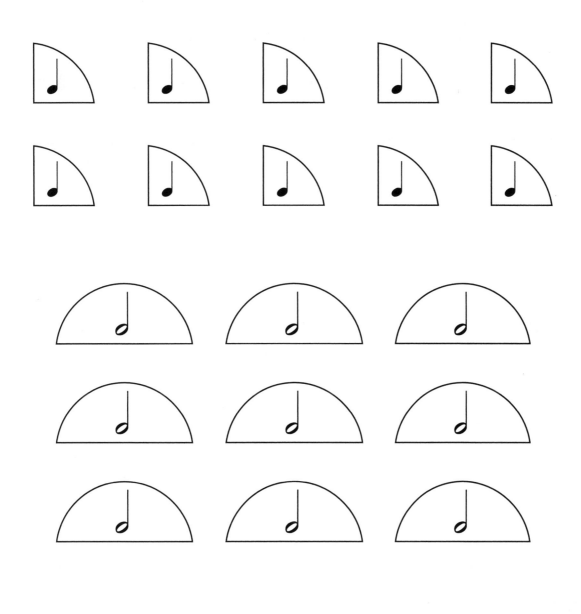

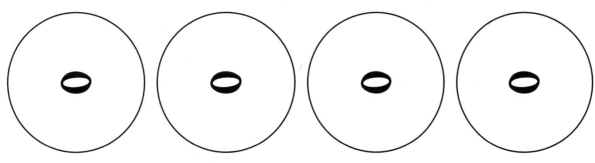

Pizza Note Slices

Rest Page

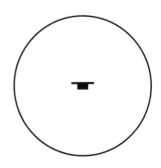 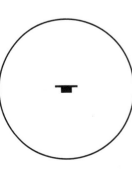 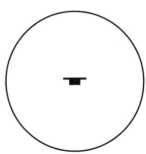 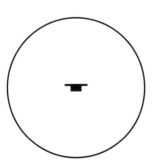

Completing Measures

Using the note values below, compose measures in 2 and 4 beats. Try performing the measures you write (using clapping, a hand drum, etc.).

o = 4 beats   ♩ = 2 beats   ♩ = 1 beat

♪   ♪ =   = 1 beat   = 2 beats

4 beats per measure

1   +   1/2   +   1/2   +   2   =   4 beats   4 beats

Two Beats per Measure

Four Beats per Measure

Try Six Beats per Measure

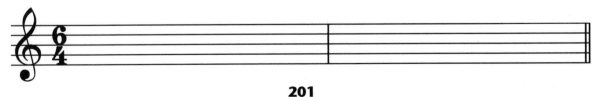

© 2001 by Parker Publishing Company

Note Values and Math

Name _____

Add the beats of each note problem.

Whole	Half	Quarter	Eighth
𝅝 = 4 beats	𝅗𝅥 = 2 beats	𝅘𝅥 = 1 beat	𝅘𝅥𝅮 = ½ beat

Ex. 𝅝 4 beats
  + 𝅝 4 beats
  _____
  8

1. 𝅝
  + 𝅗𝅥
  _____

2. 𝅗𝅥
  + 𝅗𝅥
  _____

3. 𝅘𝅥
  + 𝅗𝅥
  _____

4. 𝅘𝅥
  + 𝅘𝅥
  _____

5. 𝅘𝅥
  + 𝅘𝅥𝅮
  _____

6. 𝅘𝅥𝅮
  + 𝅘𝅥𝅮
  _____

7. 𝅗𝅥
  + 𝅘𝅥𝅮
  _____

8. 𝅘𝅥𝅮
  𝅘𝅥𝅮
  + 𝅘𝅥
  _____

9. 𝅗𝅥
  𝅘𝅥𝅮
  + 𝅝
  _____

10. 𝅘𝅥𝅮
  𝅘𝅥𝅮
  + 𝅘𝅥
  _____

Add the note values to a sum of another note value.

Ex. 𝅗𝅥 + 𝅗𝅥 = 𝅝 Whole

1. 𝅘𝅥 + 𝅘𝅥 = _____

2. 𝅘𝅥𝅮 + 𝅘𝅥𝅮 = _____

3. 𝅘𝅥 + 𝅘𝅥 + 𝅘𝅥 + 𝅘𝅥 = _____

4. 𝅗𝅥 + 𝅗𝅥 + 𝅘𝅥𝅮𝅘𝅥𝅮 = _____

© 2001 by Parker Publishing Company

Subtracting Notes

Subtract the beats of each note problem.

Whole   Half   Quarter   Eighth

○ = 4 beats   ♩ = 2 beats   ♩ = 1 beat   ♪ = ½ beat

Ex.   ○ 4 beats
    − ♩ 2 beats
       2

1. ○
   − ○
      ____

2. ♩
   − ♩
     ____

3. ♩
   − ♩
     ____

4. ♩
   − ♩
     ____

5. ♩
   − ♪
     ____

6. ♩
   − ♪
     ____

7. ♩
   − ♩
     ____

8. ♩ − ♩ − ♪ = ☐

9. ○ − ♩ − ♩ = ☐

10. ♩ − ♪ − ♪ = ☐

Subtract the notes below.

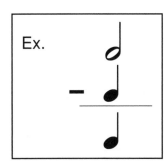

Ex.

1. ○
   − ♩
     ____

2. ♩
   − ♪
     ____

3. ○ − ♩ − ♩ = ☐

4. ♩ − ♪ − ♪ = ☐

Name _____

Table Song

Write a rhythm composition in two beats per measure. Practice clapping your music, then perform it with your partner.

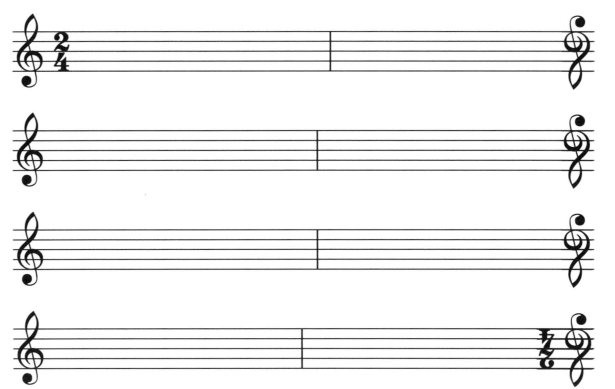

Name _____

Baseball Game
Adding and Subtracting Notes

Add or subtract the number of beats for the note problems given below. Try to hit a home run to win the game.

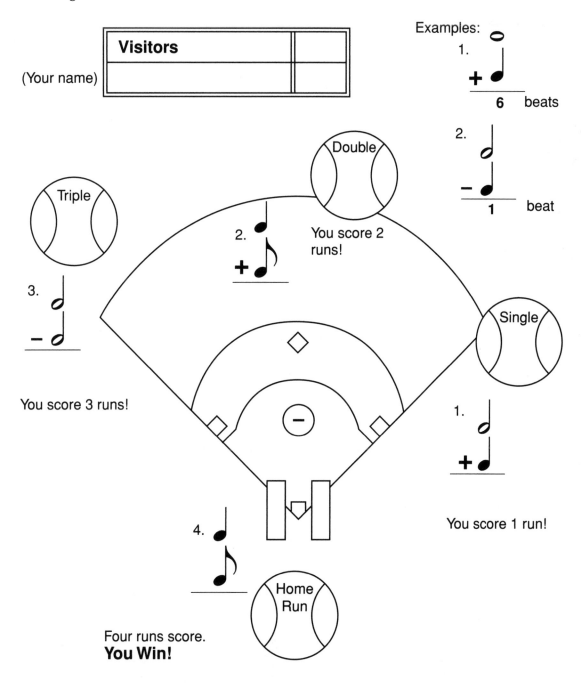

Visitors	
(Your name)	

Examples:

1. $+$ = **6** beats

2. $-$ = **1** beat

Double — You score 2 runs!

2. $+$

Triple

3. $-$

You score 3 runs!

Single

1. $+$

You score 1 run!

4.

Home Run

Four runs score.
You Win!

Petrouchka and *1812 Overture*
Music Symbols
(Fiction and Nonfiction)

LESSON PLAN

Objective: Students will identify the music symbols of the sharp (#), natural (♮), and the flat (♭).

Materials: Piano
Tone bells
A variety of bells, xylophones, piano, etc.
Pencils
Crayons or markers
Copies of: Story Page
                Music page
                Performance Game Symbols Cards
                Symbol Search page
                Music Symbol Orchard Page
                Symbol Performance Page
                Symbolized Picture Page

Procedure: 1. *Opening Activity:*

a. Tell the story of *Petrouchka*.

b. Teach the tune.

c. Hand out copies of the music page, and point out and discuss the sharp (#) symbol in *Petrouchka*.

d. Tell the story of the *1812 Overture*.

e. Teach the tune. Allow the students to follow along with the music page.

f. Discuss the story differences. One story is based on fact and the other is not.

g. Have the students point out the different symbol of flat (♭) used on the *1812 Overture*.

h. Explain that the flat (♭) lowers a pitch, and remind the students that a sharp raises a pitch.

i. Clarify that raising or lowering a pitch doesn't mean making a note louder or softer.

j. Teach the Hovhaness Symphony No. 50.

Procedure:
(Continued)

  k. Tell the story of the symphony. Explain fiction (an imaginary story—untrue) and nonfiction (a story of fact). Ask the students if the Hovhaness story is fiction or nonfiction.

  l. Lead the students to pointing out the natural symbol (♮).

  m. Explain that a natural symbol cancels a sharp or a flat by restoring or returning a note to its original pitch.

2. *Performance Game:*

  a. On a flat surface such as a desk, set up tone bells in scale order with the spaces between D, G, and A. Place the chromatic notes in the proper order but above the natural notes.

  b. Choose a student to play the bells. Make sure each student has a set of symbol cards. Have the bell player pick a student who will choose one of the cards. The bell player will perform the symbol by playing each bell's flat, sharp, or natural for each note.

  c. Have the bell player choose the next player and ask him/her to show a particular symbol card. If the guess is correct, that student will play the bells next. If not, try another student. Students will try to learn the symbols in order to play the bells.

3. *Recognition Activity:* Hand out a copy of the Symbol Search page and a set of crayons or markers to each student. Instruct the students to circle the sharps in red, the naturals in blue, and the flats in orange.

  Note: You may want to explain and add the fermata, treble clef, and the repeat signs to this activity (green box around the treble clef and a brown box around the repeat signs).

4. *Writing Activity:* Hand out a copy of the Music Symbol Orchard Page to each student and ask the students to decorate each orchard tree with the different music symbols.

5. *Performance Activity:*

  a. Place a variety of instrument stations around the room (bells, xylophone, piano, etc.). Use as many stations as possible.

  b. Copy the Symbol Performance Page for each station. Highlight or cut out each exercise strip for each station.

  c. Assign each student or groups of students to a station. After five or six minutes, rotate students to another station.

  d. Repeat the activity until each student has tried all the exercises.

Activity Page: Hand out a copy of the Symbolized Picture Page to each student, and have the students write the symbol under the picture that best describes the music symbol.

STORY PAGE

Petrouchka

A crowd of people is gathered on a square in St. Petersburg, Russia, at a fair. At one of the fair's stalls a puppeteer charms his dolls into dancing while playing his flute. Behind the scenes, Petrouchka, a jester-type puppet, is upset with his ordinary life, his slavery to his puppeteer, and his love for the puppet Ballerina. Meanwhile, a third puppet, Blackamoor, dances a waltz with the Ballerina. Petrouchka interrupts, but is tossed out. Soon different groups of people at the fair begin a variety of dances. Petrouchka begins to provoke Blackamoor, and, suddenly, the two burst into fighting. Petrouchka dies. Another puppeteer comes in and shows that Petrouchka was just a puppet. Later, Petrouchka stands up and looks around while laughing at the people's gullibility.

1812 Overture

Tchaikovsky composed this music as a dramatic portrait of the invasion of Russia by Napoleon's troops and their defeat due to the harsh Russian winter. The music was performed for the dedication of the Church of the Redeemer in Moscow in 1882.

Volcano

The music of *Volcano* comes from the third movement of Alan Hovhaness's *Mount St. Helens Symphony (No. 50)*. On the morning of May 18, 1980, the volcano at Mount St. Helens began to display its unrest. The strength and evidence of the eruption was witnessed by the entire nation, bringing attention to the state of Washington and its history-making mountain.

Petrouchka
(The Shrovetide Fair)

Stravinsky

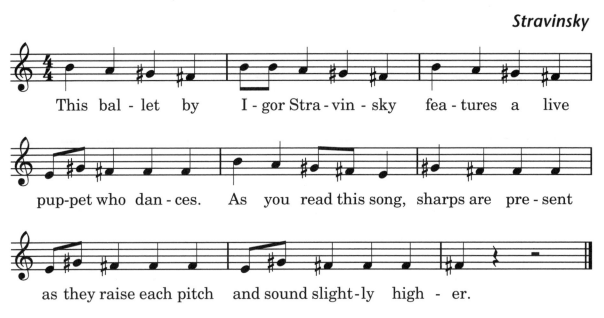

This bal - let by I - gor Stra - vin - sky fea - tures a live

pup-pet who dan - ces. As you read this song, sharps are pre - sent

as they raise each pitch and sound slight-ly high - er.

1812 Overture

Tchaikovsky

Tchai-kov - sky's Eight-een Twelve O - ver - ture.

Tchai-kov - sky's Eight-een Twelve O - ver - ture.

We wit - ness that flats low - er pit - ches slight - ly,

that low - er pit - ches slight - ly.

Symphony No. 50
(*Volcano*)

Hovhaness

Adagio

Ho - vha - ness sym - pho - ny fif - ty.

The third move-ment vol - ca - no. As you

see, nat - ur - als all change a sharp or flat ___

___ Re - store each note to its na - tural

pitch. Can you point out each one?

Performance Game

Symbols Cards

Symbol Search

Put a red (circle) around the **sharps**, a blue (circle) around the **naturals**, and an orange (circle) around the **flats**. Draw a green [box] around the **fermatas**, a yellow [box] around the **treble clefs**, and a brown [box] around the **repeat** signs.

The Fair

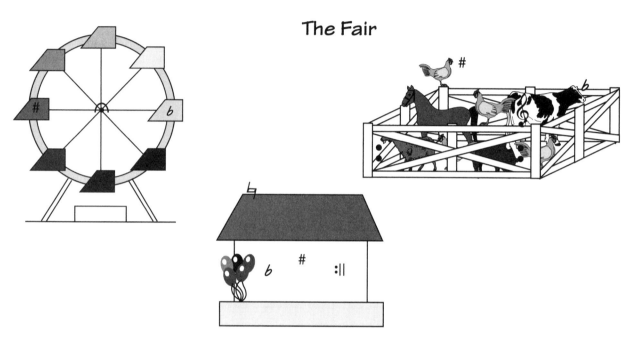

The Battle

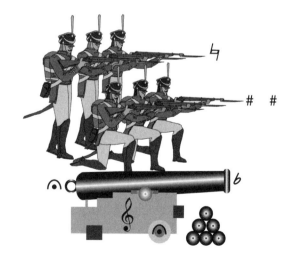
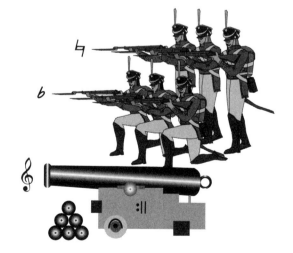

Music Symbol Orchard Page

Decorate these fictional trees with the music symbols listed below.

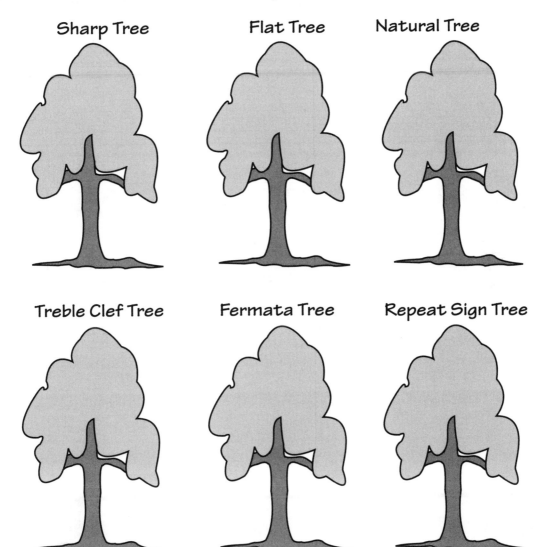

Sharp Tree · Flat Tree · Natural Tree

Treble Clef Tree · Fermata Tree · Repeat Sign Tree

\# — A **sharp** raises a pitch one-half step.

♮ — A **natural** restores a note to its regular pitch.

♭ — A **flat** lowers a pitch one-half step.

𝄐 — The **fermata** tells the musician to hold the note longer than usual or until the director indicates when to cut it off.

𝄞 — The **treble clef** appears at the beginning of each line of music.

𝄆 — This **repeat sign** tells the musician to repeat the section from the beginning or from the other repeat sign 𝄇 .

213

Symbol Performance Page

Perform the following exercises.

Symbolized Picture Page

Place the music symbol that best describes the pictures below.

Symbols

African Music
(World Culture/Africa)

LESSON PLAN

Objective: Students will distinguish slow and fast while performing and identifying characteristics of African music.

Materials: Piano
Shakers
Two different drums
Scissors
Pencils
African Music pages
Map of Africa
Copies of: African Musical Instruments page
African Music Facts Page
African Music Activity Page

Procedure: 1. *Opening Activity:* Group the students in fours. If there are two students remaining, use the alternate activity. If there are three or only one remaining, you become the extra person needed. Have the four-student groups sit with their legs crossed and have their hands point out toward the direction of their knees. As you sing "Kee-Chee," have one student from each group begin by tapping the next student's hand on the beat of the song. This will continue with each student in the circle (proceed clockwise).

   *Alternate Activity: For a group of two students, have one student sit cross-legged. One student will hold both hands out while the other taps the other's hands on beat one. The students will then turn their hands over and do the opposite side on beat two. On the third beat each student will tap his/her left shoulder with his/her right hand. On the fourth beat they will tap their right shoulders with their left hands. Sing the song at a moderate tempo. As the class continues the hand play, encourage them to sing along.

2. *Discussion Activity:* Ask the students what kind of music it is or from where the song "Kee-Chee" comes; when the students respond, ask why. Point out to the students that the song is from the Congo. Using a large current wall map or the map provided in this book (as an overhead or a handout), have the students locate the Congo. Also, have the students find Zambia. Tell the students that you are going to teach them a song from Zambia called "Mayo Nafwa."

Procedure:
(Continued)

3. ***Performance Activity:*** Sing "Mayo Nafwa" at a slow tempo to the students. Have the students tap four beats with their hands (left-right-left-right). Ask the students if the song is slower or faster than "Kee-Chee." Then have the students clap six beats. As they continue the beat, you sing "Mayo Nafwa." Teach the song to the students. Try having them tap and clap while singing the song. Choose a student to play the 6/8 meter measures and hand out shakers to the rest of the class (use African drums and shakers, if available) to play the 4/8 measures. Sing and perform the song.

4. ***Song/Game Activity:*** Teach "Obwisana." Tell the students that this song comes from Ghana. Have the students locate Ghana on the map of Africa. The Obwisana game is a stone-passing game. Crumple a piece of paper, or use a rock or some other object. Have the students sit in a circle on the floor. As the students sing the song, have one student pick the object up and place it down in front of the student next to him/her on the strong beat, then clap on the weak beat afterwards. Allow the game to continue through the entire song. Prepare the students for the game by going through the motions before doing the game with the song. Try increasing the tempo, and have the students point out the tempo change.

5. ***Instrument Game:*** Have enough copies of the African Musical Instrument Page for at least half the class. Cut along the dotted lines. Fold the tabs over so that the names of the instruments are hidden behind the illustrations. Put the students into pairs. Have one student hold and display the instrument pictures and the other student name the instrument. Check to see if the student is correct. The students continue until each student names all the instruments correctly at least once.

Activity Page: Give students copies of the African Music Facts Page and the African Music Activity Page. Have the students fill in the answers to each of the sentences or questions. This page makes a good study sheet or assessment tool.

Kee-Chee
(Congo)

Wu - ne Ku - ne cha - o wu - ni, Ah
woo - neh koo - neh chah oh woo - nee, ah

wu - me ku - ne cha - o wu - ni
woo - neh koo - neh chah - oh woo - nee

Ah yi yi yi - ki ay Kae ay - na
ah yī yī yeh - kee ay kī ay - nah

Ah yi yi yi - ki ay kae ay - na
ah yī yī yī - kee ay kī ay - nah

A ooo _____ ah dee mee kee - chee.
ah oo _____ ah dee mee kee - chee

Obwisana
(Ghana)

Ob - wi - sa - na sa - na - na Ob - wi - sa - na sa
ohb - wih - sah - nah sah - nah - nah ohb - wih - sah - nah sah

Ob - wi - sa - na sa - na - na Ob - wi - sa - na sa.
ohb - wih - sah - nah sah - nah - nah ohb - wih - sah - nah sah

Mayo Nafwa
(Zambia)

219

Map of Africa

© 2001 by Parker Publishing Company

African Musical Instruments

 AFRICAN RATTLE

 AFRICAN GUITARS

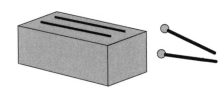 SLIT DRUM

 BAGANA

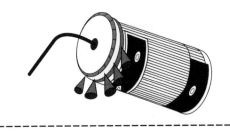 TALKING DRUM

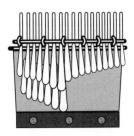 MBIRA (Kalimba, Sansa, Likemre, Kaffir)

AFRICAN MUSIC FACTS PAGE

Africa

- Africa is the second largest continent.
- It has about 800 tribes and languages, many cultures, and a population of over 400 million.

Music in African Culture

- Musicians may be trained or untrained.
- Some musicians are professional and some are amateur.
- Musicians come from royalty and the common society.
- Music is passed on orally and often changed through re-creation and improvisation.

Uses of Music

- Used for social, political, and religious events.
- Dance is usually involved.
- Songs may be performed for praising tribal chiefs, rewards, celebrating births, warnings, hunting, harvesting, work, and entertainment.

Instruments

- Drums—igbins (Nigeria), dunduns (Nigeria), batas (Nigeria), slit drums (West Africa), tuned drums (Uganda), and talking drums (Nigeria).
- Other percussion—bells, rattles (antelope ears and gourds with seeds), and mbira/thumb piano, sansa, likense, kalimba (Zimbabwe).
- Winds—horns and flutes made from animal horns, ivory, or bark.
- Strings—kora (West Africa) is the African harp, krar (Ethiopia) is the East African lyre, and zithers (Central Africa, Ruanda, and Madagascar), and guitar-like instruments (Nigeria).

History

- American jazz has its origins in African music.
- The banjo and guitar have origins in Africa.

African Music Activity Page

Fill in the blanks with terms that best fit the paragraph below.

Africa is the second largest continent in the world. There are more than 800 tribes and languages, and many cultures.

Music is used for _____, _____, and _____ purposes. Songs

may be performed for _____

_____

_____.

List some African instruments under the correct families.

PERCUSSION	WINDS	STRINGS
_____	_____	_____
_____	_____	_____
_____	_____	_____

How has African music influenced American music?

_____

_____

_____

_____

Describe African music. Think about the instruments, singing, tone color, beat, tempo, form, rhythm, and other elements.

_____

_____

_____

_____

Making Instruments
(Vibration, Cone, Cylinder, Cube, and Rectangle)

LESSON PLAN

Objective: The student will distinguish the physical attributes of the idiophone, aerophone, chordophone, and the membranophone (classifications).

Materials: Piano
A woodwind or brass instrument
A string instrument
A drum and a percussion instrument other than a drum
Chalkboard or overhead projector
Pencils
Copies of: Shapes page
      Sizes of Instruments page
      Instrument Match page
      Instruments song page
      Projects #1, #2, #3, or #4

Procedure:
1. *Opening Activity:* Ask the students to name as many instruments as they can. List each on the board or on an overhead. Hand out copies of the Shapes page and the Sizes of Instruments page. You may want to staple the two pages together for convenience. It may be helpful to put the pages on overhead sheets, also. Discuss the shapes with the class. Be quite detailed in the characteristics of each. Possibly, have the students locate objects in the room that match the shapes. Then discuss the instruments on the instrument page. Have the students find similar or matching characteristics between the parts and the instruments (classifications). Next, define and identify an aerophone, idiophone, and membranophone. Finally, have the students identify what type of instrument they had listed.

2. *Activity Page:* Distribute a copy of the Instrument Match page to each student. Direct the students to list as many instruments with matching parts in the shapes given as they can. Additionally, ask the students to design an instrument in the space provided.

3. *Singing and Listening Activity:* Teach the "Instruments" song. Perform the song on a woodwind or brass instrument, a string instrument, a drum, and a percussion instrument other than a drum. Compare and contrast the shapes of the instruments. Also, discuss why particular instruments are idiophones, chordophones, aerophones, and membranophones.

Procedure:

(Continued)

4. ***Instrument Construction Activity:*** Hand out copies of each of the projects. Assign project 1, 2, 3, or 4 to each student. You may want to do this randomly or with some method to be sure assigned projects are appropriate for each student. Be sure to have enough materials so each student can follow through with the project. Allow students to share their creations with the class. Discuss how the instrument works and why it is called what it's called.

5. ***Follow-Up Activity:*** Assign the other three projects to each student over a period of time. This will allow the student to differentiate between the instruments' constructions.

Shapes

Rectangle

Square

Circle

Triangle

Cone

Cylinder

Trapezoid

Cube

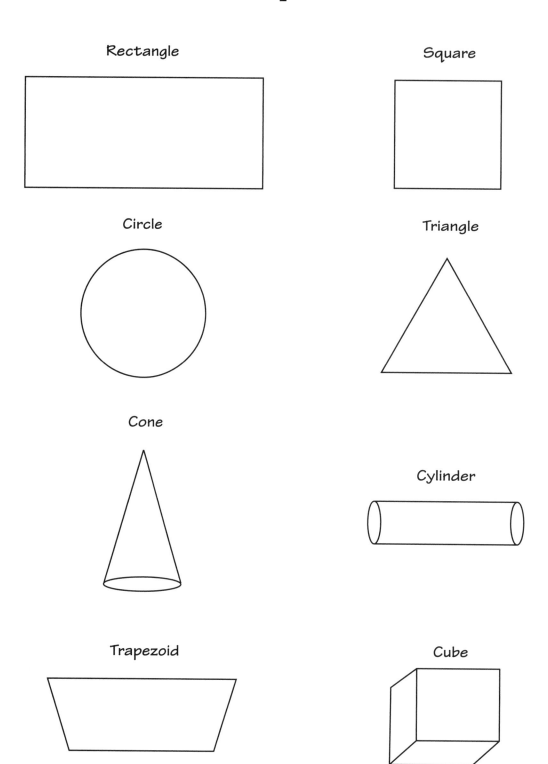

Name _____

Sizes of Instruments

Banjo
(chordophone and membranophone)

Clarinet
(aerophone)

Balalaika
(chordophone)

Trumpet
(aerophone)

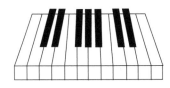

Rain Stick
(idiophone)

Keyboard
(idiophone and chordophone)

Triangle
(idiophone)

Guitar
(chordophone)

Snare Drum
(membranophone)

Chimes
(idiophone)

Instrument Match

List some instruments that are constructed of the shapes below.

Rectangle

_____
_____
_____
_____

Triangle

_____
_____
_____
_____

Cone

_____
_____
_____
_____

Circle

_____
_____
_____

Square

_____
_____

Trapezoid

_____
_____

Use the space below to create your own instrument.

Cube

_____
_____
_____

Cylinder

_____
_____
_____

What is it called?

_____

Instruments

T.F.K.

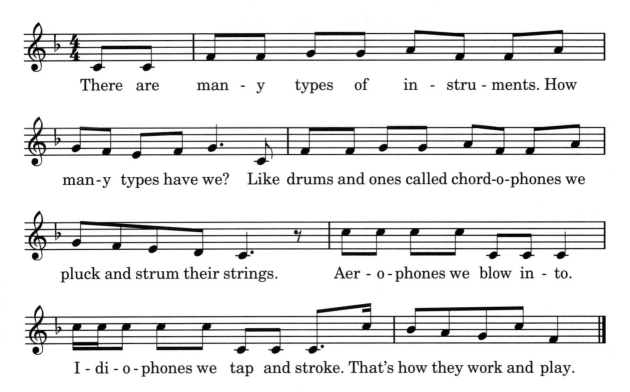

There are man-y types of in-stru-ments. How

man-y types have we? Like drums and ones called chord-o-phones we

pluck and strum their strings.   Aer-o-phones we blow in-to.

I-di-o-phones we tap and stroke. That's how they work and play.

 # Project #1

Box Guitar
(chordophone)

© 2001 by Parker Publishing Company

Materials:

Pencil
Glue
Scissors
Shoebox, cigar box, or any other cardboard box
5 Popsicle sticks
2-4 rubber bands of different thicknesses or 2-4 pieces of string
Paper towel roll center tube or a long, narrow piece of wood

Directions:

1. Cut a round or square hole in the center of the shoebox lid. Be sure it is not too small or too big of a hole.

2. Glue the lid to the shoebox by spreading the glue at the top of the box. Place the lid firmly on the box (face) to hold it in place. Put rubber bands around it to hold it until it dries.

3. Cut four or more slits of about one inch at the top of the paper towel tube and fold back each tab created by the cuts.

4. Glue the tabs of the tube on one of the shoebox sides (guitar neck).

5. Glue two Popsicle sticks together face to face (bridge). Glue the two sticks on the opposite end of the shoebox from the tube.

6. Break one Popsicle stick into three pieces. Glue each piece to the bridge. Be sure to keep each piece separate.

7. Glue two Popsicle sticks across the end of the tube (neck).

8. After allowing enough time for all glued parts to dry, tie and attach 2 or 3 strings or rubber bands to the bridge's Popsicle stick pieces. Tie the other end to the Popsicle sticks at the end of the neck.

9. The tightness or thickness of the strings will make a difference in the instrument's pitch. Be careful not to draw the strings too tight. It may break off the glued parts.

Optional Chordophone

Take a shoebox, without the lid, and wrap a few rubber bands of different thicknesses around it.

Project #2

"Air-a-net"
(aerophone)

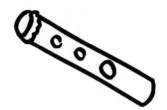

Materials:

Pencil
Phillips-head screwdriver
Hammer
Glue or masking tape
Cardboard cone or conch shell
A bottle cap

Directions:

1. Take a cardboard cone or shell and draw 3 to 4 circles the size of a nickel on one side.

2. Poke a hole in each circle with a screwdriver by placing the screwdriver in the circle and hammering it through. Try to widen the hole to the size of the circle (do not try to widen holes on a shell—shell aerophone is now finished).

3. Poke a hole in the top of the bottle cap.

4. Glue or tape the cap to the narrow open end of the cardboard cone—inside of the cap will be glued to the cone.

*To play this aerophone, buzz your lips as you blow into the cap.

Optional Aerophone

1. Take 3 bottles, and fill each with different amounts of water to create different pitches.

2. Possibly, use 3 different food colorings to color each bottle's water.

*Blow across the top of the bottle to create a sound.

Project #3

The Shake-e-bean
(idiophone)

Materials:

Glue
Beans, rice, or beads
Paper towel tube, 2 cups of the same size, a jar or can with a cover
Construction paper
Markers or crayons
2 rubber bands

Directions:

1. Glue a piece of construction paper over one end of the paper towel tube. Make sure the end is completely covered. You can also use two cups attached by wide tape.

2. Pour some beans (rice or beads) into the tube or container.

3. Glue a piece of construction paper over the other end of the tube.

4. Wrap a rubber band around each end of the tube to help hold the construction paper.

*Shake or tap the idiophone to play it.

Optional Idiophone

1. Take a few glasses and fill each with different amounts of water. Tap the glasses with a pencil to make a sound.

2. Take a piece of thick wood, and hammer numerous nails of different lengths into it. To play it, pluck the nails with your fingers.

Project #4

Drumster
(membranophone)

Materials:

Scissors
String, leather strings, or pipe cleaners
2 six-inch by six-inch pieces of leather, cloth, vinyl, or plastic (heads)
1 small piece of leather, cloth, vinyl, or plastic
1 stick or pencil six inches long
1 rubber band
1 small empty coffee can or another wide cylinder
cotton

Directions:

1. Cut or poke 2 holes in each edge of both leather pieces (heads), eight holes in all.

2. Place one head on a flat surface and put the coffee can in the center of it.

3. Place the other head on the top of the can.

4. Tie the leather string to each head. Be sure to lace the string through all eight holes on each head. Make sure the strings are tight enough to prevent the heads from sliding off the can.

5. For the drumstick, place cotton in the small piece of leather, and wrap it around one end of the stick. Wrap the rubber band around the leather and stick to hold the leather in place.

Optional Membranophone

1. Take a needlepoint ring and glue a thin piece of cloth around it.

2. Poke a hole into an even number of bottle caps.

3. Tie a short string through each of the caps.

4. Poke holes into the cloth of the ring.

5. Thread the strings with the caps through the cloth and tie each in a knot.

*Shake and tap your membranophone.

Stephen Foster
(Famous People, Biography)

LESSON PLAN

Objective: The student will identify two-section and three-section musical forms.

Materials: Piano
Pencils
Tape
Copies of: "Oh, Susanna," "Beautiful Dreamer,"
    and "Camptown Races"
    Lyrics page
    Form Shapes page
    Stephen Foster Biography
    What Song Am I? Cards page
    Who's Who? page

Procedure: 1. *Opening Activity:* Sing "Oh, Susanna" for the class. Ask the students to respond to who the composer is and what the composer intended in the words. After some response, explain to the students that "Oh, Susanna" was composed by Stephen Foster, a famous American songwriter during the 1840s to the 1860s. Explain to the class that he lived during the Civil War. Ask: "Who were some of the famous people who lived during that time?" (Abraham Lincoln, Ulysses S. Grant, Robert E. Lee, etc.). Tell the students that one historical account of the song claims that it was written to poke fun at or tease his sister, while another story says he wrote it for some song-singing friends. Nevertheless, the song is a nonsense song—the words are contradictory and nonsensical.

2. *Singing Activity:* Teach "Oh, Susanna." Afterwards, split the class in half. Have one half sing the verse and the other half the chorus. Have the chorus section stand when singing. Reverse the parts to allow the other section to stand during the verse. Ask the verse students to point to the chorus singers when the chorus part arrives.

3. *Listening Activity:* Sing "Beautiful Dreamer" to the students. Teach only the middle section, or chorus if you wish, to the students. Ask the students to sing their section of the song immediately after you sing the first. You must follow their section with the third section. Then, ask the class to generate ideas for dividing the class into sections for singing the song. Guide the class to realize that the first section is the same as the third, and maybe it should be sung by the same group. Invent a motion or movement to provide a physical application for the kinesthetic learner.

Procedure:

(Continued)

4. ***Group Activity:*** Sing "Camptown Races" to the class. Be sure the students know it well. Divide the class into teams of two to four students. Give a copy of the Camptown Races Lyrics page to each student. Have each student put the team members' names on the page. Read through and review the song with the class. Ask the students to divide the song into major sections, assign singing parts, ostinati (if using instruments), a beat or rhythm accompaniment, mark the page for sections, and use the Form Shapes page to raise or display as they divide and perform the song. Recongregate the class. Ask the students to describe, explain, and/or perform their rendition of the song. Lead the students through understanding the form.

5. ***Cooperative Activity:*** Make at least ten copies of the What Song Am I? Cards page (enough to cover your class). Cut out and laminate each song title. Have students tape a title on each other's back without revealing the title. Students will walk around the room asking only musical questions (one-word answer will work best) about the title. Each person can answer only one question. After a given time limit, or after a person asks five people, the game ends. Everyone guesses what song is on his/her back. Example questions: "In what form is this song? What is the tempo of this song? Is it a nonsense song? Is this a love song?"

6. ***Reading Activity:*** Give a copy of the biography page to each student. Assign groups of two to five students. Ask the students to read the biography and answer the following questions: "What or who may have influenced Stephen Foster's music? What famous people lived during Foster's life? Name the famous event that took place during Foster's life. List some of Foster's music titles." Reunite the class and ask the questions. You may want to put the questions on the chalkboard for the students to answer.

Activity Page: Hand out a copy of the Who's Who? activity page to all the students. Instruct the class to fill in the blanks with the name of the famous person who best fits the ten statements given.

Oh, Susanna

Foster

I come from Al - a-ba-ma with my ban-jo on my knee; I'm
going to Lou' - si-an - a my true love for to see. It
rained all night the day I left, the weath-er it was dry; The
sun so hot I froze to death, Su - san - na don't you cry.

Chorus

Oh! Su - san - na, don't you cry for me, I
come from Al - a-ba - ma with a ban - jo on my knee.

Beautiful Dreamer

Foster

Beau - ti - ful dream - er, wake un - to me, _____

Star-light and dew-drops are wait-ing for thee; _____

Sounds of the rude world heard in the day, _____

Lull'd by the moon-light have all passed a - way! _____

Beau-ti-ful dream-er, queen of my song ___ List while I woo thee with

soft mel-o - dy; ___ Gone are the cares of life's bus-y throng,

Beau - ti - ful dream-er, a - wake un - to me! _____

Beau - ti - ful dream-er, a - wake un - to me! _____

Camptown Races

Foster

The Camp-town la - dies sing this song, Doo - dah!

Doo - dah! The Camp-town race - track five miles long,

Oh! doo-dah - day! I came down here with my hat caved in,

Doo-dah! Doo-dah! I go back home with a pock-et full of tin,

Oh! doo - dah - day! Going to run all night!

Going to run all day! I'll __ bet my mo-ney on the

bob - tail nag. Some - bod - y bet on the bay.

Camptown Races Lyrics

Divide this song into major sections. Label the sections. Use the back of this sheet to explain why you divided the song the way you did.

Camptown ladies sing this song, Doo-dah! Doo-dah!

Camptown racetrack five miles long, Oh! Doo-dah day!

I come down with my hat caved in. Doo-dah! Doo-dah!

Went back home with a pocket full of tin, Oh! Doo-dah day!

Going to run all night. Going to run all day.

I'll bet my money on the bobtail nag. Somebody bet on the bay.

Why?

Form Shapes

STEPHEN FOSTER BIOGRAPHY

Stephen Foster was born on the Fourth of July in 1826 near Pittsburgh, Pennsylvania on the fiftieth anniversary of America's independence (1776). John Adams (second president of the United States) and Thomas Jefferson (third president) were two famous Americans who died on Foster's birthday.

Foster grew up in a family that loved to sing and play instruments. Although his family was involved with business and politics, Stephen was more interested in his love for music. African-American spirituals and work songs had a profound influence on Foster's music.

At fourteen, Foster was enrolled in college, but he soon left school at age sixteen to write music. He had many publications by the time he was twenty. His lack of business ability and personal problems led him to be short of money quite often during his life.

Even though Foster's songs were very popular, they did not earn him very much money. He worked for his brother briefly to become more secure, but his desire to compose was too great. Foster composed music like "Swanee River," "Oh, Susanna," "Old Folks at Home," "My Old Kentucky Home," and over two hundred more compositions before he died in 1864 (during the Civil War and Abraham Lincoln's presidency).

What Song Am I?

Cards

Oh! Susanna

Camptown Races

Beautiful Dreamer

Who's Who?

Fill in the spaces with Stephen Foster's name or the other famous person whose name best fits the statements below. At the bottom of the page you will find the other famous people listed.

1. _____ composed music during the Civil War.

2. The Pittsburgh, Pennsylvania, area was _____ 's birthplace.

3. Flying a kite during a lightning storm was _____ 's way of studying electricity.

4. The spirituals and work songs of slaves had a strong influence on

   _____ .

5. _____ was the commanding general of the southern army (rebels) during the Civil War.

6. The first president of the United States was _____ .

7. _____ was a general for the Union army during the Civil War and served as a president after the Civil War.

8. Born on the 4th of July, 1826, _____ was born on the day two other famous Americans died: John Adams and Thomas Jefferson.

9. The Gettysburg Address by _____ is one of the most famous speeches in U.S. history.

10. With his bad business sense and his personal decline, _____ was not very productive at the end of his life.

George Washington   Ben Franklin

Ulysses S. Grant

Robert E. Lee   Abraham Lincoln

Who's Who
(Answer Page)

1. **Stephen Foster** composed music during the Civil War.

2. The Pittsburgh, Pennsylvania, area was **Stephen Foster's** birthplace.

3. Flying a kite during a lightning storm was **Ben Franklin's** way of studying electricity.

4. Spirituals and work songs of slaves had a strong influence on **Stephen Foster.**

5. **Robert E. Lee** was the commanding general of the southern army (rebels) during the Civil War.

6. The first president of the United States was **George Washington.**

7. **Ulysses S. Grant** was a general for the Union army during the Civil War and served as a president after the Civil War.

8. Born on the 4th of July, 1826, **Stephen Foster** was born on the day two other famous Americans died: John Adams and Thomas Jefferson.

9. The Gettysburg Address by **Abraham Lincoln** is one of the most famous speeches in U.S. history.

10. With his lack of business sense and personal decline, **Stephen Foster** was not very productive at the end of his life.

3/4 Meter
The Music of *Sleeping Beauty*
(Fairy Tales)

LESSON PLAN

Objective: Students will perform and compose in 3/4 meter.

Materials: Piano
Rhythm sticks or any other rhythm instruments
Xylophone or bells
Pencils
Copies of: *Sleeping Beauty* Story page
"Adagio" and "Waltz" song pages
Team Composition pages for Composition, Melody,
Lyrics, Rhythm, Dynamics/Tempo, Symbols, Checker,
and Performer
Sleeping Beauty Activity Page

Procedure: 1. *Opening Activity:* Sing the "Lilac Fairy" from *Sleeping Beauty* for
the students. Then teach the song to the students. Ask the
students what kind of story *Sleeping Beauty* is (lead the class to
answer *a fairy tale*).

2. *Story Activity:* Read the *Sleeping Beauty* Story Page. Discuss the
story: "Why is it a fairy tale? What makes it a fairy tale? Name
some other fairy tales."

3. *Rhythm Activity:* Teach "Adagio" from *Sleeping Beauty*. After the
song is learned, have the students sing and clap the beat in three.
Try tap, clap, clap for a more accurate feeling of the beat. Hand
out copies of the "Adagio" song page to all the students or display
the song on an overhead projector. Review note values and
counting. Have the class play the rhythm of the song on the
rhythm sticks. Assign half the class to tap and clap the beat while
the other half plays the rhythm of the song (you may want to use
only those students who can perform the rhythm first). Rotate
parts.

4. *Performance Activity:* Teach the "Waltz." Review the treble clef
note names. Using a xylophone or set of bells with F, E, F, D, G,
A, and F# (first line to third space), select students to perform the
bell part for the waltz. Have the students sing the song and have
the bell player play when the bell part comes in. Choose
xylophone or bell players by asking them to name a fairy tale

Procedure:

(Continued)

character. After a player performs, he/she can pick someone to name a fairy tale character. This activity can involve more performers if more instruments are used at one time.

5. **Composition Activity:** This activity is best with two or three students per team (large classes may need ten or more teams). Using the Team Composition pages, have each team execute in the following order: Melody Page, Lyrics Page, Rhythm Page, Dynamics/Tempo Page, Symbols Page, Checker Page, and Performer Page. The Composition Page is the last page to be completed. It is the page that combines all the team pages in one to create a team composition. It is best for students to sing, clap, and/or tap what they compose rather than to just place notes, but this can be a start for students to develop an interest in composing. Encourage students to match words and rhythms. They may want to write the rhythm first, and then the words. This activity may take longer than one class, so you may want to plan appropriately.

Activity Page:

Give a copy to each student. You may want to use this before the Team Composition Activity as preparation. Have the students complete one exercise at a time and then perform it. Or, you may want the entire page completed, and then performed in front of the class. The mystery song is "Row, Row, Row Your Boat."

Prologue: Lilac Fairy

From *Sleeping Beauty Suite*

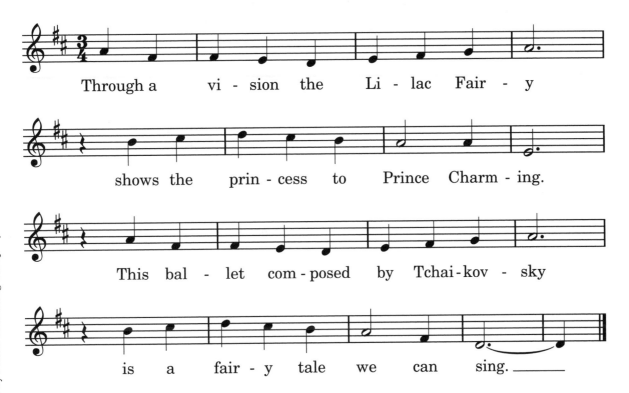

Through a vi - sion the Li - lac Fair - y

shows the prin - cess to Prince Charm - ing.

This bal - let com - posed by Tchai - kov - sky

is a fair - y tale we can sing. _____

SLEEPING BEAUTY STORY PAGE

A king and queen are holding a christening for their daughter Princess Aurora. Many guests are invited, but not the wicked fairy. The wicked fairy, however, was never invited to special events because it is believed that she is dead. Nevertheless, the wicked fairy is not dead. So when she is not invited to special festivities, she casts an evil curse. Being upset about not being invited to the princess's christening, the wicked fairy places a curse on Aurora.

Later on when the princess becomes a beautiful sixteen-year-old girl, Aurora pricks her finger on a needle while sewing, and she falls into a deep sleep. The Lilac Fairy, in the meantime, is showing Prince Charming a vision of the sleeping Princess Aurora. The Lilac Fairy leads the prince to the princess. He bestows a kiss on her and the princess awakens. The prince and the princess marry, and they live happily ever after.

Adagio

Act I

A wick - ed fair - y puts a nast - y curse on the Prin - cess Au - ro - ra when she pricks her fin - ger while she was sew - ing and puts her in a deep, deep sleep un - til Prince Charm-ing comes save her life.

Waltz

Act II

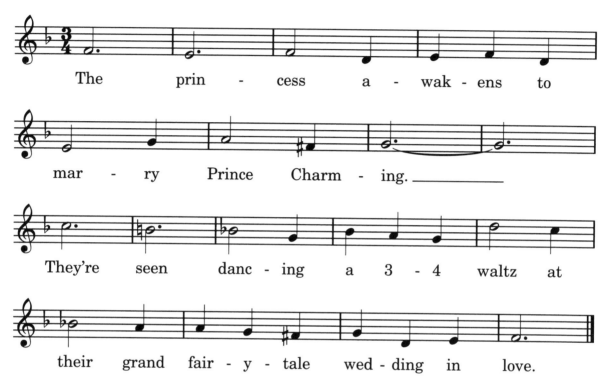

The prin - cess a - wak - ens to mar - ry Prince Charm - ing. _____

They're seen danc - ing a 3 - 4 waltz at their grand fair - y - tale wed - ding in love.

Team Composers:

_____

_____

_____

Composition Page for
Team Composition

Write a team music composition by completing the Melody Page, Lyrics Page, Rhythm Page, Dynamics/Tempo Page, Symbols Page, Checker Page, and Performer Page (in that order). Complete this team Composition Page by using the choices you made with your other pages.

_____

(Title of your composition)

MELODY PAGE FOR
TEAM COMPOSITION

Using the note banks given below, choose the notes you want to use for your composition. Place a check in the space beside the note bank you chose.

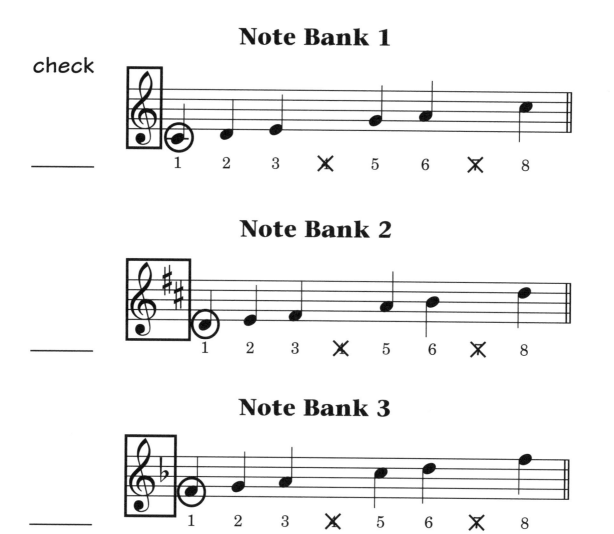

Note Bank 1

check

_____ 1 2 3 ✗ 5 6 ✗ 8

Note Bank 2

_____ 1 2 3 ✗ 5 6 ✗ 8

Note Bank 3

_____ 1 2 3 ✗ 5 6 ✗ 8

Tips for Composers

- After choosing your note bank, be sure to include your key signature.
- Try ending your composition with note 1 or 8, 3 or 5.
- Avoid large leaps between notes (low to high or high to low).

LYRICS PAGE FOR
TEAM COMPOSITION

After choosing your note bank, write down some ideas for putting lyrics to your composition. What you write about may have some influence on your composition. Complete the following questions and assignments.

1. In the box below, write down some ideas that your composition could be about. Then decide which idea you want and circle it.

2. Write four possible sentences or phrases that fit the idea you chose above in box 1 and, perhaps, make the phrase rhyme.

Tips for Composers

- Try to have your melody and rhythm fit your words.
- Have your rhythm and words work together:

    (ex. 2/4 ♩ ♫ ♩ ♮ ♪ ♫)

    Jump-ing high.   Ex-cit-ing

RHYTHM PAGE FOR
TEAM COMPOSITION

Complete the Rhythm Page by using the note bank and meter bank below.

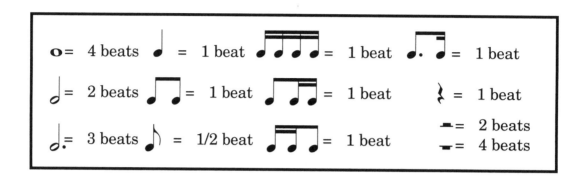

Meter Bank

2 (2 beats per measure)   3 (beats)   4 (beats)
4   4   4

Practice writing rhythms to match your works. Don't forget to add your meter (time signature). Use the first space or line to write your rhythm.

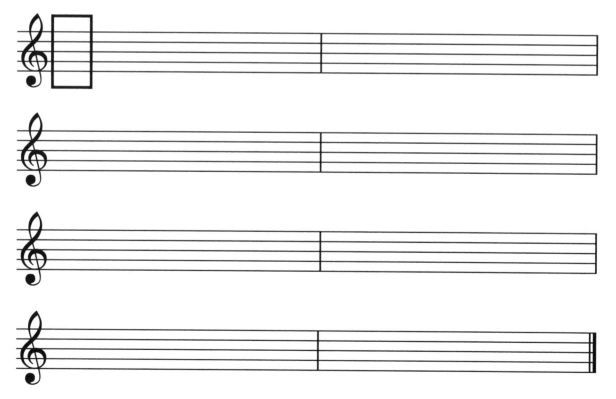

DYNAMICS/TEMPO PAGE FOR TEAM COMPOSITION

Complete the questions below. Use this page to help you complete your team composition.

Dynamics

1. How loud or soft do you want your composition?

2. Will your dynamics change throughout your composition?

Dynamics Bank

f—loud	p—soft/quiet
mf—medium loud	mp—medium soft/quiet
ff—very loud	pp—very soft/quiet

Gradually louder  Gradually softer

Tempo

3. How fast or slow do you want your composition?

4. Choose and circle the tempo for your composition.

Tempo Bank

Presto—very fast	Adagio—slow
Allegro—fast	Largo—very slow
Moderato—moderately fast	Ritardando—gradually slow down
Accelerando—gradually faster	Andante—slow/walking tempo

Tip for Composers

- Choose the Dynamics and Tempo that best fit your composition.

SYMBOLS PAGE FOR
TEAM COMPOSITION

Choose the symbols that may help express your composition.

Symbols Bank

Shows the end of a composition or section.

Repeat within these symbols.

D.C. al Fine—Repeat from the beginning and end at the **Fine.** (Don't forget to add the Fine.)

D.S. al Fine—Repeat from the sign (𝄋) and end at the **Fine.**

1.   :‖ 2.   ‖   Perform the first ending, repeat the music, skip the first ending and perform the second ending.

Fermata—Hold the note longer or until the director cuts off.

Accent—Play the note a little stronger.

Staccato—Play the note short and detached.

Tips for Composers

- Choose the symbols that best fit your composition.
- Which symbols help express your words and music?

CHECKER PAGE FOR TEAM COMPOSITION

Use this page to make sure you have completed everything needed to finish your composition. Check the box of those steps that are finished.

Composition Checklist

☐ 1. Completed the **Melody Page**

☐ 2. Completed the **Lyrics Page.**

☐ 3. Completed the **Rhythm Page.**

☐ 4. Completed the **Dynamics/Tempo Page.**

☐ 5. Completed the **Symbols Page.**

☐ 6. Completed the **Team Composition Page.**

☐ 7. Do your words and rhythm match?

☐ 8. Do your words rhyme?

☐ 9. Make sure your composition can be easily read by a performer.

☐ 10. Are you ready to perform your composition?

PERFORMER PAGE FOR
TEAM COMPOSITION

This page will assist you in performing your composition.

1. Decide which instrument you want to use. Which instrument will best express the music?

2. Practice the music measure by measure, line by line, and the entire composition.

3. Make sure to play the notes as written. Give the notes their full value.

4. Play all the symbols, tempo, and notation. How many beats in a measure? Any repeats? What accents are present? What tempo?

5. If you are playing it correctly and it doesn't sound quite right, make the necessary changes to improve your composition.

Name _____

Sleeping Beauty Activity Page

Complete the following exercises.

1. Using ♩, ♪, ♩., or ♫ compose a piece for rhythm instruments.

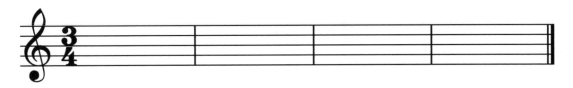

2. Add a melody to your rhythm above using F, G, A, Cm, and/or D.

3. Add the stems to the note heads to complete the music in 3/4 meter.

*Try playing these measures on a xylophone, recorder, or keyboard. Can you guess what song this is?

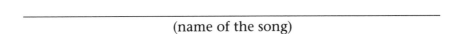

(name of the song)

Supplementary Materials
(3–4)

Dynamics (activity page)
  Dynamics (answer key)

Symbol Community (activity page)

Team Composing & Orchestration (record sheet)

Music Basketball
  Music Basketball Tournament (record sheet)
  Music Basketball Basket
  Music Basketball Basketballs

Time Signature and Meter Measuring (activity page)

A Music Recipe for Writing a Song
  A Music Recipe (activity page)
  Music Writing Page

Music Store
  The Music Store Order Page
  Music Store Money

Healthy Music and Body Organs (activity page)
  Healthy Music and Body Organs (answer key)

Healthy Music Body (activity page)

Name This Song
  Name This Song (tunes listed by melodic syllables)
  Name This Song (tunes listed by melodic notation)
  Name This Song (tunes listed by rhythm notation)

Daily Music Builders
  Daily Singing (Pitch) Skill Builders 26–50
  Daily Rhythm Skill Builders 26–50

Interdisciplinary Planner

Name _____

Dynamics

1. Place the dynamic term in the space below that best fits the size of the trumpet.

   Fortissimo   Forte   Piano   Pianissimo

_____   _____   _____   _____

2. Fill in the missing letters to complete the dynamics terms below.

   _ _ _ z _ p _ _ _ _

   F _ _ _ _ _

   _ _ a _ _ _

   _ _ _ _ _ _ _ _ _ m _

   _ _ r _ _ _ _ _ _ _

   _ e _ _ _ _ _ _ _ _

4. Unscramble the words below.

   oipan _____

   rsosoftiim _____

   ozinozaepm _____

   inaspsiomi _____

   Extra! What do crescendo and diminuendo mean?

3. Write the music term for the dynamics listed below.

   Loud _____

   Soft _____

   Medium soft _____

   Very loud _____

   Very soft _____

   Medium loud _____

5. Draw a picture in the space below that best describes the given dynamic terms.

Forte	Piano

Dynamics
(Answer Key)

1.

Piano   _Forte_   _Pianissimo_   _Fortissimo_

2. M e z z o p i a n o

Forte

Piano

Pianissimo

Fortissimo

Mezzoforte

3. Loud _____

Soft _____

Medium soft ____ Forte _____

Very loud _____ Piano _____

Very soft _____ Mezzo Piano ___

Medium loud ____ Fortissimo ____

Pianissimo

Mezzo Forte

4. oipan _____ piano _____

rsosoftiim ____ fortissimo ____

ozinozaepm ____ mezzopiano ____

inaspsiomi ____ pianissimo ____

5. Pictures will vary.

Name _____

Symbol Community

☑ Check off and circle each music symbol in this community.

263

Team Composing and Orchestration

Team Members _____

_____

_____

Directions:

1. After being assigned Theme, Ostinato, or Bass, use the assigned note bank to write four measures with four beats each. You must be able to count and perform your work.

2. Choose an instrument for your part, and practice what you wrote.

3. All three players should play their composition together.

Theme

Ostinato

Bass

Note Banks

Theme

Ostinato

Bass

Music Basketball

Objective: Students will learn the beat values of the whole note, half note, and quarter note.

Materials: Copies of: Music Basketball Tournament page
                      Music Basketball Basket page
                      Music Basketball Basketballs page
Scissors
Orange oaktag
Pencils

Preparation:
1. Copy enough Music Basketball Tournament pages for each student in the class.

2. Copy the Music Basketballs and Basket pages on orange oaktag and laminate for durability.

3. Cut out the basketballs (plastic sandwich bags work well for storing and organizing).

Procedure:
1. Pair the students. Note that the game may be played individually, however.

2. Sitting on the floor or at a table, have the students place a Basket page about two feet from each student.

3. Instruct the students to toss the basketballs onto the Basketball Basket. The balls that fall within the net will count. Students must count the total amount of beats of the balls that fall within the net.

4. The game can end after either all balls for each student have been tossed or following five minutes of play. If a timed game is played, students may need to collect the tossed balls and toss them again until time has elapsed.

5. Two baskets may be used when two students play. Also, one or two sets of basketballs may be used.

6. Paper cups may be used, if you want a more challenging game.

7. Students should use the Music Basketball Tournament page to keep score. A "best-of-five-games" series will give students a fair and fighting chance to win.

Name _____   *Players*

_____

_____

Music Basketball Tournament

Use the scoreboards to record the total points and shots of your Music Basketball games.

Game 1

Player	Score	Shots

Game 2

Player	Score	Shots

Game 3

Game 4

Game 5

Tournament Totals

Player	Points	Shots

Music Basketball Basket

Music Basketball
Basketballs

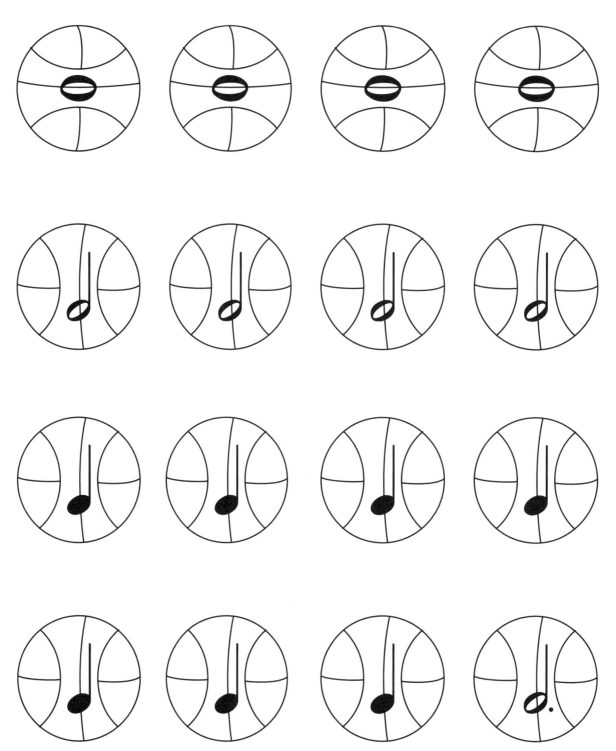

Name _____

Time Signature
and Meter Measuring

𝅝 = 4   𝅗𝅥. = 3   𝅗𝅥 = 2   ♩ = 1   𝄻 = 4   𝄼 = 2   𝄽 = 1

1. Put a ☐box☐ around the time signature/meter for the music line below.

2. Circle the (incorrect) measures.

3. In the box below, write the correct meter/time signature for the music.

4. Write a composition in 2/4 meter for these measures.

A Music Recipe for Writing a Song

Objective: Students will compose a song using the various music notations and symbols.

Materials: Pencils

Music staff paper

Copies of Music Recipe page

Procedure: 1. Give each student a copy of the Music Recipe page.

2. This activity may be done individually or in partners. Students, however, may tend to copy ideas if not carefully monitored.

3. Read and review the directions to the activity with the students. Make sure each step is being followed.

4. Assist students with good phrasing, cadences, melodic line, lyrics, and so on.

5. Perform each student's work. Put the music on overheads or just play it. Students are thrilled to hear their music performed. It is just like making or drawing something in art class.

A Music Recipe

Follow the recipe and cook up a great original song that you composed.

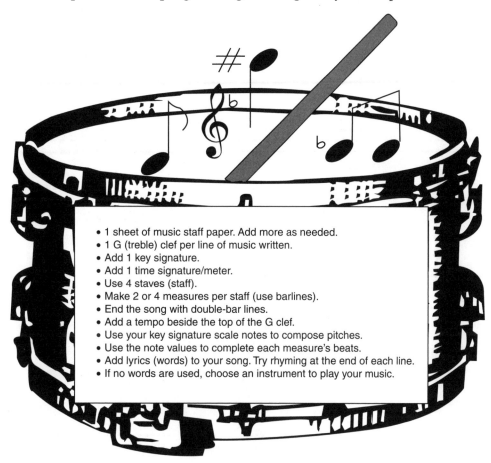

- 1 sheet of music staff paper. Add more as needed.
- 1 G (treble) clef per line of music written.
- Add 1 key signature.
- Add 1 time signature/meter.
- Use 4 staves (staff).
- Make 2 or 4 measures per staff (use barlines).
- End the song with double-bar lines.
- Add a tempo beside the top of the G clef.
- Use your key signature scale notes to compose pitches.
- Use the note values to complete each measure's beats.
- Add lyrics (words) to your song. Try rhyming at the end of each line.
- If no words are used, choose an instrument to play your music.

Ingredients

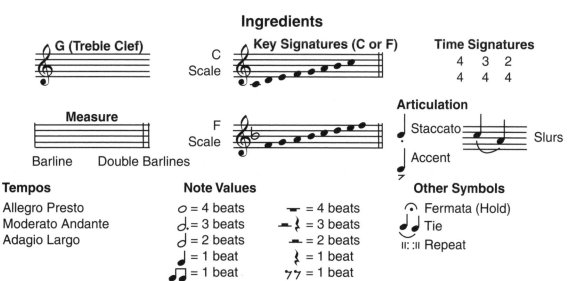

G (Treble Clef)

Measure

Barline   Double Barlines

C Scale

F Scale

Key Signatures (C or F)

Time Signatures

4	3	2
4	4	4

Articulation

Staccato

Accent

Slurs

Tempos

Allegro Presto
Moderato Andante
Adagio Largo

Note Values

○ = 4 beats   ▬ = 4 beats
♩. = 3 beats   ▬ ⁊ = 3 beats
♩ = 2 beats   ▬ = 2 beats
♩ = 1 beat   ⁊ = 1 beat
♫ = 1 beat   ⁊⁊ = 1 beat

Other Symbols

𝄐 Fermata (Hold)
♩♩ Tie
‖: :‖ Repeat

Composer _____
(Your Name)

_____
(Song Title)

Music Store

Objective: Students will demonstrate knowledge of note values and number of beats each note receives.

Materials: Pencils
Scissors
Copies of: Music Store Money page
Music Store page

Procedure: 1. Photocopy enough Music Store Money pages so that each student can be given ten music-money dollar bills. Cut out the bills. You may want to use different color paper and laminate the variety of bills.

2. Group the students in pairs. The activity can be done individually, but it is much more fun in pairs.

3. Give each student a copy of The Music Store page and ten random music-money dollar bills.

4. One student will be the customer and the other will be the clerk.

5. The customer can buy any item or items in the shop with the amount of beats he/she possesses. The clerk writes down the name of the item and its price on the Music Store Receipt. Total bill, amount paid, and change (if applicable) should also be recorded by the clerk.

6. Each student should get an opportunity to be both the clerk and the customer.

The Music Store

Customer's Name _____

Clerk _____

Directions: This Music Store has many wonderful musical items to buy. But you can use only the amount of Music Store Money beats you have to make purchases at this store. Remember: Make sure you have enough beats to buy what you want.

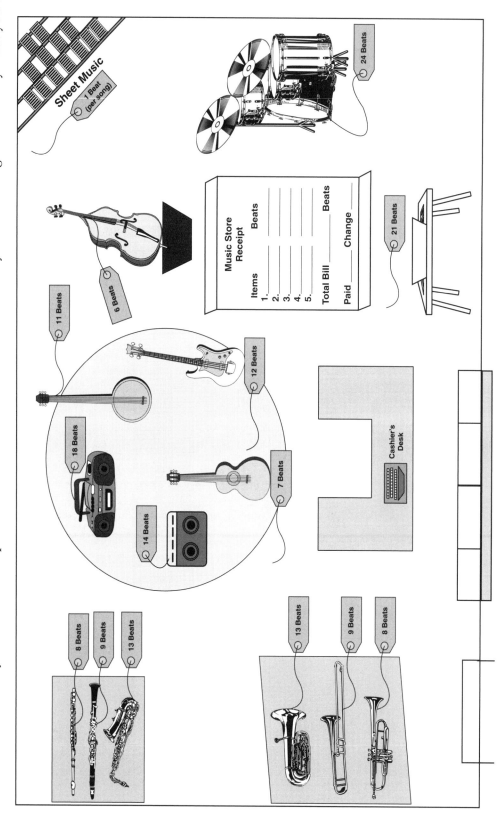

Sheet Music
1 Beat (per song)

24 Beats

6 Beats

11 Beats

Music Store Receipt

Items	Beats
1.	_____
2.	_____
3.	_____
4.	_____
5.	_____
Total Bill	_____ Beats
Paid	_____
Change	_____

21 Beats

12 Beats

18 Beats

7 Beats

14 Beats

Cashier's Desk

8 Beats
9 Beats
13 Beats

13 Beats
9 Beats
8 Beats

Music Store Money

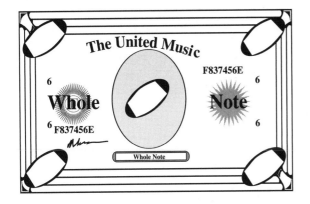

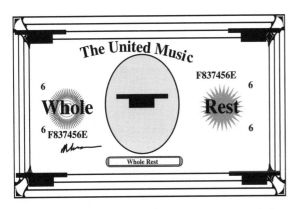

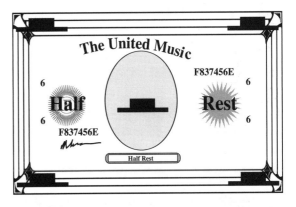

Healthy Music and Body Organs

Complete the names of the body organs by using the music notation hints. If your answer is correct, cut out the organ and glue it to the correct organ on the Healthy Music Body page.

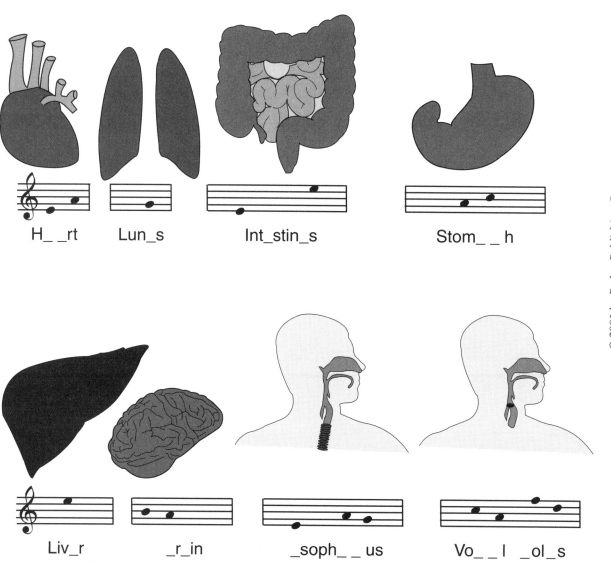

H_ _rt   Lun_s   Int_stin_s   Stom_ _ h

Liv_r   _r_in   _soph_ _ us   Vo_ _ l _ol_s

Healthy Music and Body Organs

(Answer Page)

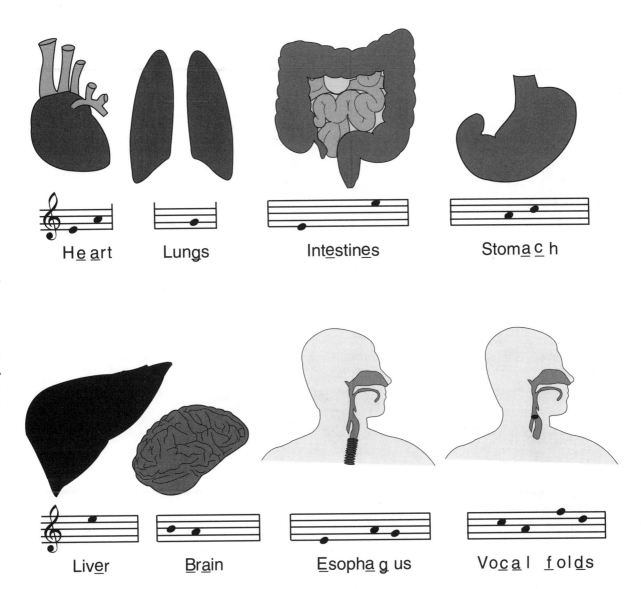

He <u>e</u> <u>ar</u> t   Lun <u>g</u> s   Int <u>e</u> st <u>in</u> es   Stom <u>a</u> <u>c</u> h

Li <u>v</u> er   <u>Br</u> <u>ai</u> n   <u>E</u> sopha <u>g</u> us   Vo <u>c</u> <u>a</u> l <u>f</u> ol <u>ds</u>

Healthy Music Body

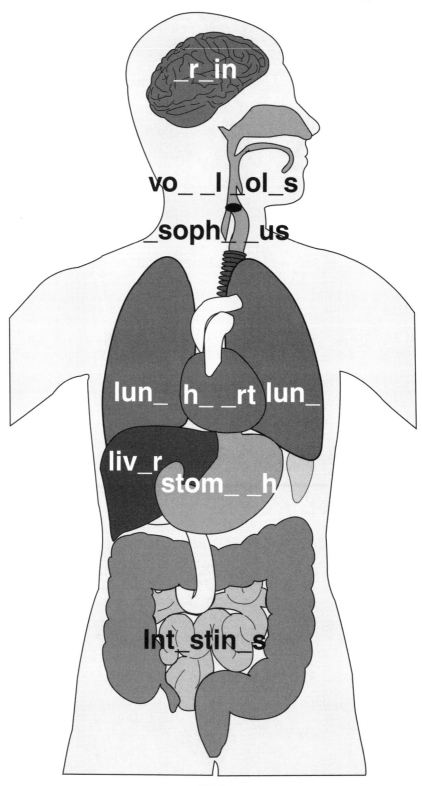

_r_in

vo_ _l_ol_s

soph _us

lun_ h_ _rt lun_

liv_r

stom_ _h

Int_stin_s

Name This Song

The following tonal and rhythm excerpts are intended to be used on a regular or occasional basis. Each excerpt comes from a well-known song and may be recognized by students. One excerpt may be displayed for a class to guess the title by reading the rhythm or melodic notation. The excerpts can be used as a school-wide "guess the tune" contest each week, possibly.

It is recommended that an excerpt be selected that coincides with rhythms, melodic syllables, or any other music concepts being promoted in your present unit or curriculum. You may possibly want to use songs more familiar to your students, other than those selected here, for more frequent use.

The Name This Song game is a good opportunity to help students develop their reading and performance skills through a challenging and fun activity.

NAME THIS SONG
(Tunes listed by melodic syllables)

1. (Hot Cross Buns)

2. (Old MacDonald)

3. (Bingo)

4. (Mary Had a Little Lamb)

5. (Ring Around the Rosy)

NAME THIS SONG
(Tunes listed by melodic notation)

1. (Twinkle, Twinkle Little Star)

2. (Frere Jacques)

3. (Ode to Joy)

4. (Star-Spangled Banner)

5. (Yankee Doodle)

NAME THIS SONG
(Tunes listed by rhythm notation)

282

DAILY SINGING SKILL BUILDERS
Do-Re-Mi

Do   Re   Mi (Rest)

Do-Re-Mi-La (Low)

Do-Re-Mi-La (Low) *(Continued)*

DAILY RHYTHM SKILL BUILDERS
Tee-Ka-Tee-Ka

© 2001 by Parker Publishing Company

Tee-Ka-Tee-Ka *(Continued)*

286

Interdisciplinary Planner

A record of the regular classroom's units, content, and concepts to be integrated with music.

Date _____

INTEGRATED SUBJECT	THIRD	FOURTH
Literature Arts		
Math		
Science		
Health		
Social Studies		
Art		
Physical Education		
Other		

LEVEL 3
(Grade Levels 5-6)

Civil War Music
(Civil War)

<u>LESSON PLAN</u>

Objective: Students will identify characteristics, composers, and music of the Civil War.

Materials: Piano
Pencils
Copies of: Music pages
      Civil War Music Facts Page
      Civil War Team Page
      Civil War Music Packet Cover
      Civil War Song page
      Civil War Music Excerpt Page
      Civil War Music Activity Page

Procedure: 1. *Opening Activity:* Teach and/or sing "Battle Hymn of the Republic." Discuss the words of the song. Ask questions about the meaning, why the song was written, who wrote it, and what war was it a product of. Lead and guide the students to the response of the Civil War. Ask, "What army, North or South, would have written this song?" After soliciting answers, explain the background of the song. "The song is a patriotic song of the North."

       2. *Listening/Discovering Activity:* Hand out the Civil War Music Facts Page. Read through and discuss (on the reverse side, photocopy "Dixie"). After discussing the facts, teach and sing "Dixie." Ask, "What is this song about? Who would have composed this song? What army sang this song?"

       3. *Team Activity:* Hand out the Civil War Music Team Page. Teach "Tramp, Tramp, Tramp." Put the students into teams of 3 or 4. Have the teams categorize "Tramp, Tramp, Tramp." Once they figure out what kind of song it is and who sang it, have the students record the answers on the Civil War Team Page.

       Afterwards, hand out the Civil War Music Packet. Teach and sing all of the songs. Have the teams categorize each song by looking at the words. They should record their answers on the Civil War Team Page.

Procedure:
(Continued)

4. ***Writing/Creating Activity:*** Hand out the My Civil War Song Page. Have the students compose two songs or poems that represent each army, one North and one South. They may use the Civil War Music Facts Page for help. Also, they may use any type of song (emancipation, battle, slave, etc.).

5. ***Extension Activity:*** Put the students in teams. Using all the learned Civil War songs, assign one song to each team. Have the teams develop a scene that would correlate and depict the theme and subject of the assigned song.

6. ***Reading Activity:*** Hand out a copy of the Civil War Excerpt Page to the students. Instruct the students to name the type of Civil War song the excerpts represent and write it in the spaces provided.

Activity Page: Give each student a copy of the Civil War Activity Page. Have the students fill in the blanks by using the answers given below each section.

CIVIL WAR MUSIC FACTS PAGE

Background: The American Civil War was a confrontation between the United States of America (Union) and the Confederate States of America (Confederacy). The Confederate States were southern states that wished to continue the practice of slavery and seceded from the Union (the United States government). In time, President Abraham Lincoln, head of the United States government, issued the Emancipation Proclamation freeing "all slaves in areas still in rebellion," but the states of the Confederacy refused to give up the use of slaves to work the plantations.

The Civil War began when the Confederates attacked and captured Fort Sumter, in Charleston, South Carolina. From 1861 to 1865 the United States was split—brother against brother, uncle against nephew, cousin against cousin. The war took a terrible toll on the country.

Whether based in people's pride in their own beliefs or in their deep hatred for their foe, music was a major force in the American culture. The music publishing business had been going strong since the 1820s. Stephen Foster was a popular composer of parlor music, the music played in people's living rooms.

The music of the American Civil War appeared in many forms within the culture. One form was slave songs, such as "Swing Low, Sweet Chariot" and other spirituals. Another was patriotic songs like "Battle Hymn of the Republic," "Dixie," "Maryland, My Maryland," and "Battle Cry for Freedom," which became popular because of people's feelings of pride and honor. Still another form of music were songs of a soldier's life, such as "Marching through Georgia," "Tramp, Tramp, Tramp," "Goober Peas," and "All Quiet Along the Potomac Tonight." The songs of a soldier's life popularized song composers like Root and Work. James Clark's "The Children of the Battlefield," Sontag's "Comrades, I Am Dying," and William Hays's "The Drummer of Shiloh" depicted some of the 600,000 deaths that occurred on the battlefield (battlefield songs).

Two other types of music during the Civil War were songs of domestic life and emancipation songs. The domestic life songs reflected those loved ones left behind when men went off to war. The lonely families and the yearning wives and mothers are the focus of many of these songs. "When Johnny Comes Marching Home," "When This Cruel War Is Over," and "O Come You from the Battlefield" were songs that clearly showed the pain and anxiousness of the soldiers' families. The emancipation /freedom songs, like "The New Emancipation Song" and "The Drinkin' Gourd," were sung to celebrate the future and hope for the abolition of slavery.

Armand Blackmar, James Clark, Luther Emerson, Daniel Emmett, William Hays, George Root, John Thomas, Henry Work, and Henry Tucker were just a few of the prominent composers during the American Civil War. These composers captured the events and feelings of the time and passed them on to us today through music and accompanying words. Their music helps us remember and appreciate our past and how we got where we are today.

Names _____   _____

_____   _____

CIVIL WAR MUSIC TEAM PAGE
What Type of Music Is This Civil War Song?

Title/Type of Song

1. _____

Composer _____

Why? _____

_____

_____

2. _____

Composer _____

Why? _____

_____

_____

3. _____

Composer _____

Why? _____

_____

_____

4. _____

Composer _____

Why? _____

_____

_____

5. _____

Composer _____

Why? _____

_____

_____

CIVIL WAR
MUSIC PACKET

Name _____

Dixie

Daniel Emmett

Battle Hymn of the Republic

William Steffe
Lyrics by Julia Ward Howe

Mine eyes have seen the glo-ry of the com-ing of the Lord. He is

tramp-ling out the vin-tage where the grapes of wrath are stored. He has

loosed the faith-ful light-ning of his ter - ri-ble swift sword. His

Chorus

truth is mar-ching on. Glo - ry, Glo-ry Hal-le - lu - jah!

Glo - ry, Glo - ry Hal - le - lu - jah! Glo - ry, Glo - ry Hal - le-

lu - jah, His truth is mar - ching on!

The Children of the Battlefield

J.G. Clark

Up - on the field of Get-tys - burg The __

sum - mer sun was high When free - dom met her

haught-y foe be - neath a north - ern sky. A -

mong the her - oes of the North, who swelled her grand ar -

ray. And rushed like moun - tain eag - les forth from

hap - py homes a - way. There stood a man of

hum - ble fame A __ sire of child - ren three And

gazed with-in a lit - tle frame their pic - tured form to

The Children of the Battlefield *(Continued)*

see. And blame him not if in the strife he

breathed a sol-dier's prayer: O Fa - ther shield the _

sol - dier's wife. And for his child - ren care. And

for _ his _ child - ren _ care.

The New Emancipation Song

E. Parkhurst
(Female)

Verse

Oh, give the slaves their free - dom. You sure-ly do not

need them. And no long-er clothe and feed them in the U-nit-ed States.

For they all sigh for free-dom. They all sigh for free-dom, for they

all sigh for free - dom in these U - nit - ed States.

298

Battle Cry of Freedom

George F. Root

Tramp, Tramp, Tramp
(The Prisoner's Hope)

George Root

In the pris-on cell I sit, Think-ing, moth-er dear, of you, And our

bright and hap - py home so far a - way, And the

tears they fill my eyes, spite of all that I can do, Though I

try to cheer my com - rades and be gay.

Tramp, Tramp, Tramp, the boys are march - ing.

Cheer up, com - rades, they will come. And be -

neath the star - ry flag we shall breathe the air a-gain of the

free - land in our own be - lov - ed home.

My Civil War Song

Compose a song or poem about the Civil War. Decide what type of song it is and list the type, title, and your name as the composer.

Type of Song

_____

Title

_____

Composer

_____

Civil War Music Excerpt Page

List the type of song each music excerpt may represent: Slave, Patriotic, Soldier's Life, Domestic, Battlefield, or Emancipation.

When Johnny Comes Marching Home

The   men   will cheer and the   boys   will shout.

Type: _____

The Drummer Boy from Shiloh

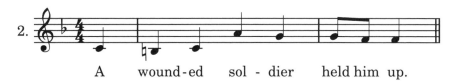

A   wound-ed   sol - dier   held him up.

Type: _____

Glory! Glory!

Glo - ry!   Glo - ry! How the Freed-men   sang!

Type: _____

Marching Through Georgia

Hur - rah!   Hur - rah!   We   bring the Ju - bi - lee!

Type: _____

© 2001 by Parker Publishing Company

Civil War Music Activity Page

Civil War Music

1. Song sung by slaves working, praying, and relaxing. _____

2. Songs of hope for freedom. _____

3. Songs performed in the living room. _____

4. Names of Civil War composers. _____

5. Music of families yearning for sons, husbands, fathers, and brothers.

   _____

6. Songs of pride and honor. _____

7. Marching music. _____

Slave Songs	**Parlor Songs**	**Root**
Emancipation Songs	**Patriotic Songs**	**Emmett**
Songs of a Soldier's Life	**Clark**	**Emerson**
Domestic Life Songs	**Hays**	**Work**

Civil War Facts

1. President during the Civil War. _____

2. Northern Army's general. _____

   Southern's. _____

3. The people held in bondage to work on plantations. _____

4. Places of great battles. _____

   _____

5. The place where the war started. _____

6. The place where the war ended. _____

Abraham Lincoln	**Gettysburg**	**Fort Sumter**
Stephen Douglas	**Antietam**	**Appomattox**
Ulysses S. Grant	**Robert E. Lee**	**Vicksburg**
Slaves		

Civil War Music Activity Page

(Answer Key)

Civil War Music

1. Songs sung by slaves working, praying, and relaxing. <u>Slave Songs</u>

2. Songs of hope for freedom. <u>Emancipation Songs</u>

3. Songs performed in the living room. <u>Parlor Songs</u>

4. Names of Civil War composers. <u>Root, Emmett, Clark, Hays, Emerson, and Work</u>

5. Music of families yearning for sons, husbands, fathers, and brothers. <u>Domestic Life Songs</u>

6. Songs of pride and honor. <u>Patriotic Songs</u>

7. Marching music. <u>Songs of a Soldier's Life</u>

Civil War Facts

1. President during the Civil War. <u>Abraham Lincoln</u>

2. Northern Army's general. <u>Ulysses S. Grant</u>; Southern's. <u>Robert E. Lee</u>

3. The people held in bondage to work on plantations. <u>Slaves</u>

4. Places of great battles. <u>Gettysburg, Antietam, and Vicksburg</u>

5. The place where the war started. <u>Fort Sumter</u>

6. The place where the war ended. <u>Appomattox</u>

Opera
(Countries and Cultures)

LESSON PLAN

Objective: Students will list or identify the parts, composers, and titles of opera.

Materials: Piano
Pencils
Copies of: Music pages
        Filling-in-the-Blanks About Opera pages
          with the Opera Facts Bank
        Opera Dots game pages
        Opera Around the World cover page
        United States, Italy, Germany, England, France,
          Russian Federation Opera pages
        My Opera activity page

Procedure:
1. *Opening Activity:* Teach "The Marriage of Figaro." Ask the students: "What kind of music is this song? Who do you think composed it?"

2. *Singing Activity:* Teach "Lucia" to the students. Ask: "What do you think about when you think of opera? Name some characteristics of opera."

3. *Singing Activity:* Teach "Madame Butterfly." Ask: "What are opera stories usually about? Where do operas come from?"

4. *Instruction Activity:* Explain that operas come from all over the world and are about many things. Operas have been written about love, telephones, tragedy, holidays, war, fantasy, bats, and even the game of baseball. Some are based on fact and some are not. Some operas take place in Egypt, France, Russia, Spain, Germany, Japan, and, yes, the Unitied States. Explain the parts of an opera (overture, aria, recitative, chorus, libretto, etc.), and types (grand, serious, tragic, comic, singspiel, etc.), and composers and their operas (Verdi/*Aida*, Puccini/*Norma*, Mozart/*Don Giovanni*, etc.). And finally, discuss the countries where opera composers have come from (United States, Italy, Germany, France, Russia, etc.).

5. *Writing Activity:* Give a copy of the Filling-in-the-Blanks About Opera page and the Opera Facts Bank page to each student. Instruct the students to fill in the blanks with the information from the Opera Facts Bank page that best fits the opera story.

Procedure:
(Continued)

6. ***Review Activity:*** This activity is a game good for reviewing. Copy, laminate, and cut out the Opera Dot game dots. Have the students stand in a circle or remain in their seats. Hand out an Opera Dot to each student. Select a student to pick another student to read his/her dot's question. If the first student answers the question correctly, the answering student then picks another student to read his/her question. This continues until a question is answered incorrectly. If a question is answered wrong, the student asking the question picks a person to read his/her dot. The game ends after a time allotment of ten to fifteen minutes (whoever has the most dots wins) or when someone holds all the dots.

7. ***Writing Activity:*** Copy enough Opera Around the World covers and Opera Country Flag pages and staple for each student. Have the students list the information about each country's opera and color its flag. Students may use their Filling-in-the-Blanks About Opera and Opera Facts Bank for assistance.

Activity Page:

Hand out a copy of My Opera page to each student. Ask each student to create a story plot, characters, costumes, scenery, title, etc., for an opera he/she thinks would be interesting. Have the students share their ideas in class.

The Marriage of Figaro

W.A. Mozart

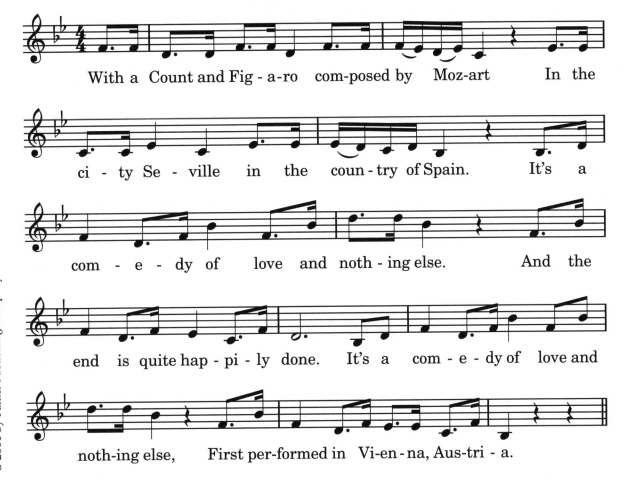

With a Count and Fig - a-ro com-posed by Moz-art In the

ci - ty Se - ville in the coun - try of Spain. It's a

com - e - dy of love and noth - ing else. And the

end is quite hap - pi - ly done. It's a com - e - dy of love and

noth-ing else, First per-formed in Vi-en - na, Aus-tri - a.

Lucia di Lammermoor

Donizetti

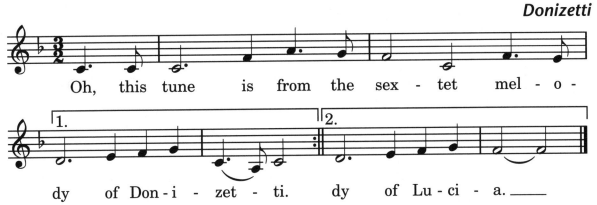

Oh, this tune is from the sex - tet mel - o -

dy of Don - i - zet - ti. dy of Lu - ci - a.

Madame Butterfly
(Un Bel Di Vedremo)

G. Bellini

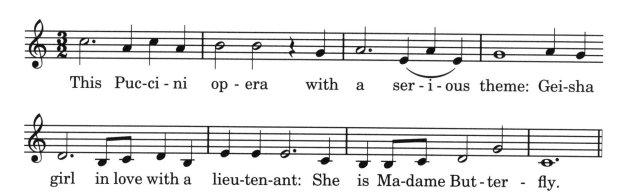

This Puc-ci-ni op - era with a ser - i - ous theme: Gei-sha

girl in love with a lieu-ten-ant: She is Ma-dame But -ter - fly.

Name _____

Filling-in-the-Blanks About Opera

Fill in the blanks about opera using the Opera Facts Bank on the next page.

Opera's roots lie in the madrigals by composer Orazio Vecchi back around _ _ _ _. By the Baroque period, opera developed from the _ _ _ _ _ _ _ which was a group of musicians who wanted to use Greek drama in music productions. About the 1590s the first opera was written. The composers _ _ _ _ and _ _ _ _ _ _ _ _ _ worked together to produce *Dafne*.

B _ _ _ _ _ opera was a music production for the common people. One of the most famous b _ _ _ _ _ operas was John Gay's *The Beggar's Opera* (1728). This type of opera led to the German opera style called _ _ _ _ _ _ _ _ which was a popular dramatic and heavy music. Composers of this style included Austrian greats _ _ _ _ _ _ , _ _ _ _ _ , and _ _ _ _ _ _ _ _ . French opera _ _ _ _ _ _ _ was light and humorous, but sometimes serious. The opera comique *La Serva Padrona* (1752) was written by P _ _ _ _ _ _ _ _ . Another type of French opera included opera _ _ _ _ _ _ . Jacques _ _ _ _ _ _ _ _ _ was a composer of this style. Other French composers include _ _ _ _ _ and _ _ _ _ _-_ _ _ _ _ . Italian opera with its bel _ _ _ _ _ style, produced a more challenging part for its voices. Italian opera included styles like _ _ _ _ _ and _ _ _ _ _ _ _ and composers like Verdi (_ _ _ _), Donizetti (_ _ _ _ _ _ _ _ _ _ _ _), Puccini (_ _ _ _ _ _ _ _ _ _ _ _ _ _ _ _), Bellini (_ _ _ _ _), and _ _ _ _ _ _ _ (*The Barber of Seville*). Although England was not known for great opera, they did produce _ _ _ _ _ _ _ / _ _ _ _ _ _ _ _ who composed operettas like *H.M.S. Pinafore* and *The Mikado*.

Other German composers, but of the Italian style, were _ _ _ _ _ _ (*Flying Dutchman*) and Weber (O _ _ _ _ _). The Dutch composer Engelbert Humperdinck wrote the opera _ _ _ _ _ _ and _ _ _ _ _ _ after the favorite children's story. The Russians _ _ _ _ _ _ (*A Life of a Czar*), _ _ _ _ _ _ _ _ _ _ (*Boris Gudunov*), Rimski-Korsakoff (_ _ _ _ _ _ _ _ _ _ _ _ _), and _ _ _ _ _ _ _ _ _ _ (*Eugen Onegin*) were nationalistic. They based their wonderful operas on folk tales and folk dances of the Russian past and present. Americans also have produced operas. Benjamin Carr (*The Archers*), John Knowles Paine (*Azara*), and Horatio Parker (*Mona*) wrote operas early in the history of the United States. But, the 20th-century Americans wrote operas on topics like the telephone (_ _ _ _ _ _ _ _ _ _ _ _ _ _ _ _) and baseball (William _ _ _ _ _ _ _ _'s _ _ _ _ _ *at the* _ _ _).

The parts of the opera are simple to remember. The music at the opening of the opera takes melodies from music throughout the opera and places it in the _ _ _ _ _ _ _ _ . The script in opera is called the _ _ _ _ _ _ _ _ _ . _ _ _ _ s are the songs of an opera, while the _ _ _ _ _ _ _ _ _ is the dialogue which is sung. When a large group of people sing, it is referred to as the _ _ _ _ _ _ . The end of the opera is the _ _ _ _ _ _ .

Opera has come a long way from its beginning during the sixteenth century. From using young boys for female characters, the oppression of monarchs like those Mozart dealt with, and the development of such great singers as Caruso, Callas, Price, and Pavarotti, opera continues to entertain audiences throughout the world in great opera houses like _ _ _ _ _ _ _ in Milan, Italy; Paris Opera House in Paris, France; Metropolitan Opera House in New York City, New York; and Bolshoi Theatre in Moscow, Russia.

309

Opera Facts Bank

aria	grand	Rossini	Gian Carlo Menotti
recitative	serious	Puccini	William Schumann
overture	comic	Bellini	Gilbert/Sullivan
chorus	tragic	Donizetti	Pergolesi
libretto	ballad	Mascagni	Schubert
finale	singspiel	Bizet	*Madame Butterfly*
1594	opera buffa	Saint-Saëns	*Aida*
Camerata	opera comique	Offenbach	*Carmen*
bel canto	Wagner	Haydn	*HMS Pinafore*
Weber	Mozart	Peri/Rinuccini	*Flying Dutchman*
Oberon	*Don Pasquale*	Tchaikovsky	*The Snow Maiden*
Norma	Glinka	Mussorgsky	*Casey at the Bat*
Hansel, Gretel		La Scala	*Orpheus in the Underworld*
Italian Opera			
German Romantic Opera			

Filling-in-the-Blanks About Opera
(Answer Key)

Fill in the blanks about opera using the Opera Facts Bank at the end.

Opera's roots lie in the madrigals by composer Orazio Vecchi back around **1594**. By the Baroque period, opera developed from the **Camerata** which was a group of musicians who wanted to use Greek drama in music productions. About the 1590s the first opera was written. The composers **Peri** and **Rinuccini** worked together to produce *Dafne*.

Ballad opera was a music production for the common people. One of the most famous **ballad** operas was John Gay's *The Beggar's Opera* (1728). This type of opera led to the German opera style called **singspiel** which was a popular dramatic and heavy music. Composers of this style included Austrian greats **Mozart**, **Haydn**, and **Schubert**. French opera **comique** was light and humorous, but sometimes serious. The opera comique *La Serva Padrona* (1752) was written by **Pergolesi**. Another type of French opera included opera **buffa**. Jacques **offenbach** was a composer of this style. Other French composers included **Bizet** and **Saint-Saëns**. Italian opera with its bel **canto** style, produced a more challenging part for its voices. Italian opera included styles like **grand** and **serious** and composers like Verdi (**Aida**), Donizetti (**Don Pasquale**), Puccini (**Madame Butterfly**), Bellini (**Norma**), and **Rossini** (*The Barber of Seville*). Although England was not known for great opera, they did produce **Gilbert**/**Sullivan** who composed operettas like *H.M.S. Pinafore* and *The Mikado*.

Other German composers, but of the Italian style, were **Wagner** (*Flying Dutchman*) and Weber (**Oberon**). The Dutch composer Engelbert Humperdinck wrote the opera **Hansel** and **Gretel** after the favorite children's story. The Russians **Glinka** (*A Life of a Czar*), **Mussorgsky** (*Boris Gudunov*), Rimski-Korsakoff (**The Snow Maiden**), and **Tchaikovsky** (*Eugen Onegin*) were nationalistic. They based their wonderful operas on folk tales and folk dances of the Russian past and present. Americans also have produced operas. Benjamin Carr (*The Archers*), John Knowles Paine (*Azara*), and Horatio Parker (*Mona*) wrote operas early in the history of the United States. But, the 20th century Americans wrote operas on topics like the telephone (**Gian Carlo Menotti**) and baseball (William **Schumann**'s *Casey* at the **Bat**).

The parts of the opera are simple to remember. The music at the opening of the opera takes melodies from music throughout the opera and places it in the **overture**. The script in opera is called the **libretto**. **Arias** are the songs of an opera, while the **recitative** is the dialogue which is sung. When a large group of people sing it is referred to as the **chorus**. The end of the opera is the **finale**.

Opera has come a long way from its beginning during the sixteenth century. From using young boys for female characters, the oppression of monarchs like those Mozart dealt with, and the development of such great singers as Caruso, Callas, Price, and Pavarotti, opera continues to entertain audiences throughout the world in great opera houses like **La Scala** in Milan, Italy; Paris Opera House in Paris, France; Metropolitan Opera House in New York City, New York; and Bolshoi Theatre in Moscow, Russia.

Opera Facts Bank

aria	grand	Rossini	Gian Carlo Menotti
recitative	serious	Puccini	William Schumann
overture	comic	Bellini	Gilbert/Sullivan
chorus	tragic	Donizetti	Pergolesi
libretto	ballad	Mascagni	Schubert
finale	singspiel	Bizet	*Madame Butterfly*
1594	opera buffa	Saint-Saëns	*Aida*
Camerata	opera comique	Offenbach	*Carmen*
bel canto	Wagner	Haydn	*HMS Pinafore*
Weber	Mozart	Peri/Rinuccini	*Flying Dutchman*
Oberon	*Don Pasquale*	Tchaikovsky	*The Snow Maiden*
Norma	Glinka	Mussorgsky	*Casey at the Bat*
Hansel, Gretel		La Scala	*Orpheus in the Underworld*
Italian Opera			
German Romantic Opera			

Opera Dots

Did Mozart compose operas?

Name an Italian opera composer

Name a Russian opera composer

Name an American opera composer

Name a German opera composer

Name a French opera composer

Opera Dots

Name an
Italian opera

What is
grand opera?

What is
tragic opera?

What is
opera buffa?

What is
singspiel opera?

In what
century did
opera begin?

Opera Dots

Define the
word libretto

What is
an aria?

The end of an
opera is called
the what?

What is
recitative?

What is it called
when a large group of
singers sing
together in opera?

Bel canto is
associated with what
country's style of
opera?

Opera Dots

The opening music to an opera is called a what?

The Beggar's Opera is known for what?

Mussorgsky is an opera composer from what country?

William Schumann is from which country?

Verdi is from what country?

Donizetti is from what country?

Opera Dots

Is England known for great opera?

Is the opera La Sonnambula about a sleepwalker or a dog?

La Scala is an opera house in what country?

The Metropolitan Opera House is in what country?

Caruso, Callas, Price, and Pavarotti are what?

The Bolshoi Theatre is in what country?

OPERA AROUND THE WORLD

Name _____

United States

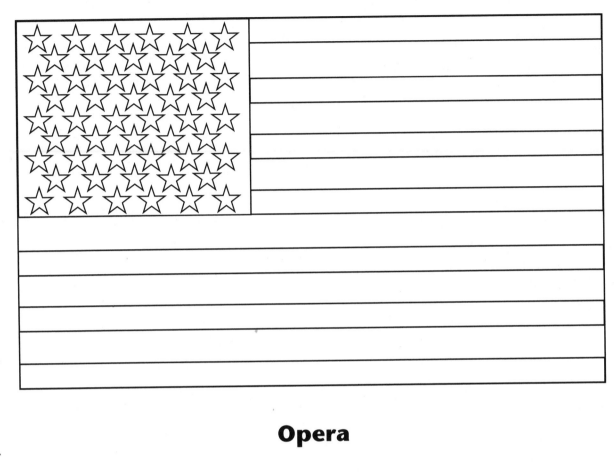

Opera

_____

_____

_____

_____

_____

_____

Italy

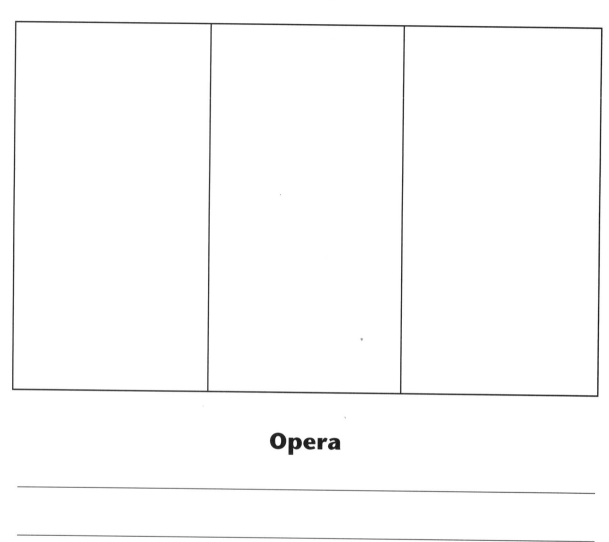

Opera

Germany

Opera

_____

_____

_____

_____

_____

_____

United Kingdom (England)

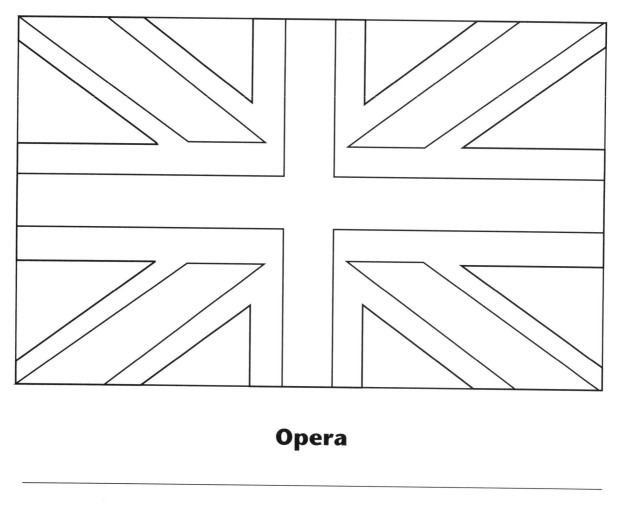

Opera

_____

_____

_____

_____

_____

_____

_____

France

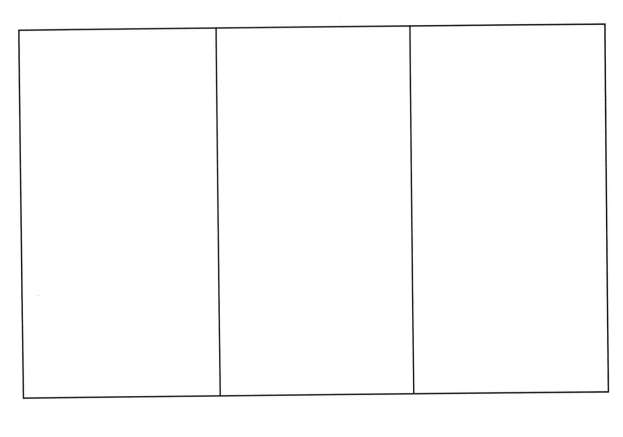

Opera

_____

_____

_____

_____

_____

_____

Russian Federation

Opera

My Opera

Title _____

Story/Plot

```



```

Characters

```



```

Costumes

```



```

Style of Music

```



```

Scenery

```



```

Tempo-Music Terms
(Italian/Windspeed, Measuring Devices)

LESSON PLAN

Objective: Students will identify the terms: presto, allegro, moderato, andante, adagio, largo, ritardando, accelerando, and a tempo.

Materials: Piano
Pencils
Scissors
Container
Copies of: Music page
          Tempo Term Cards and Tabs page
          Tempo Matching page
          Tempo Circles page
          Tempo Circle Terms and Objects page
          What Doesn't Fit? activity page

Procedure: 1. **Opening Activity:** Teach "Partita" to the students. After singing the song, ask the students, "What was the speed of the song?"

2. **Singing Activity:** Teach "Sleeping Beauty." Have the students guess the speed of this song. Then ask the students what measures the speed of a car or truck. Follow with questions pertaining to other speed measuring devices such as radar guns and anemometers (wind speed). Finally, ask the students how we know whether to play or sing music fast or slow. Explain that music developed hundreds of years ago in Italy. Many music terms we use today have been passed on through the years and are standard to most musicians.

3. **Identification Activity:** Using the Tempo Cards, identify and define the tempo terms. Cut out, laminate, and display the terms in front of the class. Explain *presto* as running fast, *allegro* as running, *moderato* as jogging, *andante* as walking, *adagio* as a slow walk, and *largo* as a very slow walk. Define *ritardando* as gradually slowing down and *accelerando* as gradually getting faster. Teach "The Tempo Song." Have the students move to the motions mentioned in the song. You may want to add other terms and other motions to enlarge the vocabulary.

Procedure:
(Continued)

4. ***Game/Activity:*** Photocopy and laminate the Tempo Tabs. Put the tempo tabs in a container from which students can easily pull one out. Split the class into two large teams, or prepare more tabs and have more teams. (You may want to try having playoffs sometime.) Choose a student to begin for one of the teams. The student must act out the tempo for his/her team to guess. If his/her team doesn't guess correctly, the tab is put back in the container and the next team sends a player up front to select a tab. Teams rotate players to act out the tabs. A point is given to the team that guesses the tempo. Only one guess is allowed, so the playing team must make it count. The game continues until all the tabs are gone. The team with the most points wins.

5. ***Matching Activity:*** Hand out copies of the Tempo Matching page. Have the students list things that can match the different tempo terms. Animals, machines, motions, etc., may be used.

6. ***Identification Activity:*** Copy, cut out, and laminate the Tempo Circles and Tempo Circles Terms and Objects. Give each student a Tempo Circle and copies of all the terms and object circles. Set a time limit of one to five minutes, and have the students place on their circle the terms and objects that match the music term you announce.

Activity Page:

Give each student a copy of the What Doesn't Fit? activity page. Have them cross out the lettered definition that least fits the tempo.

Prelude
Partita No.1

J.S. Bach
(1685 - 1750)

Allegro

It's a Pre-lude for the so-lo vi-o-lin by J. S.

Bach. He was a great com-pos-er of the eight-eenth cen-tury

Bar-oque per-i-od of time, A com-pos-er of bar-oque

times. He com-posed for the church, and taught kids in a

school. He had twen-ty-one kids. A few could real-ly com-pose well.

Sleeping Beauty

P.I. Tchaikovsky

Here's _____ Pe - ter Tchai-kov - sky's Sleep - ing Beau - ty A - da - gio. The bal - let based on the fair - y tale. The curse of a wick - ed witch and a prin-cess who loves her Prince Charm-ing ___ man.

The Tempo Song

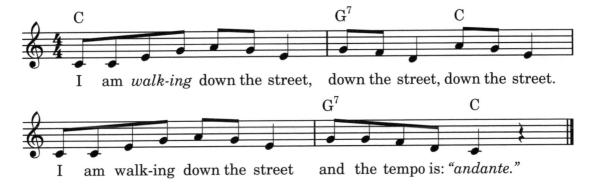

I am *walk-ing* down the street, down the street, down the street.
I am walk-ing down the street and the tempo is: *"andante."*

2. *crawling/adagio*
3. *jogging/moderato*
4. *running/allegro*
5. *sprinting/presto*
6. *dragging/largo*
7. *slowing/ritardando*
8. *speeding up the street/accelerando*

Tempo Term Cards

Presto

Allegro

Moderato

Andante

Adagio

Largo

Ritardando

Accelerando

A Tempo

Tempo Tabs

Presto	Adagio	Ritardando
Allegro	Andante	Accelerando
Moderato	Largo	A Tempo

Tempo Matching

List the things that can match the tempos below.

Presto

_____

_____

_____

_____

_____

Allegro

_____

_____

_____

_____

_____

Moderato

_____

_____

_____

_____

_____

Andante

_____

_____

_____

_____

_____

Adagio

_____

_____

_____

_____

_____

Largo

_____

_____

_____

_____

_____

Ritardando

_____

_____

_____

_____

_____

Accelerando

_____

_____

_____

_____

_____

What do the instruments below measure?

1. Anemometer _____

2. Radar Gun _____

3. Speedometer _____

4. Odometer _____

5. Barometer _____

Tempo Circles

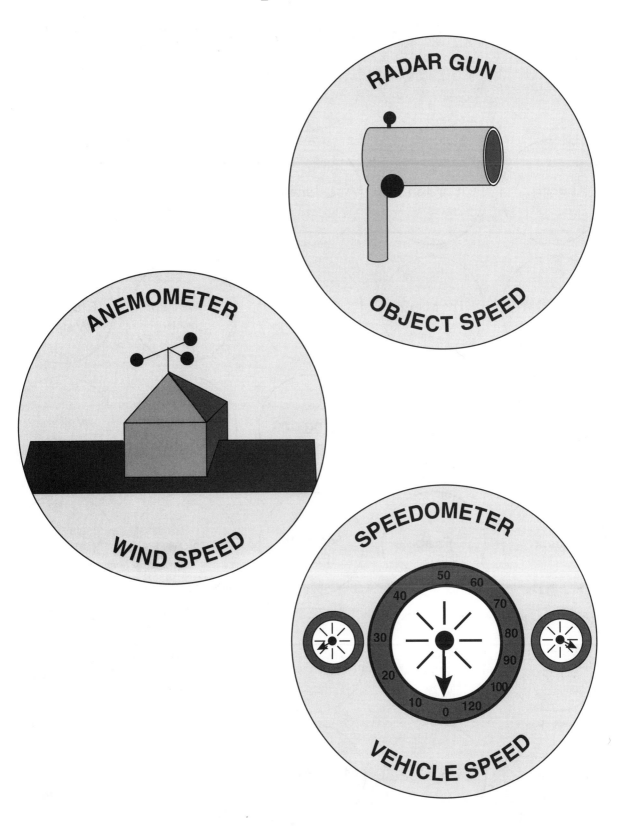

RADAR GUN

OBJECT SPEED

ANEMOMETER

WIND SPEED

SPEEDOMETER

VEHICLE SPEED

Tempo Circle Terms and Objects

Presto	Allegro	Moderato	Adagio	Andante
Largo	Ritardando	Accelerando	Speeding Jet Ski	Floating Balloon
Race Car	Trotting	Person Walking	Cheetah Running	Elephant Walking
Jogging	Crawling	Flying Jet	Skiing Downhill	Walking Slowly
Quick	Fast	Medium Fast	Slow	Very Slow
Walking Tempo	Gliding Bird	Floating Tall Ship	Losing Speed	Figure Skating
100-Mile-an-Hour Fastball	A Surfer	Molasses in January	A Tornado	Snow Falling

What Doesn't Fit?

Cross out the lettered definition that least fits the tempo.

1. **Adagio** (a) slow (b) object floating (c) racing horse (d) walking cow

2. **Allegro** (a) fastball (b) fast (c) turtle (d) running rabbit

3. **Ritardando** (a) a car running out of gas (b) gradually slowing (c) a passing car (d) a jogger slowing down

4. **Moderato** (a) a turtle (b) jogging (c) bicycling (d) skateboarding

5. **Presto** (a) a flying arrow (b) very quick (c) a turning tractor-trailer (d) a falling star

6. **Largo** (a) thick ketchup (b) a tornado (c) very slow (d) a walking cow

7. **Andante** (a) fast spinning anemometer (b) walking down the street (c) sailboat (d) a floating balloon

8. **Accelerando** (a) a rising speedometer (b) a bobsled starting down the course (c) a skydiver (d) a car running out of gas

Cross out the answer to each of the following questions:

A radar gun was pointed at several cars and trucks. Which speed fit the given tempo?*

1. **Presto** (a) 85 MPH (b) 20 MPH (c) 42 MPH (d) 35 MPH

2. **Allegro** (a) 90 MPH (b) 55 MPH (c) 15 MPH (d) 20 MPH

3. **Adagio** (a) 5 MPH (b) 80 MPH (c) 48 MPH (d) 25 MPH

4. **Accelerando** (a) 0-20 MPH (b) 70 MPH (c) 15 MPH (d) 58 MPH

_____

* If applied to driving, which term(s) would lead a police officer to give a car a ticket?

Johann Sebastian Bach
(Biography)

LESSON PLAN

Objective:	Students will identify the composer Johann Sebastian Bach.

Materials:	Piano
	Recordings of 3 Bach works
	Pencils
	Stapler
	Copies of: Music page
	           Biography of Bach
	           Composer Listening Report
	           FBI Confidential File page
	           FBI File cover page
	           MO and FBI Facts Report pages
	           Composer Facts Cover page
	           Composer Facts page
	           Writing a Biography page
	           Composer Lottery Ticket

Procedure:	1. ***Opening Activity:*** Teach "Joy of Man's Desiring." Instruct the students to pay close attention to the lyrics of the song for facts about Bach. 2. ***Reading Activity:*** Hand out copies of the Biography of Bach. Read the Biography of Bach. Ask the students the questions: "When did Bach live? Where was he born? Where did he live? What did he compose? Who were the most influential people in his life? What were some of the memorable events during his life? Any interesting stories about him?" 3. ***Listening Activity:*** Play three of Bach's works for the students. Hand out the Composer Listening Report. Have the students fill out the report as they listen to the Bach music. The students should fill out the Composer Listening Report for all three pieces of music. 4. ***Discovery Activity:*** Copy and staple enough FBI File covers, MOs and FBI Facts Reports for each student. Use a different color for the FBI File cover. Staple the cover to the MO page. Have the students read the FBI File on Bach and fill out the FBI Facts Report.

Procedure:
(Continued)

5. ***Partner Activity:*** Give a copy of the Composer Facts Cover and Composer Facts to the entire class. It is best practice to copy the Composer Facts Cover on one side of a piece of paper (or oaktag) and the Composer Facts Page on the other. Group the students in twos. If an odd amount, you can play the other partner. Have one student ask the questions while holding the Composer Facts Cover toward the student who will respond. Afterwards, have students reverse roles.

6. ***Review Activity:*** Hand out a copy of Writing a Biography for CD-Rom Encyclopedia to each student. Direct the students to write a paragraph-long biography focusing on the essential facts of Bach. Tell the students to use any of the information provided in the entire lesson.

Activity Page: Give each student a copy of the Composer Lottery Ticket. Have them scratch out those facts not true of Bach. If the student gets all the facts correct, circle the word winner.

Joy of Man's Desiring
(Cantata 146)

J.S. Bach

Bach, a com - po - ser called Jo - hann Se -
bas - tian from Ei - sen - ach, Ger - man - y,
known for his mu - sic of re - li - gious
con - tent and pur - pose for liv - ing: His
sons were quite well - known mu - si - cians, and
all com - posed mu - sic like their fa - ther.
He was one of Ger - man - y's great - est of all. ____

BIOGRAPHY OF BACH

Born on March 21, 1685 in Eisenach, Germany to a family of prominent professional musicians, Johann Sebastian Bach became one of Germany's greatest composers. The early part of his life was spent singing in church choirs. But soon he began his formal music training studying the violin and viola with his father Ambrosius Bach. Unfortunately, by age ten Johann was an orphan. He was fortunate, however, to have a brother, Johann Christoph, who was willing to take him and care for him. He began his organ studies while with his brother. But as Christoph's family grew, there became little room for Johann Sebastian, so he moved on to music positions as a professional.

Johann was a devoutly religious man, a Lutheran, and a pietist. He was also committed to new and innovative music. Bach was known to have travelled for 300 miles to hear the great organist Dietrich Buxtehade. Although devoted to music, Bach did have problems. Johann did not want to direct the choirs assigned to him, and he became quite unhappy and wanted to leave his post. The Duke, under whom Bach worked, would not release him at first. Eventually, Bach was released, and moved on.

The choir experience, nevertheless, had a profound effect on Bach's life. Through his choir directing he met his first wife, Maria. Unfortunately, she died after they had seven children together. Bach, soon after, married Anna Magdalena. About this time, Bach's life developed in Leipzig, Germany where his career began to blossom.

Johann Sebastian Bach's music included preludes, fugues, oratorios, cantatas, partitas, suites, and many more forms. Some of his most recognizable music works were *Goldberg Variations, Brandenburg Concertos, French Suite, Cello Suites, Violin Partitas, Jesu, Joy of Man's Desiring, Little Fugue in G minor, Toccata and Fugue in D minor, B minor Mass, Well-Tempered Clavier Books* and *The Art of the Fugue.*

Bach played the violin and viola. But, his talent was recognized most for his great clavier and organ performances. His legacy, however, would have to include three of his sons, Wilhelm Friedmann, Karl Phillipe Emmanuel, and Johann Christoph who all became well-known composers.

By 1749, Bach was losing his eyesight. After a couple of eye operations, he was weak and worn. From the results of a stroke and apoplexy, on July 28, 1750 Johann Sebastian Bach died. His music soon fell out of favor, but was revived by the great composers Mozart and Mendelssohn, and now continues as popular as ever.

Many great people lived and notable events occurred during Bach's lifetime. Frederick the Great, George Frederic Handel, Antonio Vivaldi, and Franz Joseph Haydn lived while Bach was alive. The Industrial Revolution, the establishment of the thirteen colonies in America, and the days of Williamsburg, Virginia were events that happened during Bach's lifetime.

Composer Listening Report

Listen to the selections and circle the items that best describe the music of the selected composer.

Composer _____

1. _____ (title)

    a. orchestra   vocal   solo instrument   small ensemble

    b. Major key   minor key

    c. secular (nonreligious)   sacred (religious)

    d. allegro   moderato   adagio

    Opinion:

2. _____ (title)

    a. orchestra   vocal   solo instrument   small ensemble

    b. Major key   minor key

    c. secular (nonreligious)   sacred (religious)

    d. allegro   moderato   adagio

    Opinion:

3. _____ (title)

    a. orchestra   vocal   solo instrument   small ensemble

    b. Major key   minor key

    c. secular (nonreligious)   sacred (religious)

    d. allegro   moderato   adagio

    Opinion:

FBI File:

Johann Sebastian Bach

MO

Name: Johann Sebastian Bach

Alias: Sebastian

Date of Birth: March 21, 1685

Parents: Ambrosius and Maria Bach

Place of Birth: Eisenach, Germany

Nationality/Citizenship:
German

Occupation: Composer, organist, teacher, musician

Last seen: Leipzig, Germany on July 28, 1750.

Family: Johann Christoph (brother), Maria (first wife), Anna Magdalena (second wife), Wilhelm Friedmann (son), Karl Phillipe Emmanuel (son), Johann Christoph (son), and Julianne (daughter) plus three other children.

Contemporaries: George Frederic Handel, Antonio Vivaldi, Franz Joseph Haydn, Frederick the Great, and Benjamin Franklin.

Residences: Eisenach, Ohrdruf, Dresden, Leipzig

Period of Time Lived: Baroque Period

Accomplishments: Great composer and organist. Composed *Little Fugue in G minor, Mass in B minor, St. Matthew Passion, Toccata and Fugue in D minor, Sheep May Safely Graze*, and six *Brandenburg Concertos*.

Name _____

FBI Facts Report

Fill out this FBI Facts Report on the suspect for which you have a confidential file.

Name of suspect: _____

Age when last seen: _____

Place last seen: _____

Suspect's occupation: _____

Employed by: _____

Accomplishments: _____

_____

_____

_____

_____

Other facts: _____

_____

_____

_____

_____

_____

Physical Description: _____

_____

_____

_____

_____

Composer Facts Cover

Johann Sebastian Bach

When did he live?

What did he compose?

Where did he live?

Who else lived and what important events took place during his life?

Composer Facts Page

1685 - 1750

Church Music
Suites
Cantatas
Mass
Prelude

B
a
r
o
q
u
e

Eisenach, Germany

George Frederic Handel

Antonio Vivaldi

Writing a Biography
for a CD-ROM Encyclopedia

You are a writer and researcher for Smartz Encyclopedia Company. It is your job and assignment to write a biography of J.S. Bach. The biography should be about one paragraph long. Only include the important facts.

Johann Sebastian Bach

_____

_____

_____

_____

_____

_____

_____

_____

_____

_____

_____

_____

_____

_____

_____

_____

Name _____

Composer Lottery Ticket

Scratch out the false facts about Bach.

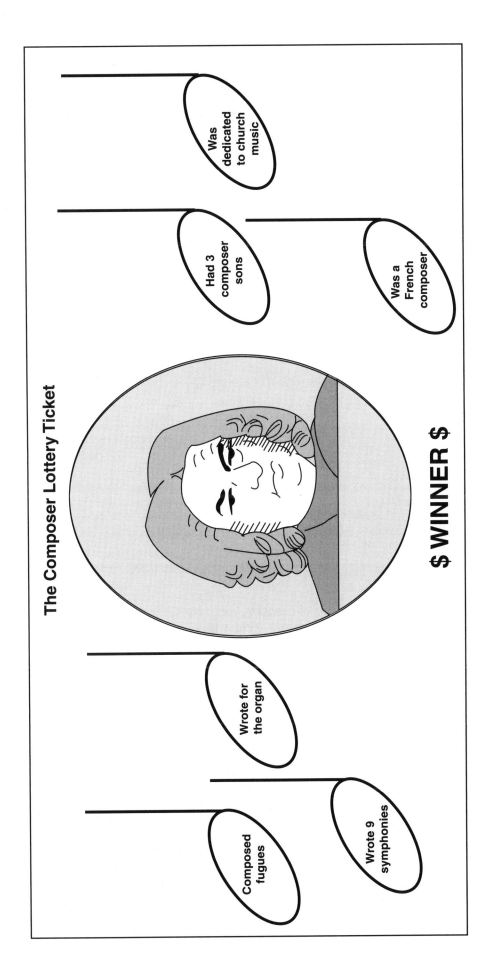

The Composer Lottery Ticket

- Was dedicated to church music
- Had 3 composer sons
- Was a French composer
- Wrote for the organ
- Composed fugues
- Wrote 9 symphonies

$ WINNER $

The Vocal Instrument
(Health)

LESSON PLAN

Objective: Students will practice various singing elements such as diction, breathing, posture, voice care, range, and quality.

Materials: Piano
Pencils
Crayons
Stapler
Copies of: Vocal music pages
          Voice Placement Exercises
          Defining the Voice Activity page
          Parts of the Vocal Instrument
          A Healthy Approach to Singing page
          Caring for Your Voice page
          Web Page for Singing

Procedure:

1. *Opening Activity/Diction:* Teach "Rocky Mountain." Repeat the song numerous times at a faster tempo each time. Ask the students what was difficult about singing the song so quickly. Guide the students to the understanding that it was getting more difficult to sing the words, to articulate, and to pronounce the words. Discuss the importance of diction and its role in music.

2. *Singing Activity/Control:* Sing "Rocky Mountain" again. Repeat the song and sing it softer each time. Afterwards, try singing it louder and louder each time. Stress the importance of singing louder—not shouting. Discuss the difference between voice uses like singing, talking, shouting, and whispering.

3. *Singing Activity/Breathing:* Again, sing "Rocky Mountain." Have the students sing the song in phrases or partial phrases. Ask the students to sing the partial or complete phrases in one breath. Slowly increase the number of phrases they sing in one breath. Discuss proper breathing. Have the strudents lie on their backs on the floor to demonstrate proper breathing. This will give the students the opportunity to witness their stomachs moving up and down as they breathe. This is what they need to develop for good breathing technique. Instruct the students to think they are breathing a bubble in and down through the mouth and windpipe. Have them picture an open ring for their voice cords/folds (larynx). Finally, discuss good posture when singing.

Procedure:
(Continued)

4. ***Singing Activity/Kinds of Voices and Vocal Cords:*** One final time, sing "Rocky Mountain." Continue singing the song higher and higher. Discuss which area (low, middle, or high) or keys were comfortable to sing. Discuss head tones and chest tones. Sing the Voice Placement Exercises with the students. Discuss where one's voice is and which examples are easier to sing. Stress the relaxation of the voice (vocal cords), particularly when the notes go much higher or much lower. Continue discussion of the voice by explaining the different kinds of voices like soprano, mezzosoprano, alto, contralto (possibly), tenor, baritone, and bass. Also, focus on the cambiata voice. This voice is one boys of the middle, intermediate, and high school ages should have some awareness of before they fall into the voice complexities of the age. Finally, read and discuss the Caring for Your Voice page.

5. ***Differentiation Activity:*** Pass out a copy of A Healthy Approach to Singing activity page. Instruct the students to circle the statements or graphics that are healthier practices for singing. Grade the papers and circle the number in the "Health Level" chart of the total number of correct responses.

Activity Page:

Give six copies of the Web Page for Singing activity page to each student (stapled). Have the students create a singing Web Page by selecting a topic, writing the topic in the allotted spot, and adding pictures and whatever else will help their pages. Be sure they color in the topic. They may want to color their pages.

Rocky Mountain

Rock-y Moun-tain, Rock-y Moun-tain, Rock-y Moun-tain high.

When you're on that Rock-y Moun-tain, hang your head and cry.

Do, do, do, do Do re-mem-ber me. Do, do, do, do Do re-mem-ber me.

C # Major

D Major

E♭ Major

F Major

F # Major

G Major

A♭ Major

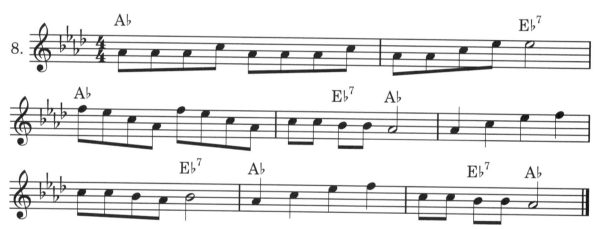

A Major

B♭ Major

B Major

C Major

Voice Placement Exercises

Which exercises are just right, a challenge, or too difficult for your voice?
Sing on melodic syllables or "loo."

354

Defining the Voice Activity Page

Voice Kinds

1. Tenor _____
2. Alto _____
3. Soprano _____
4. Mezzosoprano _____
5. Bass _____
6. Baritone _____
7. Cambiata _____
8. Head tones _____
9. Chest tones _____

Characteristics

a. The high range of a woman

b. The changing voice (range) of an adolescent boy

c. Higher voice focus and quality for resonation

d. Lowest male voice range

e. Lower voice focus with less resonating quality

f. The higher male voice range

g. The middle male voice range

h. The middle female voice range

i. The lower female voice range

Voice Usage

1. _ _ _ _ _ _ _
2. _ _ _ _ _ _ _ _
3. _ _ _ _ _ _ _
4. _ _ _ _ _ _ _
5. _ _ _ _ _ _ _ _ _

Characteristics

Enunciating, articulating, and pronouncing

Calling out, yelling, not good for your voice

Vocal, smooth, musical

Talking, saying words, communicating

Quiet, light, soft talking

Term Bank

Singing   Diction   Whispering   Shouting   Speaking

Singing Techniques

1. What can you do if the notes are getting quite high when you are singing?

2. To sing the words of a song more clearly, what can you do?

3. Describe proper breathing technique.

4. What is good singing posture?

5. Which part(s) of the mouth do you use to pronounce the "T" sound?

Defining the Voice
Activity Page
(Answer Key)

Voice Kinds

1. Tenor **f**
2. Alto **i**
3. Soprano **a**
4. Mezzosoprano **h**
5. Bass **d**
6. Baritone **g**
7. Cambiata **b**
8. Head tones **c**
9. Chest tones **e**

Voice Kinds

1. <u>D i c t i o n</u>
2. <u>S h o u t i n g</u>
3. <u>S i n g i n g</u>
4. <u>S p e a k i n g</u>
5. <u>W h i s p e r i n g</u>

Singing Techniques

1. What can you do if the notes are getting quite high when you are singing? *Relax, pretend to be stepping on steps, reach slightly higher, etc.*

2. To sing the words of a song more clearly, what can you do? *Enunciate and articulate the words, etc.*

3. Describe proper breathing technique. *Open mouth, relaxed, stomach moves outward, breathe as though you are swallowing a bubble, etc.*

4. What is good singing posture? *Standing or sitting up straight, not rigid, feet flat on the floor, etc.*

5. Which part(s) of the mouth do you use to pronounce the "T" sound? *Teeth, tongue, etc.*

Parts of the Vocal Instrument

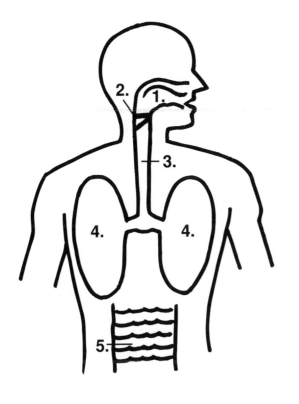

1. _____ is used to articulate words, assist air movement, and help tone.

2. _____ are used to produce vocal sound by vibrating as air moves through the two V-shaped folds.

3. _____ transports air to and from the lungs through the larynx.

4. _____ expand when filling with air and contract when expelling air.

5. _____ is the abdominal muscle that controls the force and containment of the lungs.

Diction

List the letters of the alphabet that the following mouth parts pronounce.

1. Lips _____

2. Tongue _____

3. Teeth and Tongue _____

4. Teeth and Lips _____

5. Other? _____

Parts of the Vocal Instrument
(Answer Key)

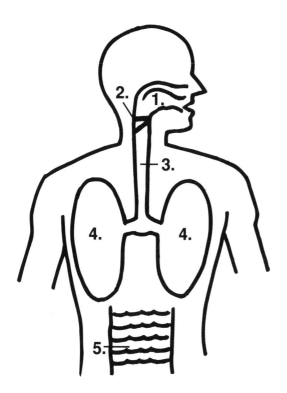

1. **Mouth** is used to articulate words, assist air movement, and help tone.

2. **Vocal Cords** are used to produce vocal sound by vibrating as air moves through the two V-shaped folds.

3. **Windpipe** transports air to and from the lungs through the larynx.

4. **Lungs** expand when filling with air and contract when expelling air.

5. **Diaphragm** is the abdominal muscle that controls the force and containment of the lungs.

Diction

1. Lips _____ B, F, M, O, P, U, V, W, Y

2. Tongue _____ C, D, G, H, J, K, L, N, Q, S, T, U, X, Z

3. Teeth and Tongue _____ C, D, G, H, J, L, N, S, T, Z

4. Teeth and Lips _____ F, V

5. Other? _____ A, E, I, R

Name _____

A Healthy Approach to Singing

1. Circle the healthy and proper approach to singing.

2. Singing High Notes

   I will:

   - Tighten my vocal cords   Relax my vocal cords

   - Put my chin on my chest   **VS.**   Keep my chin up and relaxed

   - Slide up to the high notes   Come down on the high notes as walking up steps

3. Proper Breathing

4. Which is easiest to sing?

5. It is healthier for me to sing in this voice range:

   Bass   Tenor   Soprano

Caring for Your Voice

Overview

The voice is an instrument, or sound-producing organ, used for speaking, shouting, whispering, and singing. The larynx (vocal cords or folds), diaphragm, epiglottis, lungs, and areas of the head are used for resonating and producing the voice. The singing voice is longer in duration, more intense, has a more focused quality, and covers a larger range of pitches than the speaking voice.

Breath is forced by the diaphragm upward from the lungs, through the larynx, by the epiglottis, and into the mouth for producing a singing tone. The varying tensions of the vocal cords in the larynx determine the varying pitches. Vocal cords and resonating cavities play a role in the range of voices such as soprano, mezzosoprano, alto, tenor, baritone, and bass.

The voice is a natural instrument and vulnerable to abuse and illness. Therefore, one must prevent problems, identify problems, and remedy problems. The following recommendations may be helpful when dealing with voice care.

Prevention

- Keep your voice relaxed.
- Avoid straining your voice (avoid extremes).
- Avoid making harsh vocal sounds.
- Limit shouting.
- Keep your neck warm and dry during the winter.
- Keep your mouth, throat, etc., moist (plenty of fluids).
- Limit coughing. Take care of yourself.
- Don't smoke.

Problems

- Hoarseness
- Sore throat
- Phlegm build-up
- Laryngitis (results from a cold)
- Allergies
- Infections (lungs, throat, or growths)
- Nodules (growths)

Remedies

- Voice rest (communicate with pencil and paper or type)
- Speak in a relaxed low tone, but don't whisper by force (stage whisper)
- Inhale steam (boil water, humidifier, run a hot shower)

More Tips

- Keep good general health.
- Get plenty of rest.
- Maintain a good diet.
- Avoid clearing your throat.
- Avoid talking in noisy situations.
- Use good breathing techniques.

Web Page for Singing

Complete your singing web page. Select a topic and write about it in the blank space. Continue each topic with a new page.

Singing

(Topic)

Singing

Introduction

Voice Types/Uses

Breathing

Kinds of Voices

Diction

Caring for Your Voice

The Elements of Music
(Persuasive Writing/Fact-Opinion)

LESSON PLAN

Objective: Students will demonstrate an understanding of the basic elements of music through writing.

Materials: Piano
Chalkboard or some other display board for writing
Scissors
Pencils
Copies of: Music pages
                Music Elements Cards pages
                Song Description Team Activity page
                Elements of Music Definitions
                Writing About Music page
                Which Element Is Which? page
                Elements of Music Crossword Puzzle page
Recordings of various music

Procedure: 1. *Opening Activity:* Teach the students "America." After singing it with the students, ask some questions. "How fast is this song? Should it be loud or soft? Are some pitches high, are some low? Does the song have sections or segments? How does it make you feel? What kind of music is it?"

                     2. *Identification Activity:* Play "Bridal Chorus" (original, if possible) or a favorite class song for the students. Ask the same questions as in the opening activity. This time, however, write the students' responses on the board. Make some formulations of words to describe the student responses. *Example:* The students describe the song as quiet, soft, or laid back. Have the students come up with a word to define the description of quiet/loud, such as "volume."

                     3. *Team Activity:* Place the students in groups of three to five. Play "Gymnopedie No. 1" or another class favorite for the students. Have each team answer the questions from the Song Description Team Activity page. After the teams finish, have each share its findings with the rest of the class. As the sharing is done, begin to identify the student observations as an element of music. Using the Music Elements Cards, discuss and identify each card's element. After teaching and discussing the elements, assign an

Procedure:
(Continued)

element to each group. You may need to repeat elements if you have a large class, or just make the groups larger. Copy the Music Elements Card pages and fold in half so the definitions appear on the back. Give each team a copy of the Elements of Music Definitions page.

4. *Listening Activity:* Play any selection of music or class favorite. Have the teams listen to the music and explain their assigned element of music as it pertains to the musical piece using the bottom half of the Song Description Team Activity page. When finished, have each team share its element and description of the music with the rest of the class.

5. *Writing Activity:* Play a recording of music (any style or type will do) for the class. Have each student write a description of the music using the Writing About Music page. Allow the students to use the Elements of Music Definitions page to help them with the element definitions. Remind the students of the questions that were asked at the beginning of class.

6. *Identification Activity:* Have the students complete the Which Element Is Which? activity page. Be sure that they match the element with the correct definition.

Activity Page:

Have the students complete the Elements of Music Crossword Puzzle by using the given clues. This makes a good "sponge" or review activity.

America

Smith

Bridal Chorus

Richard Wagner

Gymnopedie No. 1

Dreamy and slow

Tempo

Music Element Card
Tempo Definition

- The speed of music

- Fast, slow, or medium

- Presto, allegro, allegretto, moderato, andante, andantino, adagio, largo, ritardando, and a tempo

- Marked and found at the beginning of music, throughout the music, or as the title of a piece, movement, or section

Dynamics

- -

**Music Element Card
Dynamics Definition**

- Music's degree of loudness

- Soft, loud, medium loud, medium soft, very loud, very soft, gradually louder, and gradually softer

- Piano, forte, mezzopiano, mezzoforte, pianissimo, fortissimo, crescendo, and diminuendo (decrescendo)

- pp, p, mp, mf, f, ff, sfz, $<$ and $>$

Form

- -

Music Element Card
Form Definition

- The design and shape of a musical composition

- AB, ABA, AAvBBv, rondo, theme and variations, symphony, suite, opera, cantata, oratorio, sonata, round (circle canon), canon, fugue, and march

Texture

- -

Music Element Card
Texture Definition

- The structure and general pattern of sound created by elements of music

- Thick, thin, or mixed

- Monophonic, homophonic, and polyphonic

- Counterpoint, contrapuntal

- Many voices or parts, few voices or parts

Style

Music Element Card
Style Definition

- The features and characteristics that distinguish different types of music

- Classical, Jazz, Country, Spirituals, Blues, Folk, New Age, Rap, Rock, Rhythm and Blues, Hard Rock, Heavy Metal, Dixieland, Ragtime, etc.

Mood

- -

Music Element Card
Mood Definition

- The feeling or expressiveness of music

- Happy, sad, melancholy, fearless, fearful, angry, excited, mysterious, lively, stately, proud, etc.

- Misterioso, maestoso, and cantabile

Duration

- -

Music Element Card
Duration Definition

- The time that a sound or silence lasts

- Whole notes, half notes, quarter notes, eighth notes, sixteenth notes, etc.

- Whole rests, half rests, quarter rests, eighth rests, sixteenth rests, etc.

Tone Color

- -

Music Element Card
Tone Color Definition

- The quality of a sound that distinguishes it from another

- Instruments—violin, string bass, piano, trumpet, flute, clarinet, saxophone, harp, etc., all have a unique tone color

- Timbre

- Voice vs. instrument

- Soprano, mezzosoprano, alto, tenor, baritone, and bass have unique tone colors

- Brass, woodwinds, strings, and percussion families have unique tone colors

- The manner in which a note is played may produce a particular tone color

Timbre

Music Element Card
Timbre Definition

- The quality of a sound that distinguishes it from another

- Instruments—violin, string bass, piano, trumpet, flute, clarinet, saxophone, harp, etc., all have a unique timbre

- Tone color

- Voice vs. instrument

- Soprano, mezzosoprano, alto, tenor, baritone, and bass have unique timbres

- Brass, woodwinds, strings, and percussion families have unique timbres

- The manner in which a note is played may produce a particular timbre

Pitch

Music Element Card
Pitch Definition

- The quality of a sound

- High, low, or middle

- Can be melodic

- Pitched instruments—flute, clarinet, oboe, sax, trumpet, trombone, baritone, tuba, guitar, violin, and piano

- Nonpitched (unpitched)—snare drum, bass drum, cymbals, triangle, maracas, woodblock, and bongos

Elements of Music Definitions

Dynamics—Music degree of loudness. Soft, loud, medium soft, medium loud, very soft, crescendo, and diminuendo. Piano, forte, mezzopiano, mezzoforte, pianissimo, and fortissimo, represented by the symbols p, f, mp, mf, pp, ff, < and >

Duration—The time that a sound or silence lasts. Whole notes, half notes, quarter notes, eighth notes, sixteenth notes, whole rests, half rests, quarter rests, eighth rests, and sixteenth rests are examples of duration.

Form—The design or shape of a musical composition. AB, ABA, rondo, theme and variations, symphony, suite, opera, cantata, oratorio, sonata, round (circle round), etc., are examples of music forms.

Mood—The feeling or expressiveness of music. Happy, sad, melancholy, fearless, fearful, angry, excited, mysterious, etc., are all examples of mood in music.

Pitch—The quality of a sound. High, low, and middle are examples of pitches. A clarinet, flute, guitar, sax, and piano are examples of pitched instruments. The snare drum, bass drum, maracas, claves, and cymbals are examples of nonpitched or unpitched instruments.

Style—The features and characteristics that distinguish different types of music. Classical, Jazz, Country, Spirituals, Rock, Rap, New Age, Folk, Hip-Hop, etc., are examples of style.

Tempo—The speed of music. Fast, slow, presto, allegro, moderato, andante, adagio, largo, ritardando, and a tempo are examples of tempo.

Texture—A manner in which music interacts. The structure and general pattern of sound created by elements of music. Thick, thin, mixed, polyphonic, homophonic, monophonic, counterpoint, contrapuntality, and a round are all examples of texture.

Timbre—Tone color. The quality of a sound that distinguishes it from another. Instruments and voices each have a unique timbre (pronounced: tam-ber), or tone color.

Tone color—Timbre. The quality of a sound that distinguishes it from another. Instruments and voices each have a unique timbre, or tone color.

Team Members _____
_____
_____
_____

Song Description Team Activity

Answer the questions below about the music you heard.

1. How fast or slow was the song?

2. Was the song loud, soft, or other?

3. What instrument(s) and/or voices were used?

4. Were instrument(s) and/or voices bright or dark sounding?

5. Did the music sound thick or thin? Have many or few parts?

6. How many sections were there in the music?

Element of Music Description

Element _____

Describe the music you heard using your assigned element.

Writing About Music

A Few of the Facts and Some Opinions

Write about and describe the music you have just heard. Use your Elements of Music Definitions to help you with the music terms.

_____

_____

_____

_____

_____

_____

_____

_____

_____

_____

_____

_____

_____

_____

_____

Which Element Is Which?

Place the letter of the definition beside the correct element.

1. Texture _____
2. Tone Color _____
3. Dynamics _____
4. Mood _____
5. Tempo _____
6. Style _____
7. Pitch _____
8. Form _____
9. Duration _____

a. Genre; features that characterize the music type; Jazz, Country, Hip-Hop, etc.

b. Happy, sad, excited, melancholy

c. Thick, thin, polyphonic; a general pattern of sound

d. The design or layout of music; rondo, round, AB, ABA

e. High, low; the relationship and quality of sound

f. Bright/dark; instrument or voice sound quality

g. Loud, soft, forte, pianissimo; the volume of music

h. Fast, slow, allegro, largo; the speed of music

i. Long/short; how long a sound lasts; whole note, half note, etc.

Connect the element with its definition.

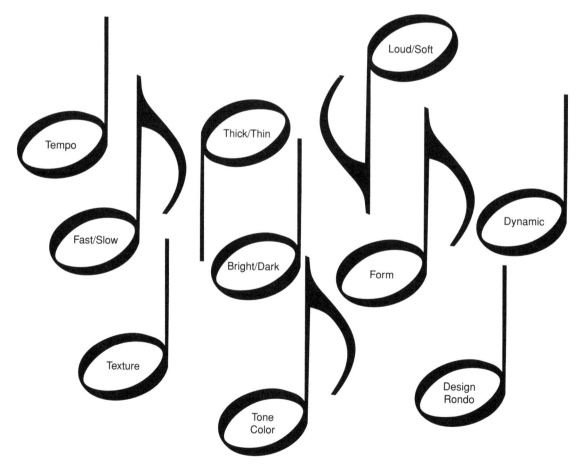

Which Element Is Which?

(Answer Key)

1. Texture _c_
2. Tone Color _f_
3. Dynamics _g_
4. Mood _b_
5. Tempo _h_
6. Style _a_
7. Pitch _e_
8. Form _d_
9. Duration _i_

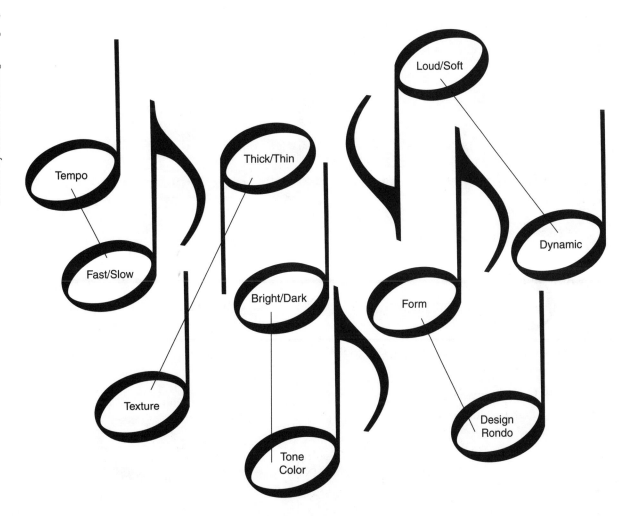

Elements of Music
Crossword Puzzle

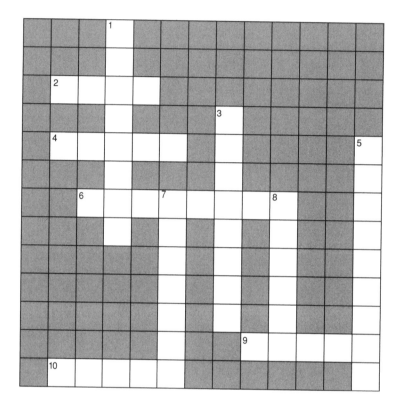

ACROSS

2. The design of music/AB/Rondo

4. High/low

6. Differences/Opposites/Dark-light/ loud-soft

9. Speed of music/Allegro/Largo

10. Type of music/Blues/Classical

DOWN

1. The length of a sound

3. Volume of music/loud/forte

5. Bright/dark/instruments/voice/timbre

7. Thick/thin

8. Bright/dark/instruments/voice/ tone color

Elements of Music

(Answer Key)

		¹D								
		U								
²F	O	R	M							
		A		³D						
⁴P	I	T	C	H	Y				⁵T	
		I		N				O		
	⁶C	O	N	⁷T	R	A	S	⁸T		N
		N		E		M		I		E
			X		I		M	C		
			T		C		B	O		
			U		S		R	L		
			R			⁹T	E	M	P	O
¹⁰S	T	Y	L	E				R	

An Eighth Note Gets a Beat
(Fractions)

LESSON PLAN

Objective: Students will read and perform in the meters of 6/8 and 3/8.

Materials: Piano
Pencils
Copies of: Music pages
    Music Pizzas (page 176)
    Big Meter Cards
    Small Meter Cards
    Music Math page
    Eighth Notes and More activity page

Procedure: 1. *Opening Activity:* Teach "Row, Row, Row Your Boat." While singing it through in its entirety, have the students tap on the first and fourth beats and snap their fingers on the second, third, fifth, and sixth beats.

2. *Singing Activity:* Hand out the music to "Over the Sea to Skye." Teach the song. While singing the song, have the students point to the notes in rhythm. Also, try "Joy of Man's Desiring" on page 338.

3. *Demonstration Activity:* Copy numerous Big Meter Cards on pages 387–392 and a set of Music Pizzas from Level 2 (3–4) pp. 173-176. Using the Meter Cards for 6/8, display the cards on the board (use tape, magnets, clips, etc.) or use a couple of music stands. Show the eighth note to students. Explain that the 8 on the bottom of the meter means an eighth note gets a beat. Discuss that a quarter = 2 beats, dotted-quarter = 3, dotted-half = 6 beats, etc. Use the Music Pizzas to show the fractions. Also, compare the slices with the corresponding note. Finally, compose some sample 6/8 and 3/8 measures using the Big Meter Cards.

Perhaps, select students to come forward to compose a measure on 6/8 or 3/8 with the Big Meter Cards. Have the rest of the class give a thumbs up for a correctly composed measure and thumbs down for an incorrect one. Continue the activity until you use a few students. Have the class clap the rhythms.

Procedure:
(Continued)

4. ***Composition Activity:*** Copy enough Small Meter Cards to have a large pack of cards for each student. Have the students compose a measure in 6/8 or 3/8. Be sure to have each student clap or tap his/her measure. This activity can continue through a number of measure compositions by each student.

5. ***Listening/Dictation Activity:*** Continuing to hold on to their cards, have the students dictate the following rhythm for you to clap. The students will use the Small Meter Cards to write the clapped rhythm.

You perhaps may want to use other 6/8 and 3/8 meter combinations to expand on the practice.

6. ***Reading Activity:*** Give each student a copy of Music Math. Instruct the students to color in the amount of the fraction listed above the item. Then have the students write the corresponding music notation on the line provided below the item. This is a great activity for students to learn and understand note values.

Activity Page: Copy and distribute the Eighth Notes and More activity page. Have the students complete the exercises for adding and subtracting notes with note answers, adding/subtracting fractions with note answers, and adding/subtracting notes and fractions with note answers.

Row, Row, Row Your Boat

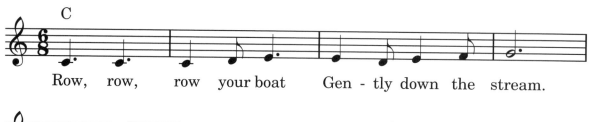

Row, row, row your boat Gen - tly down the stream.

Mer-ri - ly, mer-ri - ly, mer-ri - ly, mer-ri - ly, Life is but a dream.

Over the Sea to Skye

MacLeod/Stevenson

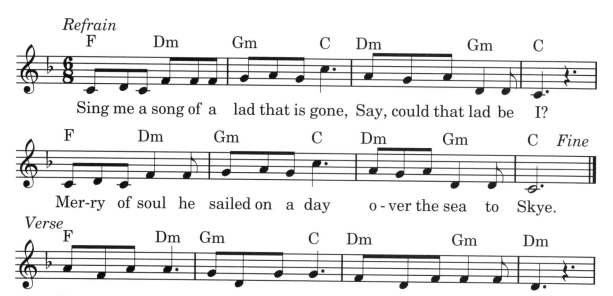

Refrain

Sing me a song of a lad that is gone, Say, could that lad be I?

Mer-ry of soul he sailed on a day o - ver the sea to Skye.

Verse

1. Give me a - gain all that was there, give me the sun that shone.
2. Bil - low and breeze, is-lands and seas, moun-tains of rain and snow.

D.C al Fine (last time)

Give me the eyes, give me the soul, give me the lad that's gone.
All that was good, all that was fair, all that was me is gone.

Big Meter Cards

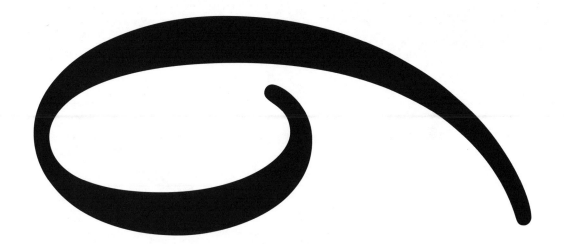

Big Meter Cards

Big Meter Cards

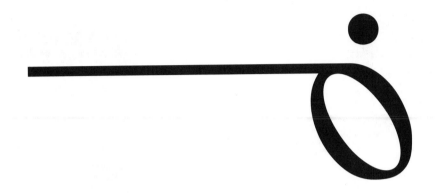

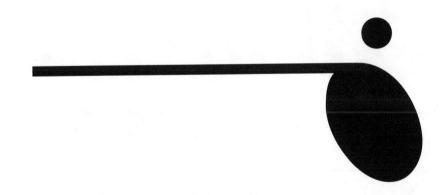

Big Meter Cards

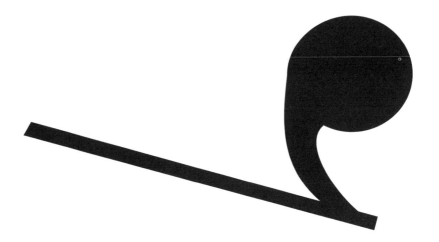

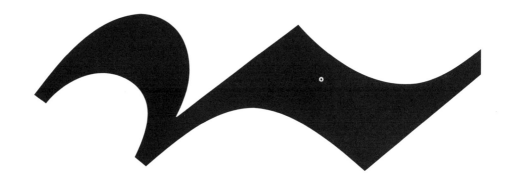

Big Meter Cards

Big Meter Cards

Small Meter Cards

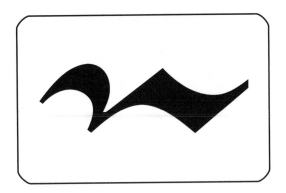

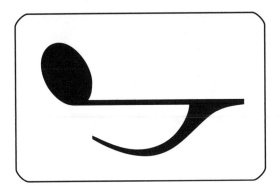

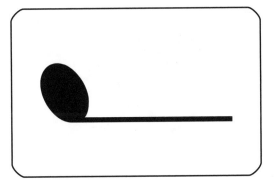

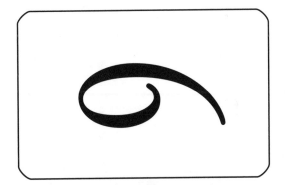

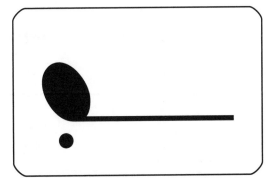

Small Meter Cards

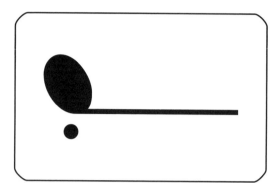

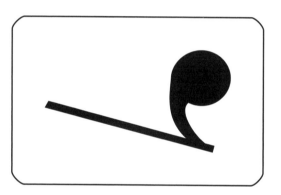

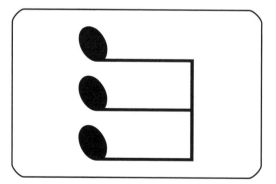

Name _____

Music Math

Color the fraction amount and write the matching music note below on the line provided.

$\frac{1}{2}$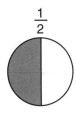

$\frac{1}{4}$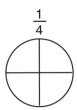

$\frac{1}{8}$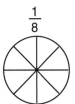

  ♩ _____

_____

_____

$\frac{3}{8}$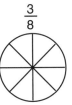

$\frac{1}{2}$

$\frac{6}{8}$

_____

_____

_____

$\frac{1}{2}$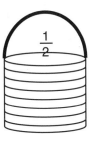

$\frac{1}{4}$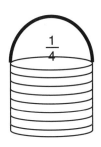

$\frac{3}{8}$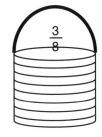

$\frac{6}{8}$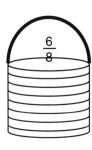

_____

_____

_____

_____

$\frac{1}{2}$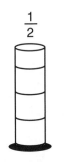

1

$\frac{1}{4}$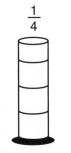

$\frac{4}{8}$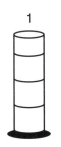

_____

_____

_____

_____

Name _____

Eighth Notes and More

Complete the following exercises.

♩ + ♩ = ___𝅗𝅥___   ♪ + ♪ + ♪ = _____   𝅗𝅥 – ♪ = _____

♪ + ♪ = _____   ♩ + ♪ + ♪ = _____   𝅗𝅥 – ♩ = _____

𝅗𝅥 + ♩ = _____   𝅗𝅥 + ♪ + ♪ = _____   𝅝 – ♪ = _____

♪ + ♩ = _____   ♫♫ + ♩. = _____   𝅝 – ♩ – 𝅗𝅥 = _____

Complete the fraction math with the correct music note(s) answer.
*Hint—Write the music note beside the fraction to help you figure out the answer.

$\frac{1}{4} + \frac{1}{4} = $ ___𝅗𝅥___ $\frac{1}{8} + \frac{3}{8} = $ _____ $\frac{3}{4} - \frac{1}{4} = $ _____

$\frac{1}{8} + \frac{1}{8} = $ _____ $\frac{5}{8} + \frac{3}{8} = $ _____ $\frac{1}{2} - \frac{1}{4} = $ _____

$\frac{1}{2} + \frac{1}{2} = $ _____ $\frac{3}{8} + \frac{3}{8} = $ _____ $1 - \frac{1}{2} = $ _____

$\frac{1}{8} + \frac{1}{8} + \frac{1}{8} = $ _____ $\frac{1}{4} + \frac{1}{8} + \frac{1}{8} = $ _____ $\frac{3}{4} - \frac{1}{2} = $ _____

Answer the music note/fraction math with the correct music note(s).

♩ + $\frac{1}{4}$ = ___𝅗𝅥___   ♪ + $\frac{1}{4}$ = _____   𝅝 – $\frac{1}{2}$ = _____

♪. + $\frac{1}{8}$ = _____   ♩ + $\frac{1}{2}$ = _____   𝅗𝅥 – $\frac{1}{4}$ = _____

♪ + $\frac{1}{8}$ = _____   ♪ + ♪ + $\frac{1}{4}$ = _____   ♩ – $\frac{1}{8}$ = _____

♪ + $\frac{1}{8}$ = _____   ♩ + $\frac{1}{4}$ + $\frac{1}{2}$ = _____   ♫♫ – $\frac{1}{8}$ = _____

Bass Clef Notation
(Suffixes and Parts of Words)

LESSON PLAN

Objective: Students will identify and name notes of the bass clef.

Materials: Piano
Chalkboard
Pencils
Copies of: Music page
      Bach's Bouree
      Bass Clef Staff
      Bass Clef page
      Bass Clef Staff Notes and Barlines
      Learning the Bass Clef page
      Bass Clef in Words page
      Only in the Words story page
      Treble to Bass page

Procedure: 1. *Opening Activity:* Teach "Perry Merry Dictum" (treble clef). Ask the students to point out the treble clef in the song. Also ask the students: "What if we wanted to sing the song in a lower key—a key where the notes actually are below the staff that we usually use? Who can name the notes of 'Perry Merry Dictum'? How can one figure out the note names? How many letters do we use in music?" Help the students arrive at the answers to these questions. Finally, have the students look at the bass clef version of "Perry Merry Dictum" while you play it on the piano. "How does it differ from the first version?" Discuss the differences.

2. *Identification Activity:* Teach Bach's "Bouree." Have the students sing the treble clef and play the bass part on the piano at the same time. Have the students name instruments, aside from the piano, that use bass clef (tuba, timbre, bassoon, string bass, cello, and bass guitar).

3. *Reading Activity:* Using the Bass Clef Staff, the Bass Clef page, and Bass Clef Staff Notes, demonstrate and explain the bass clef notation. Good Boys Do Fine Always (lines) and All Cows Eat Grass (spaces) are good mnemonics. After making a presentation to the students, give each student a copy of the bass clef staff and several bass clef staff notes. Pair students and have one student place a note on the staff and the other student name it. Have the partners switch places and repeat the activity.

Procedure:
(Continued)

4. **Performance Activity:** Using the bass clef staff, have two to four class members place one note on the staff. Select a student to perform the bass clef notes on an xylophone or a set of bells. Have the note placers pick students to replace them on the xylophone next. This activity can be done with more people. Student performers must be able to name the notes.

5. **Reading and Writing Activity:** Copy enough pages of the Learning the Bass Clef page for the entire class. This page is in two parts. Have the students fill in the top part with the correct letter for the given bass notes. At the bottom have the students write the note in bass clef of the letter.

6. **Reading and Writing Activity:** Copy enough pages of the Bass Clef in Words for the class. Have the students complete the words by filling in the letters of the given notes. At the bottom, have the students write the bass note on the staff of the underlined letters of the given words.

7. **Identification Activity:** Give each student a copy of Only in the Words story activity page. Have the students complete the story by filling in the missing letters of the words by using the bass note clues.

Activity Page:

Give each student a copy of the Treble to Bass activity page. Have the students transcribe the treble clef music line to bass clef and the bass clef line to treble clef. Keep in mind that the transcription may be an octave or so higher or lower.

Perry Merry Dictum

(Treble Clef)

I had four bro - thers o - ver the sea.

Per - ry Mer - ry Dict - um Do - mi - nee. And they

each sent a pres - ent un - to me.

Par - tum quar - tum Per - ry di - cen - tum
(chen)

Per - ry Mer - ry Dict - um Do - mi - nee.

J. S. Bach

(Bass Clef)

Bach's Bouree

J. S. Bach

Voice: It's a tune of a dance, and it's called a bour-

Piano

eé. It is French, from a suite, and by J. S. Bach they say. As we sing this old tune we will hope to learn soon the bass clef and its notes will do.

Bass Clef Staff

Bass Clef

(F Clef)

Bass Clef Staff Notes
and Barlines

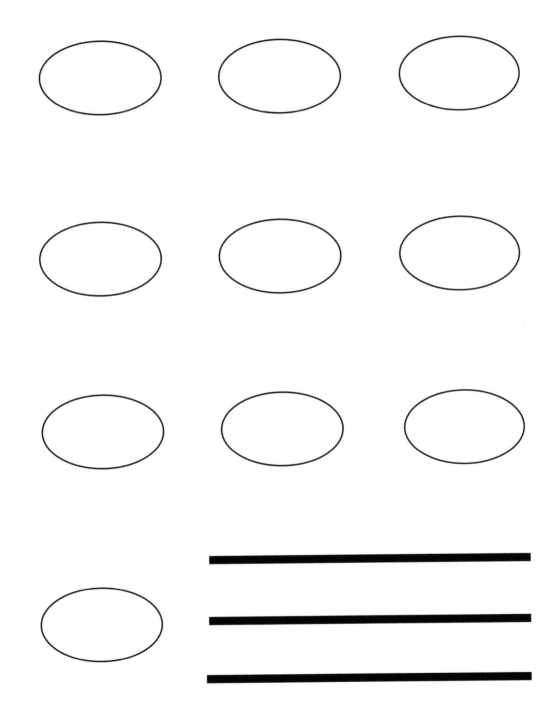

Learning the Bass Clef

Fill in the correct name of the bass notes.

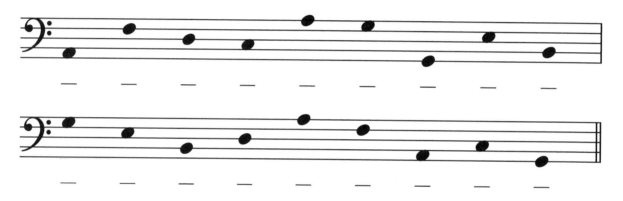

Write the note on the staff of the given letter.

F   G   C   A   D   B   E

C   B   E   F   D   G   B

Name _____

Bass Clef in Words

Complete the following words by using the bass note hints.

_ _ K _ _ _ _ _ _ _ _ R _ _ _ _ _

_ _ U _ H T P _ I _ R _ _ _ I V _ _

_ _ S _ _ O U _ T P N _ U M O N I _

Write in the notes of the underlined letters.

Prefixes and Suffixes

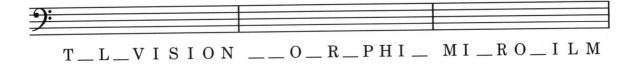

T _ L _ V I S I O N _ _ O _ R _ P H I _ M I _ R O _ I L M

_ U T O M _ T _ _ _ U T O _ R _ P H _ U T O _ R _ T

Only in the Words

Complete the story by filling in the missing letters using the note clues.

Trying to l __ __ rn the __ __ ss __ l __ __ staff can be simpl__. But one must

learn the lines and the spaces of the staff. It is not mi__ ro __ iolo __ y or

__ __ o __ r __ phy. The bass clef is as easy as remembering the sentences

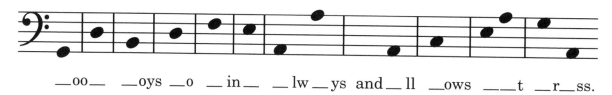

__oo__ __oys __o __ in__ __lw__ys and__ ll __ows ___t __r__ss.

With all you've l__ __rn___ and all you've__on__ in school the bass clef is not

too tough. After some practice it becomes __utom__ti__.

© 2001 by Parker Publishing Company

Name _____

Treble to Bass
Bass to Treble

Transcribe the treble clef line of music to bass clef.

Transcribe the bass clef line of music to treble clef.

Women Composers
(Role Change of Women)

LESSON PLAN

Objective: Students will identify various women composers and their music.

Materials: Piano
Pencils
Copies of: Music pages
        Five composer biographies
        Who, What, When, and Where Activity Page
        Women Composers Timeline
        Women Composers Crossword Puzzle
        Women Composers Wordsearch

Procedure:

1. ***Opening Activity:*** Ask the students the following questions: "Who was Aaron Copland's (American composer) composition teacher?" (Nadia Boulanger), "Which composer had a brother who was a great composer?" (Fanny Mendelssohn), "What composer wrote the opera *Cabildo*?" (Amy Beach), and "What composer earned a doctorate degree from Julliard School of Music and won a Pulitzer Prize for music?" (Ellen Taaffe Zwilich). Finally, "Who was married to a composer?" (Clara Schumann). Ask all these questions first; save the answers until later. Then ask: "What do all the composers have in common?"—"They are all women." Teach "Mazurka."

2. ***Discussion Activity:*** Ask the students the following questions: What other great women have there been and what did they do? (Joan of Arc/Leader of France, Molly Pitcher/American Revolution Hero, Rosa Parks/Civil Rights, C. J. Walker/First Woman Millionaire, and Amelia Earhart/Pilot). Teach "Melodie."

3. ***Reading Activity:*** Give each student copies of the women composers biographies. Read each biography. Teach "The Returning Hunter." Allow the students to color the composer pictures.

4. ***Research Activity:*** Give each student one, two, three, four, or five Who, What, When and Where Page(s). Allow the students to fill in the pages by using the information provided in the women composers biographies.

5. ***Writing Activity:*** Hand out a Women Composers Timeline to each student. With the women composers biographies, have the students fill in the empty lines on the chart.

6. ***Crossword Activity:*** Pass out a Women Composers Crossword Puzzle to each student. Instruct the students to complete the crossword puzzle.

Activity Page: Hand out a Women Composers Wordsearch to each student for completion.

Mazurka

Clara Wieck Schumann
(1819 - 1896)

This Ma-zur-ka, by Schu-mann. Not by Ro-bert, but his wife. Cla-ra

Schu-mann com-posed quite well. Mu-sic for the pi - a - no.

The Returning Hunter
(Eskimos—Four Characters)

Amy Beach
(1867 - 1944)

A-my Mar-cy Beach was per-form-ing at the age of sev-en-teen.

Com-posed her Gae-lic Sym-pho-ny. Toured in Eur-ope. Gained the re-spect

of all Eu - rope. Lived in New York, U. S. A.

409

Melodie
(op. 4, no. 2)

Fanny Mendelssohn Hensel
(1805 - 1847)

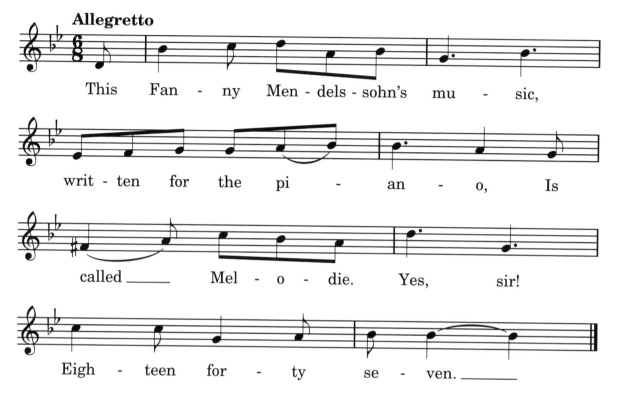

Allegretto

This Fan - ny Men - dels - sohn's mu - sic,

writ - ten for the pi - an - o, Is

called ____ Mel - o - die. Yes, sir!

Eigh - teen for - ty se - ven. ____

Ellen Taaffe Zwilich

(b.1939)

Ellen Taaffe Zwilich was born in Miami, Florida, in 1939. She was the first woman to earn a doctorate degree in music composition from Julliard School of Music. She was also the first woman to win a Pulitzer Prize for music. Zwilich continues to compose successfully for audiences around the world.

By the age of ten Zwilich was composing. She studied piano, trumpet, and violin. She also conducted and composed for her high school band. Ellen majored in music at Florida State University and played in different student performance groups. She later moved to New York in the 1960s and soon joined the American Symphony Orchestra.

During the 1970s Zwilich entered the Julliard School of Music where she studied composing with Elliot Carter and Roger Sessions. Interestingly, she worked as an usher at Carnegie Hall for a season.

Soon Zwilich earned money and financing for her music compositions. Her music is considered to be neo-Romantic like Shostakovich and Schoenberg. She is known for her compositions *Symposium for Orchestra, String Quartet, Chamber Symphony, Symphony No. 1, Celebration,* and *Prologue and Variations.*

Fanny Mendelssohn Hensel
(1805–1847)

Born in Hamburg, Germany, in 1805, Fanny Mendelssohn Hensel was a child prodigy. However, Fanny fell into the shadow of someone who was even more gifted—her brother, Felix Mendelssohn. The Mendelssohns were a prominent German-Jewish family. Fanny's grandfather was the famous German philosopher Moses Mendelssohn. In 1811 the Mendelssohn family fled to Berlin due to the French invasion.

Fanny's music education began with piano lessons from her mother. Mrs. Mendelssohn soon recognized Fanny's talent. By age 13, Fanny could play Bach's "Well-Tempered Clavier." But Fanny faced the hurdles of anti-semitism and the fact she was a female in a male's profession. Fanny, however, continued to perform, compose, and publish music.

Fanny Mendelssohn married William Hensel, an artist but no musician, who encouraged her to continue her musical endeavors. She composed songs, oratorios, and operas.

Felix and Fanny Mendelssohn were very close. While rehearsing for a performance, Fanny died suddenly. Felix lost his zest, drive, and will to continue living, let alone compose. Within the next six months, Felix died.

Clara Wieck Schumann

(1819–1896)

Clara Schumann was born in Leipzig, Germany, to a well-known music teacher father, Friedrich Wieck. She began piano lessons at age five with her father. Her first concert was at age nine at the Leipzig Gewandhaus. As she continued in music, Clara studied voice, violin, and, certainly, piano. She also worked in music theory, score reading, and composition.

Clara's father encouraged her pursuit of music, although few women enjoyed successful music careers in her time. Nevertheless, Clara toured playing the piano. Famous composers like Paganini, Mendelssohn, Chopin, and Robert Schumann had great admiration and respect for her.

In 1840, against her father's wishes, Clara married Robert Schumann, the great German pianist and composer. The couple had eight children. Clara felt commitment and duty to her family, but her family life wasn't easy. Even though Robert Schumann supported her dedication to music and loved her undyingly, he suffered from mental illness and health problems. This made Clara's life difficult. Composer Johannes Brahms, a student of Schumann, became a close companion to Clara, and helped her through many difficult times.

Clara Schumann composed piano pieces, a piano concerto, and numerous songs. She became quite influential in some of Robert Schumann's and Johannes Brahm's music. Unfortunately, Clara Schumann was probably born too early to fully appreciate and develop the greatness that was very apparent and noticed by many of history's great composers.

Amy Beach

(1867–1944)

In 1882, for the first time, the New York Philharmonic Society performed the work of an American woman—a fifteen-year-old woman. Amy (Cheyney) Beach was a child prodigy. At age sixteen she debuted in Boston in concert as a pianist. By age seventeen she was playing solo with the Boston Symphony Orchestra. Her *Gaelic Symphony* and *Mass in E-Flat* set the path for a wonderful future as a composer.

Amy married Dr. H. H. Beach, a surgeon, by the time she was eighteen. After the death of her husband, she toured Europe playing the romantic music of Brahms, Chopin, Liszt, and Schumann. She gained a wonderful reputation and respect from the tough European audiences.

Amy Beach composed over 150 pieces including works for chorus and orchestra, her opera *Cabildo,* a violin sonata, a piano quintet, and a mass. She spent the end of her life in New York, an accomplished composer.

Cecile Chaminade

(1857–1944)

Chaminade, born in Paris, France, began composing by the age of eight, and by eighteen she made her debut as a pianist with much success in the concert halls of Europe. Unfortunately, the road to success was difficult. Having brought up their daughter as a proper, well-finished young woman, her parents resisted her desire to become a professional musician. In Chaminade's day, it was proper for a young woman to gain the skills to run a household and marry a well-off suitor.

The career of Chaminade was destined to be successful. Her parents were friends with the great French composer Bizet. The composer realized the ability and talent in the young woman, and he encouraged Cecile, as well as her parents, to pursue her aspirations as a composer. She became the first woman to make a career of composing. Chaminade is accredited for writing orchestral suites, an opera comique, two piano trios, music for piano and orchestra, a choral symphony, and more than 200 piano pieces. She also composed four ballets—including her "Scarf Dance."

Unfairly, during the time of World War I, her music came to be regarded as light-weight and superficial, but Chaminade continued to gather new listeners and retain the devoted fans she entertained during her entire career. She died in 1944 in Monte Carlo.

Name _____

Who, What, When, and Where
Activity Page

Respond to the following.

Composer's name _____

   Who were the significant people in the composer's life?

   What did the composer write?

   When did the composer write?

   When did the composer live?

   Where was the composer's life spent?

   Other important events occurred during the life of the composer.

Name _____

Women Composers Timeline

Fill in the lines with the correct names and information.

Great Women Composers

1. _____
Woman composer in Florence, Italy.

2. 1882 New York Philharmonic
Society performed the work of an
American woman composer for
the first time. _____

_____

3. _____ married Robert
Schumann.

4. The younger brother of
_____
was born. A great composer, he over-
shadowed his sister.

5. After WW I, _____'s
music was dismissed as light-weight.

6. _____ was the
younger sister of a female composer.

7. _____ was the
1st woman to win the Prix de Rome.

8. Aaron Copland studied with
_____.

9. The stepson of _____
became a well-known folksinger.

10. _____ won the
Pulitzer Prize in 1983.

Great Women

1500	— Joan of Arc (French Leader)
	— Elizabeth I (Queen of England)
1600	
1700	— Marie Antoinette (Queen of France)
	— Molly Pitcher (American Revolution)
	— Jane Austin (author)
1800	— Mary Shelley (author of *Frankenstein*)
1900	— Harriet Tubman (Underground RR)
	— Emily Dickinson (author/poet)
	— Elizabeth Cady Stanton (Suffrage)
	— Susan B. Anthony (Women's Rights)
	— Mother Teresa (Missionary)
	— Martha Graham (Dance)
	— Rosa Parks (Civil Rights)
1999	— Valentina Tereshkova (1st Woman in Space)
	— C.J. Walker (1st Woman Millionaire)
	— Sandra Day O'Connor (1st Woman Supreme Court Justice)

21st Century

Fanny Mendelssohn   Lili Boulanger   Ellen Taaffe Zwilich
Chaminade   Francesca Caccini   Amy Beach
Nadia Boulanger   Clara Schumann   Ruth Crawford Seeger

Women Composers Crossword Puzzle

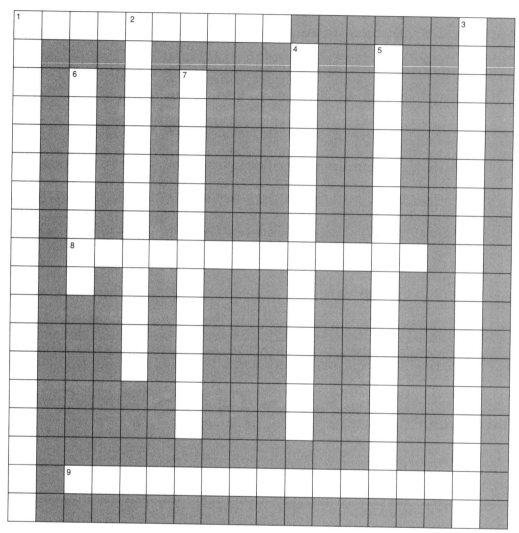

ACROSS

1. Wrote 6 operas including "The Wrecker"

8. Married to Robert Schumann

9. Bizet was a friend of her parents

DOWN

1. First woman to win a Pulitzer Prize for music

2. Her sister was her music teacher

3. Her stepson became a well-known folksinger

4. Aaron Copland studied with her

5. Her brother was a composer

6. Wrote the *Gaelic Symphony*

7. Studied at the Royal College of Music in London

COMPOSER BANK

Cecile Chaminade
Ruth Crawford Seeger
Nadia Boulanger
Lili Boulanger
Rebecca Clarke

Ethel Smyth
Amy Beach
Ellen Taaffe Zwilich
Fanny Mendelssohn
Clara Schumann

Women Composers

(Answer key)

¹E	T	H	E	²L	S	M	Y	T	H					³R	
L				I				⁴N		⁵F				U	
L		⁶A		L		⁷R		A		A				T	
E		M		I		E		D		N				H	
N		Y		B		B		I		N				C	
T		B		O		E		A		Y				R	
A		E		U		C		B		M				A	
A		A		L		C		O		E				W	
F		⁸C	L	A	R	A	S	C	H	U	M	A	N	N	F
F		H		C				L		D				O	
E		G		L				A		E				R	
Z		E		A				N		L				D	
W		R		R				G		S				S	
I				K				E		S				E	
L				E				R		O				E	
I										H				G	
C	⁹C	E	C	I	L	E	C	H	A	M	I	N	A	D	E
H														R	

Women Composers Wordsearch

```
E  F  Z  F  J  P  V  T  O  A  Y  E  O  Q  K  C  B  N  R  F
E  N  K  R  A  W  R  P  H  V  M  G  M  H  I  T  A  A  V  I
B  D  S  J  D  N  S  Y  Y  R  R  Y  R  P  P  I  E  D  C  J
B  I  N  G  E  N  N  O  S  O  I  V  B  U  I  D  V  I  A  P
B  D  U  E  U  M  C  Y  N  I  X  F  E  E  A  U  T  A  K  H
I  H  S  C  H  Y  P  D  M  K  M  Q  E  N  A  F  U  B  S  M
L  E  F  V  M  T  A  X  H  E  B  W  I  Q  P  C  V  O  W  A
W  M  M  M  H  H  Y  Q  I  T  N  M  R  C  D  O  H  U  O  R
F  E  J  R  L  G  J  M  D  N  A  D  L  I  N  P  N  L  N  T
E  R  R  E  U  G  A  L  S  H  I  A  E  E  G  R  R  A  A  I
J  U  S  W  Z  C  A  H  C  L  R  C  R  L  L  G  L  N  M  N
G  A  I  L  S  M  I  T  H  A  E  R  C  J  S  Q  K  G  Y  E
R  B  D  J  O  O  P  L  S  K  A  H  U  A  O  S  S  E  Z  Z
X  U  A  N  H  G  B  C  D  C  L  Z  T  M  C  L  O  R  S  L
D  M  R  R  C  O  H  B  K  L  F  L  P  E  G  Y  A  H  B  O
C  J  A  C  P  U  S  O  O  Q  V  K  K  W  Y  J  S  N  N
L  O  P  S  M  R  E  G  N  A  L  U  O  B  I  L  I  L  E  Q
T  F  U  A  Y  O  C  D  D  Y  H  R  E  W  S  B  L  G  M  K
S  R  N  O  J  L  B  B  G  Y  K  R  N  D  A  M  M  M  Q  Y
G  N  H  C  I  L  I  W  Z  E  F  F  A  A  T  N  E  L  L  E
```

AMY BEACH
CARRENO
ELLEN TAAFFE ZWILICH
GAIL SMITH
LAGUERRE
NADIA BOULANGER

BINGEN
CHAMINADE
ETHEL SMYTH
GRONDAHL
LILI BOULANGER
PARADIS

CACCINI
CLARA SCHUMANN
FANNY MENDELSSOHN
JOLAS
MARTINEZ
SZYMANOWSKA

Women Composers

(Answer Key)

421

Keys/Mood
(Mystery, Fantasy, Drama, and Comedy)

LESSON PLAN

Objective: Students will identify minor key signatures.
*This lesson is an extension to major key signatures. Students need to know how to figure out major keys and read note names.

Materials: Piano
Pencils
Chalkboard
Copies of: Keys Music Page
          Mood Examples Page
          Mood and Literature page
          Relative Minor Keys page
          Literature and Key page
          Naming the Key page
          A Key to Literature page

Procedure: 1. *Opening Activity:* Play "If You're Happy" for the students. You can have them sing it, but some students at this age find the song childish. However, you could use another happiness song that the students like. After playing the song, ask why the song is about being happy. Responses will vary, but most will say it is the word happy. Also, ask if the song still would sound happy if the words were eliminated.

2. *Listening Activity:* Play Symphony No. 9, "Ode to Joy." Have the students discuss what the music sounds like. "What does it sound like it could be called? Does it sound mysterious, humorous, joyful, sad, melancholy, etc.?" Play numerous songs and pieces. Have the students categorize the tunes. Discuss stories that are mysteries, comedies, dramas, adventures, fantasies, etc. Ask, "What makes stories fall into these types? What makes music fall into these categories?" Use the Mood and Literature page to give students a reference.

3. *Singing Activity:* Sing "Pavane for a Dead Princess." "How would you describe this music? What is it that makes this music fit your description?" At this time discuss key signatures and keys. Stress the importance of the key to the music and the mood it presents. Play *Symphony No. 7*. Using the Mood and Literature page, have the student fit the tunes into a literature category. Play many examples.

Procedure:
(Continued)

4. ***Discovery Activity:*** Give each student a copy of the Mood Examples page. Have the students point out where to find the key signature. Review with the students how to find the major scale and key. Have the students name the keys to each tune. Possibly, give each student a music textbook, and name the keys to music selections. Have the students search for a song in the selected key (pick either flats or sharps to simplify).

5. ***Discussion Activity:*** Put a "C" major scale on the board. Ask the students what scale, or key, the scale represents. When "C" is established, show the process for counting up to the sixth step of the scale to find the relative minor key. Hand out a copy of the Relative Minor Keys page to the students. Have them find the minor key to each scale.

6. ***Recognition Activity:*** Give each student a copy of the Literature and Key page. Have the students name major and minor for the key that best fits the literature type. Under the stories section, have the students name major or minor and how they feel the music should sound to best fit the story.

7. ***Identification Activity:*** Hand out a copy of the Naming the Key page to each student. Review the process for figuring out the major key. Then, show the students how to find the relative minor key. Instruct the students to identify each key signature.

Activity Page:

Give each student a copy of A Key to Literature page. Instruct the students to decide whether the literature type should be major or minor, and name it.

If You're Happy

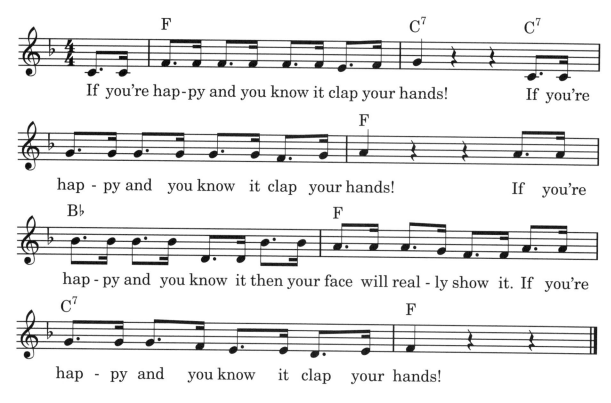

If you're hap-py and you know it clap your hands! If you're
hap - py and you know it clap your hands! If you're
hap - py and you know it then your face will real - ly show it. If you're
hap - py and you know it clap your hands!

Ode to Joy

L. van Beethoven

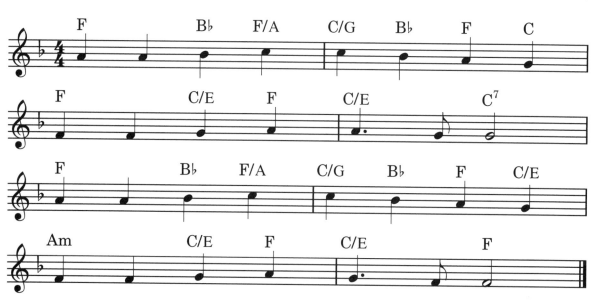

Pavane for a Dead Princess

M. Ravel

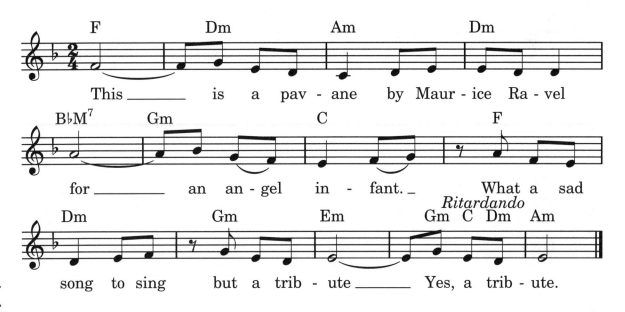

| F | Dm | Am | Dm |

This _____ is a pav - ane by Maur - ice Ra - vel

| B♭M⁷ | Gm | | C | | F |

for _____ an an - gel in - fant. ___ What a sad

Ritardando

| Dm | Gm | Em | Gm C Dm Am |

song to sing but a trib - ute _____ Yes, a trib - ute.

Symphony No. 7
(Allegretto)

L. van Beethoven

Mood Examples Page

426

Mood and Literature

Mystery

Drama

Comedy

Fantasy

Adventure

Relative Minor Keys

Find the major and minor keys for each scale.

C Major = A minor (relative minor)

Example

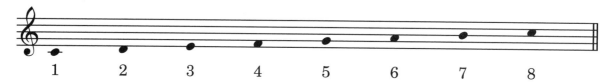

*Hints—Count up six or back three letters for the relative minor key name.

Name _____

Literature and Key

Give a major or minor key to the type of literature and stories below.

Mystery _____   Comedy _____

Drama _____   Fantasy _____

Stories

1. A busy-body barber tries to play matchmaker for a count and young lady who each want to meet. But because of the girl's guardian, they are afraid to meet in public. Her guardian wants to marry her for her dowry. Silly and comical things happen during the story. Nevertheless, the count and the girl do finally get together at the end.

   Key: _____

   How do you think the music should sound?

2. This story takes place hundreds of years ago. A man goes hunting too far from home and he becomes lost. He ends up in a territory where he stumbles across a dragon. The queen of this particular kingdom has three ladies who save him from the dragon. The queen asks the hunter to join one of her people, a man dressed like a bird—the birdcatcher—to help rescue her daughter from an evil knight who has abducted her.

   Key: _____

   How do you think the music should sound?

Name _____

Naming the Key

Name the minor key to each key signature.

Examples:

D Major
D E F# G A ⓑ C# D
1 2 3 4 5 ⑥ 7 8

__B minor__

Bb Major
Bb C D Eb F ⓖ A Bb
1 2 3 4 5 ⑥ 7 8

__G Minor__

1.
_____

2.
_____

3.
_____

4.
_____

5.
_____

6.
_____

7.
_____

8.
_____

9.
_____

10.
_____

11. _____

12. _____

A Key to Literature

Name the key signature. Determine whether the key is major or minor using the literature type listed. There is not necessarily a correct answer as far as major or minor.

Mystery   Comedy   Adventure

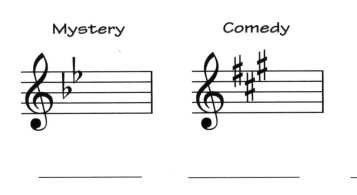

_____   _____   _____

Drama   Fantasy   Mystery

_____   _____   _____

Comedy   Drama   Fantasy

_____   _____   _____

Supplementary Materials
(5–6)

Adding Words/Lyrics (Similes, Metaphors, and Alliteration)
   Adding Lyrics (activity sheet)

Web Page Designer
   Web Page (design pattern)

Who Am I? (American composers)
   Aaron Copland (1900–1990)
   George Gershwin (1898–1937)
   John Philip Sousa (1854–1932)
   Scott Joplin (1868–1917)
   Ellen Taaffe Zwilich (b. 1939)
   Composer Questions
   Composer Selections Page

Musical Football
   Music Football Scoreboards
   Music Football Questions
   Music Football Questions (continued)
   Music Football Questions (continued)
   Music Football Football Field

16th Notes (Fractions)
   Music Pizza (16ths)

MASCAR Racing (game to review music concepts)
   MASCAR Racetrack
   MASCAR Racecars
   MASCAR Response Pages
   MASCAR Example Questions

Daily Music Skill Builders
   Daily Singing Skill Builders 51–75
   Daily Rhythm Skill Builders 51–75

Interdisciplinary Planner

Adding Words/Lyrics
(Similes, Metaphors, and Alliteration)

Objective: Students will compose lyrics to popular tunes.

Materials: Pencils
Lined writing paper (composition paper)
Copies of the Adding Lyrics page

Procedure: 1. Teach the students about similes, metaphors, and alliteration.

2. Give each student a piece of lined writing paper. Have the students practice writing similes, metaphors, and alliteration.

3. Finally, give each student a copy of the Adding Lyrics page. Have them do an example of each style with the tunes provided.

Adding Lyrics

Add words to these tunes in the form of similes, metaphors, and alliteration.

1.

2.

3.

Web Page Designer

Objective: Students will be able to write about a topic in music.

Materials: Pencil
Copies of the Web Page

Procedure:
1. This activity may be used with any music concept that can be discussed through writing.

2. Give each student a copy of the Web Page. Have the students fill out the subject, subtitle, and topics fields. Also, the students can blacken the circle to the topic which is being written about in the text field.

3. If there are numerous topics, several copies of the Web Page may be needed.

4. Students may want to color their pages for added effects.

Name _____

_____

Web Page

(Subject)

(Subject)

(Topics)

◯

◯

◯

◯

◯

◯

(Subtitle)

(Text)

Who Am I?

Objective: Students will identify characteristics and the work of various American composers.

Materials: Pencils
Copies of: five composer biographies
           Composer Selections page
           Composer Questions page

Procedure:

1. Select five students to portray the given American composers. Seat the students in front of the class. Give each of the five students a copy of the biography of a composer. Have each of the five students silently read his/her biography to prepare for questions. Also, give the composers a copy of the Questions page for more assistance. If information to respond to the questions is not in the biography, the student can say: "I can't anwer that question at this time."

2. Hand out a copy of the Composer Questions to each student in the class. Have the students take turns asking questions. The questions should not be ones that ask the composer's name or some similar variation.

3. After each member of the class has had the opportunity to ask a question or two, have a vote on which student is what composer. Students may use the Composer Selections page to take notes. Collect the response sheets, and have the composers tell the whole class who is who.

AARON COPLAND
(1900–1990)

In his youth, Aaron Copland almost didn't get the opportunity to study music. He had older brothers and sisters who studied piano but were not very good, so his parents were reluctant to allow Aaron to take lessons. He first learned piano from his sister until he decided he wanted an actual piano teacher. By 13, he was studying with a professional teacher.

At 21, in 1921, Aaron traveled to France to study music. He wanted to learn about modern and contemporary music by the composers of the day. While in France he studied with the renowned French composition teacher Nadia Boulanger. The techniques and styles he learned in France remained an influence in his music we hear today. But, although influenced by French style, Copland's music became very American. He also kept some of the characteristics of the old classics that people wanted to hear in the 1930s. His music was simple and widely enjoyed by his American audiences as well as by people throughout the world.

Among his compositions are "The Red Pony" (a score for the movie *The Red Pony),* ballets (*Appalachian Spring, Rodeo,* and *Billy the Kid*), "Lincoln Portrait" (filmscore), "Connotations," and his "Music for the Theater." Copland's music was contemporary, but it included old favorite classical styles, American folk music, jazz, and blues. He was certainly a diverse composer.

Born in Brooklyn, New York in 1900, Copland became one of America's foremost and respected composers of all time. He died in 1990 after a great career which established him as a beloved icon in American history.

Contemporaries

- Roger Sessions, composer
- Paul Hindemith, composer
- George Gershwin, composer
- William Faulkner, writer
- Ernest Hemingway, writer
- Jackson Pollack, artist

Events and People of His Lifetime

- World War I
- World War II
- Korean War
- Vietnam War
- Theodore Roosevelt
- Woodrow Wilson
- Franklin D. Roosevelt
- John F. Kennedy
- Ronald Reagan
- George Bush
- Computer technology

GEORGE GERSHWIN
(1898–1937)

George Gershwin, a son of Russian-Jewish immigrant parents, was born in 1898 on the Lower East Side of Manhattan in New York. On his neighbor's piano, he taught himself to play the hit tunes of his boyhood. At 13, he began studying piano with a teacher who introduced him to the great composers like Bach, Liszt, and Debussy. He left school at 15 to become a pianist who demonstrated new songs in the salesroom of a music publisher. By 18, he was starting a career writing his own songs. In 1919 he wrote his first Broadway musical, *La, La, Lucille.* The next year, when he was 21, his song "Swanee," sung by Al Jolson, became a hit. During the 1920s and 1930s he wrote the Broadway musicals *Lady, Be Good; Funny Face* and *Of Thee I Sing;* and his renowned film music *The Jazz Singer.*

Gershwin's brother Ira was also a composer and musician. However, Ira was considered more the lyricist for the brilliant musicals that the Gershwin brothers produced. George also composed concertos for piano and orchestra, including "Rhapsody in Blue," and "Concert in F." He composed an opera, *Porgy and Bess,* and a symphonic poem called *American in Paris.*

George loved the outdoors, art, and he even tried to paint. He went from Tin Pan Alley to being a wealthy musician. His style was a fusion of popular, jazz, and classical. He broke new ground in American music, and he was considered a musical genius.

Gershwin played tennis with the composer Arnold Schoenberg on occasion. Gershwin stated that he wanted to be as good a composer as Schoenberg. Schoenberg said: "Why do you want to be like Schoenberg, when you make such a good George Gershwin?"

George Gershwin died in Hollywood, California, at the age of 38 of a brain tumor. His music and style had broken ground never before trodden, and created its own place in the world's music.

Contemporaries

- Schoenberg, composer
- Stravinsky, composer
- Berg, composer
- Ravel, composer
- Charles Ives, American composer
- T.S. Elliot, writer
- Pablo Picasso, artist

Events and People of His Lifetime

- Spanish-American War
- World War I
- Theodore Roosevelt
- Woodrow Wilson
- Thomas Edison, inventor

JOHN PHILIP SOUSA
(1854–1932)

John Philip Sousa was born in 1854 in Washington, D.C., a fitting birthplace for a man whose music was known throughout the world as "American." He studied in Washington, D.C., and at the age of 13 became a member of the Marine Corps Band. The rest of his life was spent directing and composing for bands.

Sousa became world renowned for his marches and patriotic songs. He also composed operas and waltzes and wrote a few books. His most famous works include "The Stars and Stripes Forever," "El Capitan," and "High School Cadets."

Because of his marches, which were loved by many, Sousa became known as the "March King." Very few parades take place in the United States during which one doesn't hear a marching band playing Sousa. And one surely can't attend a Fourth of July celebration without hearing that wonderful piccolo part during the Trio of "The Stars and Stripes Forever."

In 1932, Sousa died leaving a wealth of marches and other music that is labeled, and will always remain, "American."

Contemporaries

- George Gershwin, composer
- Giacomo Puccini, composer
- Igor Stravinsky, composer
- Bela Bartok, composer
- Maurice Ravel, composer
- Virginia Woolf, writer
- Henri Matisse, artist
- Pablo Picasso, artist
- Vincent Van Gogh, artist

Events and People of His Lifetime

- American Civil War
- Spanish-American War
- World War I
- Abraham Lincoln
- Ulysses S. Grant
- Woodrow Wilson

SCOTT JOPLIN
(1868–1917)

Born in Texas, about 1867–68, Scott Joplin was the son of a former slave. He taught himself the basics while playing a piano in the home of a white family where his mother worked. The family moved to Texarkana where Scott had the opportunity to study with Julius Weiss. He studied classical music with Weiss, and it had a great influence on his music. Joplin lived in Sedalia, Missouri for a few years, but soon moved to St. Louis, which was becoming a ragtime center.

Scott played cornet and sang with bands like Queen City Cornet Band and Texas Medley Quartette. He performed in clubs, opera houses, and other establishments. One such club was the Maple Leaf, fitting for his most famous work "Maple Leaf Rag."

Among his compositions were "The Entertainer," a dance called "The Ragtime Dance," "Cake Walk," "Palm Leaf Rag," an opera titled *Treemonisha*, waltzes, and many more. He was considered the King of Ragtime.

About 1916, Scott suffered physical and mental distress due to a disease. By January, 1917, he was hospitalized and soon put in a mental institution where he died three months later.

Scott Joplin was a quiet, serious, well-mannered, and articulate man who had a wonderful influence on music history, and, particularly, African-American music for which all Americans can be proud and thankful. His contributions will be felt in music forever.

Contemporaries

- George Gershwin, composer
- Claude Debussy, composer
- Arnold Schoenberg, composer
- Henri Matisse, artist
- Thomas Edison, inventor
- James Joyce, writer
- Sigmund Freud, psychoanalyst

Events and People of His Lifetime

- Spanish-American War
- World War I
- Einstein's Theory of Relativity
- Theodore Roosevelt
- Woodrow Wilson

ELLEN TAAFFE ZWILICH
(b. 1939)

Ellen Taaffe Zwilich was born in Miami, Florida in 1939. During her childhood she began to make up music, and she was putting it on paper by the age of ten. She studied piano, trumpet, and violin. She composed and conducted for her high school band. While studying at Florida State University, she majored in composition, and chose the violin as her principal instrument, playing and performing with a student orchestra conducted by Hungarian composer Ernst von Dohnanyni. In 1964 Ellen moved to New York where she continued to study the violin. She joined the American Symphony Orchestra, conducted by Leopold Stokowski, which had an enormous influence on her compositions.

While in New York, in 1972, Ellen was accepted to study with American composers Elliot Carter and Roger Sessions. She earned her doctorate of music in 1975. Her "Symposium for Orchestra" was premiered the summer of 1975. Her abilities and reputation soon earned commissions and awards. The music of Ellen Taaffe Zwilich was making its mark in history.

Ellen composed a string quartet, two symphonies, a chamber symphony, Concerto Grosso, and much more. She was the first woman to earn a doctoral degree in composition from Julliard, and the first woman to win the Pulitzer Prize for music. She is one of America's leading composers, and her music has certainly made its mark on history.

Contemporaries

- Aaron Copland, composer
- Leonard Bernstein, composer/conductor
- William Schumann, composer
- Phillip Glass, composer
- Norman Mailer, writer
- Andrew Wyeth, artist
- David Hockney, artist

Events and People of Her Lifetime

- World War I
- Korean War
- Vietnam War
- Persian Gulf War
- Watergate scandal
- Presidents F. D. Roosevelt, Truman, Eisenhower, Kennedy, Johnson, Nixon, Ford, Carter, Reagan, Bush, and Clinton
- First man on the moon
- Space Shuttle

Composer Questions

1. What year were you born?

2. What year did you die?

3. Where are you from?

4. Who were some significant people in your life?

5. What music did you compose?

6. For what instruments did you compose?

7. Did you compose any symphonies?

8. Did you compose any operas?

9. Have you composed any ballets?

10. Name a significant event in your life.

11. Did you compose _____?

12. Were you from _____?

13. Were you the composer of _____?

14. Did you have any brothers or sisters? Did they compose?

15. What famous person lived or what event took place during your life?

Name _____

Composers Selections Page

Student Name		**Composer**
1. _____	is	_____
2. _____	is	_____
3. _____	is	_____
4. _____	is	_____
5. _____	is	_____

Notes

Music Football

Objective: Students will practice, learn, or review information about music.

Materials: Pencils
Scissors
Scratch paper
Copies of: Music Football Questions pages
Music Football Field
Music Football Scoreboards

Procedure:

1. Pair the students (one student could play both teams). Students may want to give themselves team names. Give each pair of students a copy of the Music Football Field, a Music Football Question page, a copy of the Music Football Scoreboards, and a pencil. The football from the Scoreboard page needs to be cut out (oaktag and lamination work best). Each team needs a football.

2. The game is based on principles of football. This is a good review and form of assessment that is fun and enjoyable for students.

3. A student is selected to begin. The football is placed on the 20-yard line. Each possession of the ball is for 4 downs. For each down the defense student gives the offense student (person with the ball) a question from the question page. For each correct answer the football moves 10 yards to the other side of the field. If it is fourth down, a student may punt automatically for 40 yards, where the other student begins. If the ball ends up in the end zone the ball should be placed on the 20-yard line of the other student. If it is fourth down and the ball is within 30 yards or less, a student may go for a field goal. The question on fourth down must be correct for the field goal to be good. If the student wants to keep going for the touchdown, the student must get 4 consecutively correct answers in order to get another first down. This process can continue until the ball ends up in the end zone.

4. The length of the game is flexible. You may want to time the game or allow so many plays, or possessions.

5. Each pair of players must have a set of questions and answers. The same questions may be asked more than once. This will help students learn and review. The questions can be connected to a specific concept, numerous concepts, or a specific number of questions.

6. You may want to keep a win-loss record and go the whole way to playoffs and a Super Bowl, but the activity itself will work well from September through January.

7. Give each student a piece of scratch paper for drawing symbols.

Music Football Scoreboards

Team/Coach   Score

Team	
Your Name	

Team/Coach   Score

Team/Coach   Score

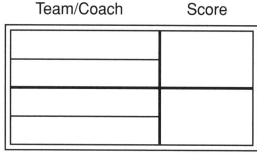

Team/Coach   Score

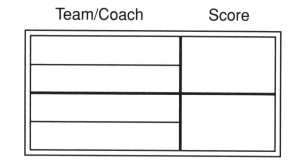

Team/Coach   Score

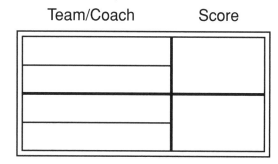

Team/Coach   Score

Team/Coach   Score

Team/Coach   Score

Music Football Questions

Dynamics

1. What does forte mean? (loud)
2. Define the dynamic term *piano*. (soft, quiet)
3. What is a crescendo? (sign for gradually getting louder)
4. What is a decrescendo? (sign for gradually getting softer)
5. What is diminuendo? (gradually getting softer)
6. Define fortissimo. (very loud)
7. What is the music (Italian) term for very soft? (pianissimo)
8. What is mezzoforte? (medium loud)
9. Give the music term for medium soft. (mezzopiano)
10. What is the term used for volume/loud and soft in music? (dynamics)

Tempo

1. What does the term *largo* mean? (very slow)
2. Allegro tells the musician to play the music how? (very fast)
3. What is the term that means to gradually get slower? (ritardando)
4. To return to the regular tempo, the term _____ is used. (a tempo)
5. Presto means what? (quick, quite fast)
6. A song that is moderato goes how in regards to tempo? (moderately fast, medium)
7. How would someone move if they move andante? (slow, walking)
8. Adagio means what? (slow)
9. Vivace means what? (lively)
10. What is the term used for speed of music? (tempo)

Composers

1. What German composer composed the tune "Ode to Joy"? (Beethoven)
2. Did the German composer Johann Sebastian Bach write mostly for the stage or church? (church)
3. Name an American composer. (Copland, Gershwin, Sousa, Joplin, Foster, Schumann)
4. Name a woman composer. (Zwilich, Fanny Mendelssohn, Clara Schumann, Beach)
5. Name an African-American composer. (Joplin, R. Nathaniel Dett, William Grant Still)
6. Name a Russian composer of ballets. (Tchaikovsky, Stravinsky)
7. Which American composer wrote the ballet *Rodeo?* (Copland)
8. Which Austrian composer wrote *The Magic Flute?* (Mozart)
9. Give the name of an Italian opera composer. (Verdi, Rossini, Puccini)
10. Name two operas. (*The Magic Flute, Don Giovanni, Aida, Rigoletto, Carmen*, etc.)

Music Football Questions (page 2)

Instruments

1. The trumpet belongs to which family of instruments? (brass)
2. The flute belongs to which family of instruments? (woodwinds)
3. Which instrument is made of brass but belongs to the woodwind family? (saxophone)
4. What does the trombone use to change pitches? (slide)
5. The bass drum is included in what family? (percussion)
6. The bigger the instrument, the _____ the sound. (lower)
7. What is the stick called used to play the violin? (bow)
8. The clarinet, saxophone, oboe, and bassoon use what wooden item to produce a sound? (a reed)
9. What makes a snare drum different from other drums? (snares)
10. Name the four families of instruments in the orchestra. (strings, woodwinds, brass, and percussion)

Notation

1. What is a sentence used to remember the treble clef lines? (Every Good Boy Does Fine)
2. What are the names of the spaces on the treble clef? (F A C E)
3. Name the note on the third line of the treble clef staff. (B)
4. Name the note on the third space of the treble clef staff. (C)
5. Name the note on the fifth line of the treble clef staff. (F)
6. Name the notes on the lines of the bass clef staff. (G, B, D, F, A)
7. What are the names of the spaces on the bass clef staff? (A, C, E, G)
8. How many different letters of the alphabet does music use? (7)
9. Name the note on the third line of the bass clef staff. (D)
10. Name the note on the third space of the bass clef staff. (E)

Scales/Keys

1. What is a sharp? (raises a note a half step)
2. What is a flat? (lowers a note a half step)
3. What is a natural? (restores a sharp, flat, or natural to its original state)
4. Where is the key signature located in a piece of music? (at the beginning)
5. What key has one sharp? (G Major or E minor)
6. Which sharp is the first one listed in a sharp key signature? (F#)
7. What key has two flats? (B-flat Major/G minor)
8. What key has no flats or sharps? (C Major/A minor)
9. F Major has how many flats? (1)
10. What minor key is the relative to C Major? (A minor)

© 2001 by Parker Publishing Company

Music Football Questions *(page 3)*

Rhythm

1. A whole note receives how many beats in 4/4 time signature? (4)
2. What note receives one beat in 4/4 time? (quarter note)
3. How many half notes equal a whole note? (2)
4. Two eighth notes equal how many quarter notes? (1)
5. What does the top number of a time signature mean? (number of beats per measure)
6. What does the bottom of a meter mean? (what kind of note receives one beat)
7. Define meter. (Time signature. Tells how many beats per measure and what note gets a beat)
8. Where can the meter of a song be found? (at the beginning)
9. What kind of note gets one beat in 6/8 meter? (an eighth note)
10. In 6/8 meter a dotted-half note receives how many beats? (6)

Symbols

1. What does this symbol mean > ? (accent a note)
2. Draw a sharp. (#)
3. Draw a flat. ♭
4. Draw a natural. (♮)
5. Draw a treble clef. (𝄞)
6. What is this symbol? (𝄢)
7. What does a musician do when performing a fermata? (hold a note longer than its usual value or until the director cuts him/her off)
8. What is this symbol ⌢ ?(fermata, bird's eye, hold sign)
9. What is a staccato? ♪ (short, detached note)
10. Draw a slur. (♩＿♩)

Other

1. What is a round, or circle canon? (a song or piece that repeats the melody in parts, starting at different points)
2. What is legato? (to play smoothly)
3. A tie does what? (ties one note to another, adding the number of beats of the two or more notes together)
4. Conduct the pattern for 2 beats per measure. (↙↖)
   1   2
5. What is cut time? ¢ (the time is cut in half ∨ 2 beats per measure, a half note equals one beat)

Music Football Field

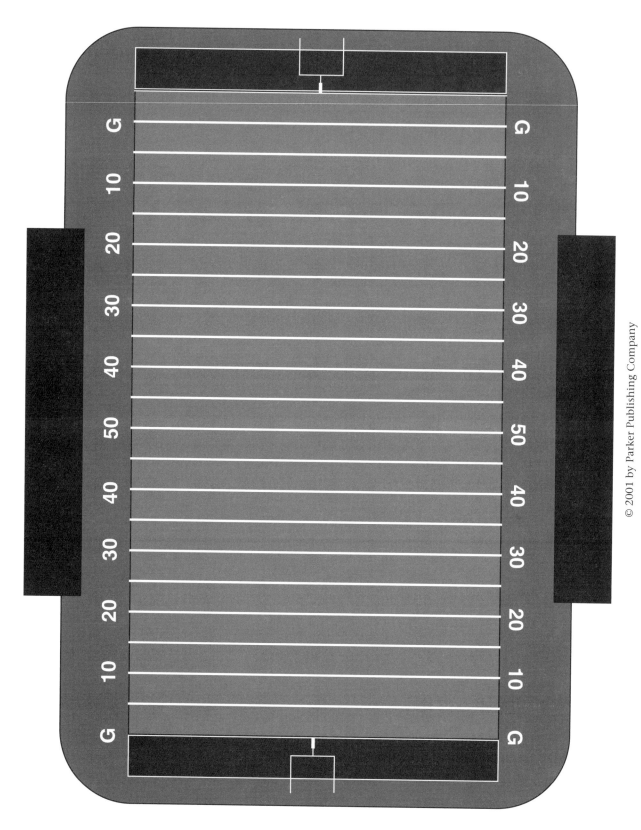

16th Notes
(Fractions)

Complete the following exercises.

○ = 4   ♩ = 2   ♩ = 1   ♪ = 1/2   ♫ = 1   𝅘𝅥𝅯𝅘𝅥𝅯𝅘𝅥𝅯𝅘𝅥𝅯 = 1   𝅘𝅥𝅯𝅘𝅥𝅯♪ = 1

𝅘𝅥𝅯𝅘𝅥𝅯♪ = 1   ♩.♪ = 1   𝅘𝅥𝅯 = 1/4   ♫ = 1/2   ♩. = 1 1/2   ♩. = 3   ♪. = 3/4 of a beat

1. ♩ + 𝅘𝅥𝅯𝅘𝅥𝅯𝅘𝅥𝅯𝅘𝅥𝅯 = _____ beats

2. 𝅘𝅥𝅯𝅘𝅥𝅯𝅘𝅥𝅯𝅘𝅥𝅯 + 𝅘𝅥𝅯𝅘𝅥𝅯♪ + ♩ = _____ beats

3. 𝅘𝅥𝅯𝅘𝅥𝅯♪ + 𝅘𝅥𝅯𝅘𝅥𝅯♪ + ♩ = _____ beats

4. 𝅘𝅥𝅯𝅘𝅥𝅯 + ♪ + ♪ = _____ beats

5. ♪ + 𝅘𝅥𝅯𝅘𝅥𝅯 + ♪ = _____ beats

6. ♩ − ♩ − ♪ = _____ beats

7. ○ − ♫ − ♪ − ♪ = _____ beats

8. ♩ − ♪ − ♪ − ♪ = _____ beats

9. ♩ + ♫ − ♪ − 𝅘𝅥𝅯𝅘𝅥𝅯 = _____ (note)

10. ♩ + ♩ + ♫ + 𝅘𝅥𝅯𝅘𝅥𝅯𝅘𝅥𝅯𝅘𝅥𝅯 = _____ (note)

11. ♩ + 1/2 = _____ beats

12. ♩ + ♪ + 1/2 = _____ beats

13. 1/2 + 1/2 − ♪ = _____ beats

14. ○ − 3/4 − ♪ = _____ beats

15. ♩.
     + ♪
     _____
     (note)

16. ♩.
     + ♩
     _____
     (note)

17. 𝅘𝅥𝅯𝅘𝅥𝅯♪
     + 𝅘𝅥𝅯𝅘𝅥𝅯♪
     _____
     (note)

18. 𝅘𝅥𝅯𝅘𝅥𝅯𝅘𝅥𝅯𝅘𝅥𝅯
     − 𝅘𝅥𝅯𝅘𝅥𝅯♪
     _____
     (beats)

19. 𝅘𝅥𝅯𝅘𝅥𝅯♪
     + 𝅘𝅥𝅯𝅘𝅥𝅯♪
     _____
     (beats)

20. 𝅘𝅥𝅯𝅘𝅥𝅯♪
     − ♪
     _____
     (beats)

451

Music Pizza
16ths

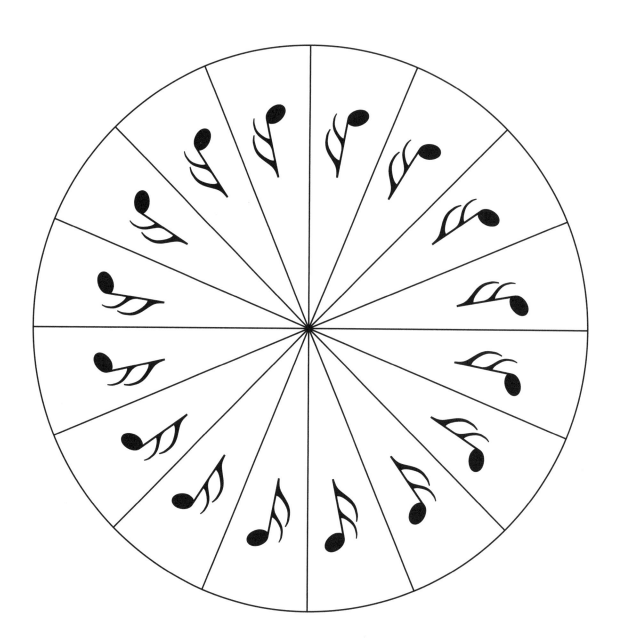

MASCAR Racing
(Music Association of Stock Car Racing)

Objective: Students will practice, learn, or review concepts of music. This activity is a good alternative assessment device.

Materials: Pencils
Music Questions for MASCAR Racing
Copies of: MASCAR Race Track
MASCAR Racecars page
MASCAR Response Page
MASCAR Sample Questions

Preparation: Give each student copies of the Race Track, Racecars, Response Page, and the Sample Questions page. Have the students cut out and color the racecars.

Procedure:
1. Each student will place his/her racecar on the start line. Ask ten questions about music. Students will respond on the racing response page. Check to see if the response is correct. If the response is correct, the student moves his/her car one section of the track. The race track has ten sections. If the student answers all ten questions correctly, the student wins the race. If nine are correct, second place; eight correct, third; etc.

2. The race can be done as a topic like dynamics. The Dynamics 100, if it consists of 10 questions. If you want to go to 20 questions, it would be The Dynamics 200, and so on. If the questions are general, the race can be called The Music 100, or whatever you wish. For every ten correct responses, the student moves around the track one lap.

3. Placing: *10* questions: 1st = 10 correct, 2nd = 9 correct, 3rd = 8 correct, etc. *20* questions: 1st = 18-20 correct, 2nd = 17 correct, 3rd = 15 correct. *30* questions: 1st = 27 correct, 2nd = 24 correct, 3rd = 21, and so on. The award provided on the response page may be given to the students as a trophy for winning a place in the race. Write the place the student won.

4. You may want to have a tournament. Students will accumulate points after several races. The student with the most points is the MASCAR Champion.

5. *Extension:* To integrate your curriculum, you may want to add questions about other topics and subjects. Fractions work well. Example: "If you have one half of a tank of gas and you need a whole tank to finish the race, how much more gas do you need?" (another half of a tank)

MASCAR Race Track

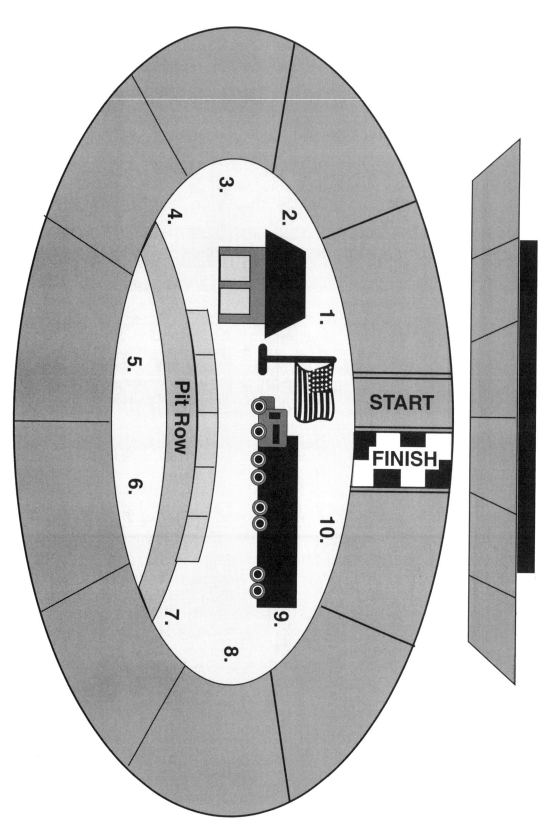

MASCAR Racecars

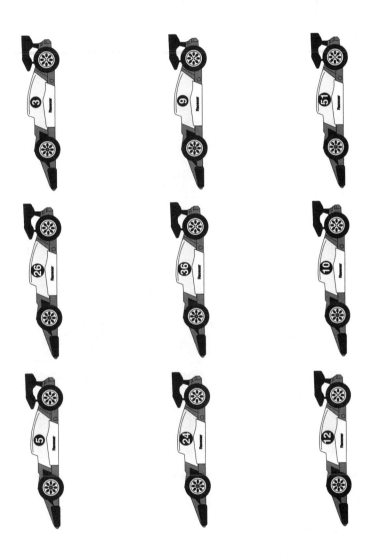

MASCAR Response Page

The MASCAR   Name _____   Placed

_____
(Topic)

1. _____
2. _____
3. _____
4. _____
5. _____

_____
(Length)

6. _____
7. _____
8. _____
9. _____
10. _____

The MASCAR   Name _____

_____
(Topic)

1. _____
2. _____
3. _____
4. _____
5. _____
6. _____
7. _____
8. _____
9. _____
10. _____

_____
(Length)

11. _____
12. _____
13. _____
14. _____
15. _____
16. _____
17. _____
18. _____
19. _____
20. _____

The MASCAR   Name _____

_____
(Topic)

1. _____
2. _____
3. _____
4. _____
5. _____
6. _____
7. _____
8. _____
9. _____
10. _____
11. _____
12. _____
13. _____
14. _____
15. _____

_____
(Length)

16. _____
17. _____
18. _____
19. _____
20. _____
21. _____
22. _____
23. _____
24. _____
25. _____
26. _____
27. _____
28. _____
29. _____
30. _____

MASCAR Sample Questions

Race: The MASCAR Dynamic 100

1. What does forte mean?

2. What does this symbol (pp) represent?

3. ⟨———⟩ tells a musician to do what?

4. How should you sing when the director tells you to be pianissimo?

5. f equals?

6. What does diminuendo mean?

7. Define mezzopiano.

8. How should fortissimo be performed?

9. What is the symbol for decrescendo?

10. What are the music (Italian) terms for medium loud?

Daily Singing Skill Builders

Ti

458

Daily Singing Skill Builders *(Continued)*

Daily Rhythm Skill Builders

Daily Rhythm Skill Builders *(Continued)*

Interdisciplinary Planner

A record of the regular classroom's units, content, and concepts to be integrated with music.

Date _____

INTEGRATED SUBJECT	FIFTH	SIXTH
Literature Arts		
Math		
Science		
Health		
Social Studies		
Art		
Physical Education		
Other		